Leader's Guide

I HAVE GOOD NEWS FOR YOU

by Rev. Donald F. Ginkel

Contents

CHURCH PRESS
Rev. Donald F. Ginkel
7818 W. Oxford Circle
Lakewood, CO 80235-1936
Toll Free: 1-888-772-8878

I Have Good News For You Leader's Guide
Copyright © by Donald F. Ginkel, 1996
All rights reserved

ISBN O-9642122-3-4

Printed in the United States of America

Before The Class

Set the date for the new class early and begin to publicize it early. Usually it is not best to wait to start a class when "there are some people who are interested." Ideas for promotion:

1. Order a good supply of *I Have Good News For You* books, accompanying cassette tapes, adults class tract cards, adult class bulletin inserts, and posters.

2. **Place posters in prominent places with a sign-up sheet placed to the side of each poster.** *Well placed posters and sign-up sheets are really indispensable.*

3. Speak of the class in sermons (It's easy to work this into most texts), prayers in the worship service, bulletin paragraphs, bulletin inserts, newsletter, etc.

4. Develop a list of individuals who should be contacted for the class and another list of those who have indicated they plan to attend. Aim to expand both lists. Ask certain members to invite and bring certain prospects. Develop and maintain a regular Prospect List (Ask for one of our Prospect Cards).

5. Beside non-Lutherans, be sure to invite Lutheran transfers to go through for a refresher and get to know you better and for you to become better acquainted with them. Two things happen here:

   a. The new member usually enters into a new and higher level of discipleship, and

   b. The discipling bond between pastor and member increases. Another excellent opportunity to do all this is when the pastor has a new congregation. Many pastors do this early in a new parish during the Sunday morning Bible class. One brother simply said, "It helps insure that we are all marching to the same drum beat."

6. All members of the congregation should be invited and challenged to attend and to bring a friend. We know of congregations that systematically put their entire membership through this course with tremendous benefits. The adult class bulletin insert helps greatly with member enrollment with a section on the insert for this purpose.

7. Pastor and people should work hard at ***bringing*** people to the class, not just inviting them. The prospect may have many fears about studying the Bible and, of all things, "Going to a Lutheran Church." A delightful Christian in my first parish always insisted on bringing his prospects. When they responded, "What's wrong? We'll be there. Don't you trust us?", he always said with a smile, "Oh, I trust you! I just don't trust the devil." I remember one class to which he personally brought 26 people. Guess how many trips he had to make for that one! Inviting ***and bringing*** is always best.

8. Use the promotional letters to members on pages 3 and 4 and to prospects on pages 5 and 6. People who have already attended the class are excellent candidates to bring others to the new class. Endeavor to involve them in outreach to their friends to build the new class.

Promotional Letters To Members

Letter # 1

Dear Member of God's Beloved Family:

On October 1, at 6:00 p.m., we will begin another _____ Class in the _____ Room. Once again I am emphasizing that each of us needs to reach out and bring at least one person to the Class.

Why? Well, the invitation of St. Paul to his people was: "Come, help change the world for Christ!" That's my invitation to you. "Come, help change the world for Christ!"

We need to bring as many people as possible to this Class because all of the people we know will some day stand before the judgment seat of God – our neighbors, our fellow workers, our boss, our close friends, our more distant friends – everyone! Those without Christ will be condemned to an eternity without God, in total darkness, dying every day but not getting the job done, no comforts, no relief, no conversation, no joking, no vacations. As children of our beloved Father we must have compassion on all those not yet prepared for this awesome day.

"Come, help change the world for Christ" because God is in the forgiveness of sins business! God is satisfied with the payment that has been made for the sin of all these people you know. God has been made happy about them by Jesus. But this Good News will do them no good whatever unless they know it and believe it! Remember the parting words of Jesus to us? "Go and make disciples of all nations... teaching them to obey everything I have commanded you" *(Matthew 28:19-20).* This is our business. Jesus says so.

Pick out three or four people as "prospects." Pray for each of them. Speak to them about the Class and what it does. Give them one of the enclosed tract cards on the course, *I Have Good News For You.* Offer to bring them to the first session and attend with them. If they like it, they can attend the second session on their own. Remind them that there is nothing to lose and everything to gain, including a new life here and a perfect one in heaven. Tell them about the impact of this Class on your life. "Love them" into the Class. Let me know if I can help.

I look forward to seeing you October 1 with the people you are bringing!

All my love in Jesus,

Pastor

Dear Fellow Redeemed:

> *I love to tell the story - 'Tis pleasant to repeat What seems each time I tell it,*
> *More wonderfully sweet; I love to tell the story - For some have never heard*
> *The message of salvation From God's own holy Word. I love to tell the story!*
> *'Twill be my theme in glory - To tell the old, old story Of Jesus and His love.*

Some of us have never had the joy of being an instrument in the hand of the Holy Spirit to bring a soul to Jesus. We have no idea of what we're missing. We have no idea of what our non-believing friends are missing.

Fortunately for all of us, we have a golden opportunity right before us to tell the story – to give a very important invitation. On Sunday, June 2, at 6:00 p.m., our _____ Class begins in the _____ Room of the Church.

There are many things we can do to share Jesus with people who are so precious to the Lord. Here are just three suggestions.

1. Jot down the names of three people who either do not know the Lord or who need to know Him better.
2. Briefly tell each of these people what Jesus means to you in your own words. Share with them the nature and purpose of our _____ Class. Give them one of the enclosed tract cards on the course, *I Have Good News For You*. Remind them that it is an exciting study on the basics of Christianity right from the Bible. They will not be put on the spot in the Class. There is nothing to lose, the class is free, and there is everything to gain in this world and in the world to come. Tape cassettes are available for those who have to miss a lesson.
3. Tell them, "I really want to personally bring you to the first session on June 2. I'll pick you up and bring you home afterward. If you like the class, come back; if not – don't." *Do not let them come on their own.* The chances are great that they will not make it.

Does this approach work? Sure it does. I am using it myself with a number of prospects. I have learned that you really have to ask them to attend and then lovingly nudge them along. We must remember that they are sheep, very precious sheep. By this we let Jesus know we love Him. By this we let our friends and neighbors know we love them.

"We are therefore Christ's ambassadors, as though God were making His appeal through us. We implore you on Christ's behalf: Be reconciled to God" *(2 Corinthians 5:20).*

I look forward to seeing you June 2nd at 6:00 and meeting the people you bring with you.

In His love and mine,

Pastor

Promotional Letters To Prospects

Letter # 1

Dear Joe and Mary:

This is the day of bad news, world-wide, across America, locally, and many times in our own lives. But there is some Good News around; in fact, next Sunday, January 20, I will begin what is called the _____ Class. We will meet in the _____ Room right inside the double doors of our Church at 7:00.

The _____ Class will be using a special ten-week Bible study entitled, *I Have Good News For You!* And it truly is Good News. It is a course designed for those who do not know Christ, for those who do but want to know Him better, and for those who are looking for a church home. We encourage everyone interested in the possibility of joining our Christian fellowship, including Lutherans who wish to transfer their membership, to attend this exciting course.

This study is informal, but it is intensive and right from the Bible. I am the teacher. You may listen or ask questions. Cassette tapes are available for make-up in case of sickness, work, or vacation. No memory work is required. There are no obligations to join our Church when the course is finished. These sessions will undoubtedly be the most lively Bible study classes you have ever attended in your life. People from all types of church backgrounds and some with no church background will be in attendance.

Please feel free to bring your friends with you. The classes are open to everyone. I am enclosing a tract card which describes the study, *I Have Good News For You.* Remember, we begin this Sunday evening at 7:00 in the _____ Room which is directly inside the front double doors of our Church.

I sincerely hope I can have the pleasure of meeting you at the door.

Yours in Christ,

GROWING IN THE SON

Pastor

Letter # 2

Dear Fred and Susan:

Next Sunday, October 4, a new _____ Class will begin at 7:00 p.m. in the _____ Room of our Church. In this course we will go into an exciting Bible study entitled, *I Have Good News For You.* This in-depth study reveals God's answers on subjects like: Marriage, Divorce, Baptism, Communion, the Holy Spirit, the Person of Christ, Death, Hell, Heaven, and many others. Above all it answers these two important questions:

1. Does God really care about me?
2. How can I know the way to heaven and be sure about it?

If you are not a Christian you can come to know Jesus in a very personal way by the time the course is finished. If you are a Christian you can get much closer to Christ and better understand His will for your life.

We believe that God has a special plan for each of His children. That plan will be revealed to the child of God as he or she searches the Scriptures, begins to understand the plan, and then joyfully becomes obedient to it. The joy and new life that has come to thousands of others through this course can also be yours in greater measure – it's His promise!

We meet each Sunday evening for ten weeks. You may ask questions or just listen. This exciting Bible study is required for people interested in membership. In fact everyone, including Lutherans, are encouraged to go through this course before joining. All sessions are on tape for those who may be out of town for a lesson.

We are living in very difficult times, and indications are that they will become even more trying. Surely we need a Savior for our sins and an Almighty God who loves us, forgives us, strengthens and guides us, and finally, when life is over, takes us to His home in heaven forever. That is really what this Bible study course is all about. I hope to see you Sunday!

Your friend and His,

For the Word of God
is sharper than any
two-edged sword –
is a lamp unto my feet and
a light unto my path

the
Bible

Pastor

Promotional Paragraphs For Bulletins And Newsletter

HOW WOULD YOU LIKE to be instrumental in changing for the better the welfare of another human being for the rest of their life on earth and for all eternity? Well, that is exactly the opportunity before you this week. Next Sunday, February 6th, at 6:00 p.m., we will begin the next _____ Class in the _____ Room. *You have the opportunity to bring someone for a life-changing experience!* What can happen in that Class can change their entire life now and forever. Some of the people you know may never have another opportunity to get right with God. Time is critical for many people. Please invite and bring as many as you can. If you don't, who will?

OUR NEXT _____ Class begins Sunday, March 4, at 6:00 p.m., in the _____ Room. We will study a course which over 250,000 people have gone through: *I Have Good News For You*. It's a ten week Bible study which covers all the basic teaching of the New Testament. The student grows immensely in knowledge, but even more important, he moves closer to God, knows it, and likes it. That's very important in any Bible study. People from various church backgrounds are usually in attendance which promotes good discussion and excellent questions. Students are made to feel comfortable knowing that they can ask questions without any embarrassment. The sessions are informal, which makes for a better learning situation. A good dose of humor is also used. This helps even more. Tape cassettes are available when a student must miss, which means that one can easily keep up with the class. This course helps people know what this church and pastor believe and teach. So many times people join a church without this knowledge. At the close of the class those who wish may become members of our church. That is a nice approach. You may attend just the first lesson or all ten of them. Why not give it a try? We are sure you will discover that this Bible study is unlike any you've ever attended before. The impact it will have on your life will be surprising and pleasant.

NEXT SUNDAY EVENING we begin our next _____ Class at 6:00 in the _____ Room. Those of you who have attended one of these classes know how people found new life and forgiveness from God. Now that you are a Christian and are on your way to heaven, what about that neighbor, friend, or relative of yours who does not have this yet? You can help him. You can invite and bring him to this Class. Be sure that you reach out for someone even as someone reached out to you. The love of Jesus constrains us!

"EACH ONE REACH ONE!" This phase was popular with evangelism-minded believers years ago. The phrase is still a good one. If every adult member of our congregation would bring just one person to the new _____ Class which begins April 26 at 6:00 in the _____ Room, we would have a class of _____ people! If each family would bring just one unchurched person to this Class we would have a Class of _____ people. "Each One Reach One!" Possible? Yes! All things are possible with God who wants all men to be saved. Who can you reach and bring? A neighbor, a friend? Do it!

Conducting The Class

1. Have the class in the proper size room: small class = small room; large class = large room. If possible, use tables. Arrange students in a circle or a U shaped pattern. Supply pencils. Try to have no more chairs than students. Use an erasable marker board and bright color erasable markers. Be sure the room temperature is comfortable; lighting should be good.

2. At the first session strive to make the group comfortable. Ask everyone to share their name, where they live, and what they do. Then ask each person to tell why they are present; this will prove to be interesting and positive. Supply each student with their own book (no sharing). Pass an information sheet around for each student to fill in: Name, address, phone, church background, baptized? During the course you can keep track of individual attendance on this sheet.

3. Share the following information and goals:

    a. We will be informal and everyone should feel free to ask questions.

    b. Three goals for this course are –
       (1) To experience new birth in Jesus Christ.
       (2) To grow mightily in Christian discipleship (explain word).
       (3) To safely reach our eternal home in heaven.

    c. Briefly emphasize the three needs on pages 2 and 3 of the study guide.

    d. Try to attend all classes rain or shine. If you are sick or will be out of town, you will want to use our cassette tapes (hold up a copy of Tape 1).

    e. Try to faithfully do the weekly assignments. Turn to page 11, middle of the page. We want to develop the good habit of daily Bible reading. Read just one chapter a day, thoughtfully and quietly. Try to do this at the same time each day. Fill out the worksheet questions on pages 11 and 12. Do the best you can with the questions. At the beginning of the next session we will quickly review our answers. • before a verse indicates a verse for suggested memorization; this is not required, but encouraged.

    f. During the ten weeks of the course try to worship with us each Sunday and attend our adult Bible class. This will assist in helping you understand what you are learning and what we believe and teach.

    g. As we go into each lesson try to be open minded, unbiased, and honest as God speaks through His Word.

4. Encourage discussion. Be challenging and excited as you present God's marvelous story. Exude enthusiasm for the Lord Jesus.

5. Begin on time with prayer and then go directly to the worksheet of the previous lesson and check answers. Then go to the next lesson. Have class members assist you in reading the Scripture verses and conclusions. Be sensitive to the fact that a few people would rather not read.

6. Basic questions for all Bible study are:

    a. What does the text say?

    b. What does it mean?

    c. What does it mean to me?

    Be sure that Scripture verses studied are applied to everyday life – make it practical.

7. Avoid lecturing. Use illustrations freely. Be sure to keep the discussion moving. Endeavor to bring everyone in the group into the discussion. Guide the discussion into the practical and personal sharing of experience. Demonstrate loving leadership. Put in real preparation before the session. Make the most of the physical surroundings to create an atmosphere of quiet, intimate, informal study and sharing. Bring the session to a close with a sense of catharsis or "high point."

8. At various times in the ten week study (especially Lesson 2, Question 1 and all of Lesson 7), **vigorously stress the need and benefits of regular Bible study and that in our congregation we encourage everyone to be active in the following Bible study settings:**

   a. Every Sunday worship including vacations, when out-of-town company arrives, etc.

   b. Every Sunday adult Bible class attendance.

   c. Daily family devotions and/or personal devotions at home (Make devotional aids available when studying Lessons 2 and 7).

   d. Participation in a small Bible study group during the week.

9. Learning involves a number of very important steps.

   a. There must be knowledge of *facts and principals*. This element is frequently missing in the learning process today. A person who does not understand the basics of the Christian faith will have difficulty without special guidance and encouragement from the teacher.

   b. There must be *comprehension* where possible. This simply means that we must have an understanding of the facts and principles.

   c. There must be *application* of the above points into every day life. This step needs special and constant emphasis by the teacher during the learning process.

10. Questions for the instructor: Will I –

   a. Lead and teach the class with love and humility?

   b. Encourage students when they are having difficulty?

   c. Endeavor to use some humor in teaching?

   d. Commend the class as it struggles, learns, and grows?

   e. Not allow any bashing of church, pastor or people who might be absent?

   f. Pray regularly for each person in the class?

11. Make sure that refreshments are provided either during the class or at the end for the purpose of additional fellowship. Solicit members to take turns doing this and/or have class members take turns providing refreshments.

12. This Leader's Guide carries the entire text of *I Have Good News For You*. The instructor may, therefore, use this Guide to teach the course. The actual page numbers of the student's guide are indicated in this Guide as follows: page 1 is **[1]**.

End Of Course

1. Distribute "Application for Membership" and an "Identification and Talent Card" to each student (See sample for both on pages 11 and 12). These two items should be filled out and returned a week after the last lesson at the "Review and Orientation Night."

2. Discuss the next adult membership class with the present class. Who can they bring? Give each person several Adult Class Tract Cards with the time of the new class on the card.

3. Should any people in this class join your evangelism or outreach group?

4. Make plans to have this group form their own small Bible study group. Assist them in getting a group leader (teacher) and good Bible study materials (*The Many Wonders of Heaven* and *A Time To Laugh or Cry* are excellent studies for a new study group like this.)

5. Review and Orientation Night. One week after Lesson 10 meet at the regular time. Have a 45 minute oral review on the highlights of all ten lessons. Remind the class that this is not a test but an important mini-review. After coffee break have an informal 30-45 minute review of the past history of the congregation together with present and future plans in the areas of education, evangelism, stewardship, and other related areas such as organizations, building programs, constitution, etc.

6. Have a tea at the church or pastor's home honoring the class. For this the pastor can invite "select" members (one member for each person in the class) to join the group.

    a. Pastor has brief inspirational opening.

    b. Pastor gives everyone a copy of these four questions:

        (1) How did you come to believe in Jesus as your Savior?
        (2) What do you want your church to do for you?
        (3) What will you do for your church?
        (4) Why did you (do you want to) join Family of Christ Lutheran Church? First ask the members why they did and then new members why they want to.

    c. Pastor pairs up an "old member" with a "new member." When everyone is paired up, have these teams go off by themselves. Have "old member" share answers to these four questions with the "new member." Then "new member" shares answers to these questions with the "old member." The witnessing and building between these two believers will be delightful. Allow about twenty minutes for this. Pastor should then bring everyone back together again and have some interesting highlights of the team sharing passed on to the entire group. Plans should be shared on the next adult membership class. Make sure that each person present receives several copies of the Adult Class Tract Card with starting time of new class.

7. Receive new members into membership at the next worship service with warm expressions of welcome and prayer. Provide each new member with a corsage (Let's make a big deal of this!) Have them sit together as a group in the front of the sanctuary. Be sure each new member receives an appropriate membership certificate (Request a copy of our certificate for examination).

8. Have the new members sit together as a group in adult Bible class. Have the chairman of the congregation give them a welcome. You might also ask if any of the new members would like to respond.

Application For Membership In
Family Of Christ Lutheran Church

My Commitment to the Lord Jesus Christ and His Church

I. BAPTISM, PREVIOUS CHURCH MEMBERSHIP

1. I have been baptized in the Name of the Triune God (Yes or No): _____

2. Denomination in which baptized: _____

II. STATEMENT OF FAITH

3. I believe that the Bible is God's Word and therefore the only sure guide to eternal life in heaven through Jesus Christ: _____

4. I believe in God the Father, Son, and Holy Spirit and am resolved to suffer all things, even death, rather than fall away from the Triune God: _____

5. I believe that I am a sinner and that by my sins I deserve to be eternally lost: _____

6. I believe that by faith in Christ I am given a pure white robe of His righteousness so that I can appear holy and innocent before God in Judgment: _____

7. To me, personally, Jesus Christ is: _____

_____

III. DECISION, PETITION, AND PROMISE

8. I wish to be a member of Family of Christ Lutheran Church: _____

9. It is my sincere purpose to be faithful in Sunday church attendance, Bible class attendance, and in Holy Communion attendance: _____

10. I will endeavor to be a good student of Scripture at home and will regularly pray for my pastor and members of the congregation: _____

11. I will strive for purity in the Church by avoiding false doctrine and ungodly living: _____

12. I will try to bring as many people into Jesus' Kingdom as possible by prayer and witnessing: _____

13. I am a member of a secret organization or lodge: _____

    If yes, please state name of organization: _____

    I am ready, in the interest of undivided loyalty to Christ, to give up such membership: ____

14. Specifically, I am willing to try to help build and expand the Kingdom of my Savior and my Church in the following ways: _____

_____

_____

Sign (name) _____

Identification And Talent Card

Full name _____ Address _____ Phone _____

Date of birth _____ Where born _____

Father's name _____ Mother's given name _____

When baptized _____ Where _____ Pastor _____

When confirmed _____ Where _____ Pastor _____

When married _____ To whom _____ Pastor _____

Formal education received _____

Where employed _____ Phone _____

Job title and description _____

Hobbies _____ Musical instruments _____

Past work in church _____

In what church work will you be willing to serve the Lord in the future? _____
_____

(Back side of 5" x 8 ½" card)

NOTE: Mother, please fill in this side

Child's full name _____ Date of birth _____

Where born _____ Date baptized _____ Where _____

Sponsors_____

Father's name _____ Mother's maiden name _____

(Repeat child information about three or four times. Most of this form comes from various LCMS congregations.)

To the instructor:

    The entire text of *I Have Good News For You* is laid out in this Leader's Guide.

    You can highlight the notes and illustrations you wish to use in your presentation and then make additional notes as you see fit. Or, you can take notes and illustrations from the Leader's Guide and write them down in a student's book.

    May the Holy Spirit enable you to teach the Word with wisdom and enthusiasm.

Your co-worker in the Lord,

Don Gilal

Name: _____

I HAVE GOOD NEWS FOR YOU

By Rev. Donald F. Ginkel

MORE THAN 700,000 COPIES

SOLD WORLD WIDE

The love of God is greater far Than tongue or pen can ever tell;
It goes beyond the highest star, And reaches to the lowest hell;
The guilty pair, bowed down with care, God gave His Son to win;
His erring child He reconciled, And pardoned from his sin.
O love of God, how rich and pure! How measureless and strong!
It shall for evermore endure The saints' and angels' song.

- F. M. Lehman

Additional copies of this book plus other Bible studies for children and adults, confirmation, stewardship and evangelism materials may be ordered from the address below. Ask for a brochure.

CHURCH PRESS
Rev. Donald F. Ginkel
4809 W. 121st Street
Overland Park, KS 66209
Phone & Fax 913-491-6264

[1]

A Word of Introduction

On a dark night on a road from Jackson to Vicksburg, MS, heavy rains washed a bridge away. When a truck driver saw the tail lights of the car ahead of him disappear, he knew something was wrong. Suddenly his own truck sailed silently through the black void where a bridge once stood, and he crashed into the river below. He made it out of the cab, swam to shore, and sat there in the darkness. Car after car zoomed into the gap and crashed into the swirling water below. Sixteen people died that night. Each of them had faith in a bridge that was no longer there.

Spiritually, there are millions of people today who have faith in a bridge that isn't there. So many people believe that by their good works, their character, their church membership, their morality, they will somehow cross the river of death to heaven. But the bridge is out! From Genesis to Revelation the message is the same. It is that God's Son, Jesus, has come, and He is the sure and only Bridge to heaven.

The bottom line of Christianity is that Jesus Christ satisfies in life and in death! People cannot give the satisfaction that man desires. Human nature says that a lot of friends, a lot of companionship, a lot of fellowship satisfies. But every friend will let you down. Every fellowship finally breaks up. Then you are alone – with your thoughts, your feelings, your desires.

The famous words of St. Augustine are still true today: "God, Thou hast made us for Thyself, and our hearts are restless until they rest in Thee."

You have at least three needs.

Need No. 1: You need to know who you are. A woman said, "I don't know who I am. I don't know why I am here. And I don't know where I am going." You know the feeling. Jesus came from the Father into this world to tell you that His Father made you and that the Son redeemed you on the cross so that you might have new life. He comes to give you worth, self-esteem, joy, peace, forgiveness, and a place in the family of God!

Need No. 2: You need to know that you are loved. Someone said, "Just put your arm around me once in a while when I get mean." We all get mean. The Good News is that God is so powerful and His love so unlimited that He can hug you no matter how mean or hurting [2] you may be. He loves you perfectly. He loves you totally. And He wants you to study the Bible from cover to cover to discover just how great His love is for you!

Need No. 3: You need heaven. You are not going to be here very long. The Bible teaches that your life is like a flower and the grass, here today and cut down tomorrow. The Good News is that you are not going to disappear. You are going to live with God in eternity, on a new earth and in a mansion that He is already preparing for you. You possess this and own this now as your very own by faith in Jesus. He promises, "I tell you the truth, he who believes has everlasting life" *(John 6:47)*.

There are two basic objectives for this exciting course: 1. To learn about your needs and the solutions, especially, to learn to truly trust Jesus Christ as your personal Savior from sin and to receive that new and abundant life which comes only from Him. 2. To prepare you for meaningful membership in the Lutheran Church if you are not a member, and if you are, to better equip you for full-time service to Christ, to others, and to self.

We claim to be a Bible-centered, Bible-believing, and Bible-confessing Church. Our chief aim is to bring people to Christ. The most important question before you is: What am I going to do with Christ? Why did He die on the cross? How do I believe in Him as my Savior? What do I do after I come to faith?

We encourage you to participate fully in the lessons. React honestly and candidly. Be open to God's message to you. Ask questions: Is this really what God says? What does this Church believe? And listen. Listen carefully. God has some incredibly Good News for you.

Carefully complete the worksheets at the end of the lessons. Review your answers at the beginning of the next class. Faithfully follow the daily Bible reading schedule. Set aside a little quiet time each day for this. • indicates a Bible verse for suggested memorization.

May God the Father, Son, and Holy Spirit instruct and direct you in your study.

Soli Deo Gloria!

[3]

Contents

I HAVE GOOD NEWS FOR YOU

WELCOME

[4]

Instructor's Opening Comments At Start Of A New Class

Have students write their names on top of page 1. Please turn to page 2. Very briefly review these **three basic needs** on pages 2 and 3: 1. You need to know *who you are*. 2. You to know that *you are loved.* 3. *You need heaven.*

The Table of Contents is on page 4. We will be taking one lesson each week.

We have **two goals**: 1. That you may come to know Jesus personally and intimately as your personal Savior. 2. Get to know this church and its pastor.

To this end –

1. **Attend all classes** rain or shine. Use tapes for makeup.

2. **Faithfully do your assignments**: Turn to page 9 and note the • in front of John 3:16. There will be two or three verses in each lesson marked like this for suggested memorization. Turn to page 11. Follow the Bible reading schedule and read just one chapter a day. Answer the worksheet questions on pages 11 and 12. Try to answer *every* question. At the start of our next session we will quickly review our answers.

3. **Worship regularly** with us during the course and **attend our adult Bible class** Sunday mornings. This will help you understand what we are studying and what we believe.

4. **Try to be open minded, unbiased, and honest** as you study; this can be difficult because we all carry with us baggage that isn't always correct. Please feel free to ask questions and to make notes in your book as we study.

Let's bow our heads for prayer:

Almighty God, tonight we are gathered together in this room, and we have come to search out the truth of Your Holy Word. We would know Your will for our lives. O God, please help us and bless us. Please send Your Holy Spirit into this room and into every heart. Speak to each of us in this Bible study. Give us faith and give us understanding. Above all, give us repentance over our sin and a genuine faith in Jesus as our personal Savior that we may have and appreciate the full forgiveness of our many sins. When life is over may we join You in Your Home to live with You forever. We pray in the precious and wonderful name of Jesus Christ, our Lord and Savior. Amen.

Lesson 1

I HAVE GOOD NEWS FOR YOU

About A God Who Cares For You

1. How can we know that there is a God?

> In Genesis Chapter 1 God makes no attempt to prove His existence. He assumes that people will naturally know that He exists.

PSALM 109:1 The *heavens* <u>declare</u> the glory of God; the *skies* <u>proclaim</u> the work of His hands.

> We spend too much time looking at cement and asphalt. Just look up. The heavenly bodies shout the glory of God. They proclaim His vast wisdom. Here we see the folly of atheists who see the heavens and yet say, "There is no God," who see the effect and yet say, "There is no cause" or "It happened all by itself." For the next verse underline all italicized words as we come to them.

ROMANS 1:19-20 What may be known about God is <u>*plain to them*</u>, because God has made it plain to them. For since the creation of the world *God's* <u>*invisible qualities*</u> – His eternal power and divine nature – *have been* <u>*clearly seen*</u>, being <u>*understood from what has been made*</u>, so that men are *without excuse*.

God has left imprints of Himself on what He created. Just a glance at this building tells you that it did not get here by itself. What do you naturally conclude? Someone built it. So also this world. When looking at it you can only conclude that a powerful God made it. **God has made Himself very clear in this world so that men would seek Him and find Him**.

No one will be able to say on Judgment Day, "God, we had no idea that You existed!" There will be no atheists on Judgment Day; there should be none today! The Bible says that on Judgment Day every knee will bow before Jesus. My suggestion to people is to bow willingly before Jesus now so that they will not have to do it unwillingly then. Will you crown Him Lord of lords and King of kings tonight? *This is the NATURAL KNOWLEDGE of God in contrast to the Bible which is called the REVEALED KNOWLEDGE of God* (Ask students to write these two down on the bottom of page 1).

ROMANS 2:15 Gentiles show that the *requirements of the law* (what is left of the image of God in the heart of men after the fall into sin in the Garden) *are written on their hearts*, their *consciences* also *bearing witness*, and their thoughts now *accusing*, now even *defending* them.

Above the word "Gentiles" write the word "Unbelievers." Do you have a little voice inside of you that talks to you? When you are tempted to do something bad it says, "Don't you do that." And when you are tempted to do something good what does that voice say? "Yes, that's good – do it!" We call this voice our conscience. It can accuse us or defend us. We call this the remnant of the moral Law originally written in Adam and Eve's heart at creation. They knew this Law perfectly and obeyed it perfectly until the fall. Today, because of sin, it is no longer perfect in our hearts, but a remnant remains. **Our conscience is still to be our guide, but it is no longer a perfect guide.** That is why we go back to the Word of God to clear up this blurred writing.

PSALM 14:1 The *fool* says in his heart, *"There is no God."* They are corrupt, their deeds are vile; there is no one who does good. [5]

Let's get a quick definition of a fool. A fool is a person who has the capacity to think, to come to objective conclusions, but refuses to listen to those conclusions. A moron, however, does not have the capacity to think and cannot come to proper conclusions. Now **when God sees someone who says that He does not exist, what does He call him? A fool!** An atheist is a fool. That's a pretty nasty word to get from God, that He should have to call a human being a fool. Kids today quickly call one another a fool, but it's not a compliment when God calls you that.

"It's not a compliment when God calls you a fool"

Nature (Underline "nature" and above it write "Everyone sees") is dynamic proof that there is a God. The conscience (Underline "conscience" and above it write "everyone has"), placed in every human by God, also declares that God exists. We call this the natural knowledge of God; it is there for all. The American Indians, the ancient Egyptians, and heathen throughout the world down through time have been convinced in the reality of God. Only fools (atheists and agnostics) deny the overwhelming evidence (The atheist says there is no God; an agnostic says there may be).

2. **Who is the one true God?**

Behind the word **"God"** write the word **"idol."** This word has many different meanings in Hebrew, some of which are these: "**An empty thing**," "**a non-entity**," "**a terrifying thing**," "**a horrible thing**," "**a shameful thing**," "**a detestable thing**." I like to summarize these various meanings with this little definition: "Good for nothing." You can write that behind the word "idol." So if your idol is yourself, what is it good for? Nothing! If your money is your idol, what is it good for? Nothing! If your husband or wife is your idol, what is he or she good for? Nothing! Wow! I had a woman confess to me in tears one time, "I have made of my husband a god. I have worshiped at his feet for years. It has brought me nothing but anguish and turmoil. I confess to my God that I have sinned." Despite all this idolatry she still lost her husband in divorce. How sad. But she now has found the one true God. And she is happy.

MATTHEW 3:16-17 As soon as *Jesus* was baptized, He went up out of the water. At that moment heaven was opened, and He saw the *Spirit of God* descending like a dove and lighting on Him. And a *voice* from heaven said, "This is My Son, whom I love; with Him I am well pleased."

This is the first time that the three persons of the Trinity are openly manifested. Which person of the Trinity is standing in the water? Jesus, the Son! Which person is speaking audibly from heaven? The Father! Which person is descending in the form of a dove? The Holy Spirit! Let's look at this erasable marker board. Let me write one word: G-O-D. In this one word we have three separate and distinct letters. If we remove just one letter we no longer have GOD. We must have all three letters to have GOD. We have to have all three persons, Father, Son, and Holy Spirit, to have the one true GOD. Further, the "G" is not a "D" or the "D" an "O." This word has three separate letters that make up the one word. Remove just one person and you have an idol, a false God. Or let's put it in the form of a triangle. Let's write GOD in the middle of the triangle. Let's put an "F" on one side for the Father, a "S" on another side for the Son, and a "HS" on the third side for the Holy Spirit. We must have all three sides for a triangle and all three persons to have GOD. **Each person is separate and distinct from the other, yet, together, they form the one true GOD.** They may think, speak, and act by themselves or in concert with each other.

MATTHEW 28:19 Therefore go and make disciples of all nations, baptizing them in the name of the *Father* and of the *Son* and of the *Holy Spirit*.

The three separate and distinct persons are each preceded by the definite article "the." The true God is the Triune God. We believe that all who deny the Trinity automatically place themselves outside of Christendom.

DEUTERONOMY 6:4 Hear, O Israel: The LORD our God, the LORD is *one*.

The true God is one God. The Bible emphatically teaches monotheism (one God) and not polytheism (many gods).

There is only one true God but there are three distinct and separate Persons (Triune, meaning three ("tri") in one ("unus"). The Father made us, the Son redeemed us, and the Holy Spirit brings us to saving faith in Christ (The two well known creeds are the Apostles' Creed and the Nicene Creed which are carried on page 83).

Please make a note here suggesting that students study these two creeds on page 83 at home.

3. **What is God like?**

People who sometimes refer to God as "The Man upstairs" are in for a huge surprise. Some people who glibly say, "I am ready to meet my Maker," have no idea of the inexpressible splendor and glory of the invisible, immortal God. What an immense shock they are in for when they meet God for judgment in the moment of death! What is God like? This is an interesting question. Some times people who don't know me will ask one of our members: "What is Pastor Ginkel (use your name) like?" And then to explain what I am like they will say, "Well, he is tall, good looking, very intelligent, wealthy, and has a charming personality." Ha, ha! Seriously now, sometimes we ask, "What is so and so like?" And then the answer comes, "He or she is like this and this and they are sure not like that!" We want to find out what they are like by a verbal description. That is what we're going to do right now with God. We're going to go to Scripture and say, "God, what are You like?" Notice we're asking God, not a church or denomination or preacher because they can err. We are going to ask, "God, what are You like so that we can better understand You with our little finite minds?" God delights in defining His being! Listen to what Jesus says about God –

JOHN 4:24 God is *spirit*, and His worshipers must worship in spirit and in truth.

Above the word "spirit" write "personal being, without flesh and blood." The exception would be Jesus who assumed flesh and blood to be our Savior. God is not a ghost. **He is a being with entity, reality and personality.**

When God spoke to Moses from the burning bush He was a real personal being with real feelings. Moses got closer and closer. God told him to take the sandals off his feet for the ground he was walking on was holy ground. God told Moses to lead His people out of captivity in Egypt to the Promised Land where they would be His people and where the Messiah would finally be born. Moses gave God a rough time; he didn't want to go, so he offered excuses. God finally said, "Go!" Moses replied again, "But they won't believe me. Who shall I say told me to do this?" And then God, with His patience wearing thin, said, "Moses, you tell My people that I AM WHAT I AM. You say to them I AM has sent you to them." I AM! This is part of what God is like.

JOHN 1:18 No one has ever *seen* God.

That is in this world. Why is that? Let's use an analogy. Have you ever looked into the sun? What did you see? Nothing. How come? It's too bright. The Bible tells us that God dwells in a light that is so bright that if a man in this world did see it he would be consumed instantly. How bright is God? **The sun is a small example of what it is like to see the brightness of God**. On the mount of transfiguration Jesus revealed some of His heavenly glory to the disciples. His face and garment shined with a brilliant light. It was beautiful, and Peter, James, and John didn't want to leave. **Once you see God in heaven you'll never want to leave**.

A Sunday School teacher asked her class to draw a picture from the Bible, any picture they wanted. When she asked one boy what he was drawing he said, "God." So she explained, "But no one has seen Him. We don't know what God looks like." To which the boy replied, "We will when I get done." Well, here on earth it cannot be done. We can see the manifestation of God at times, like when we see sparks, we say, "Look at the electricity." But what we're seeing is only the presence of electricity. Here there are moments when God shows that He is around, but He cannot be seen here. **What a great day awaits us when we enter the sunshine of heaven and see Him!**

PSALM 90:1-2 Lord, You have been our dwelling place throughout all generations. *Before* the mountains were born or You brought forth the earth and the world, *from everlasting to everlasting* You are God.

Underline "from everlasting to everlasting." God had no beginning and will have no end. You had a beginning but will have no end. How long is eternity? This illustration takes a stab at it: Suppose that a bird came to a granite mountain one mile high to whet its beak once every 1,000 years. When that little bird has worn that granite mountain down, then one second of eternity has passed. But eternity is even longer. **No beginning, no end. That's one of the characteristics of God.**

MALACHI 3:6 I the LORD *do not change.*

Do you ever change? Sure. You get smarter, more beautiful with time, promotion after promotion at work. We live in a state of constant change, but not all of it is good. Everything about us is changing – except God who doesn't change. Would you be comfortable with a God who changed? No, because He might change to something you might not like. How wonderful, when you study the Old Testament, that the God described there is the same God who exists today. In fact, we Christians have a hymn we love to sing:

Swift to its close ebbs out life's little day; Earth's joys grow dim, its glories pass away; Change and decay in all around I see; O Thou who changest not, abide with me.

What a comfort that should be to us.

MATTHEW 19:26 With God *all things are possible.*

Who can measure what God can do? He can do anything. There isn't a sinner that He cannot save. He is omnipotent. This characteristic of God makes our minds swim in confusion. The story is told of Martin Luther who was lecturing one day at a university. After class a student came up to him and asked, "Dr. Luther, could God make a rock so big He couldn't lift it?" Luther thought for a long moment and, looking right at the student, said, "Young man, God made hell for people who ask such stupid questions." God's characteristics do amaze us. **Never forget that God can do anything!**

JEREMIAH 23:24 "Can anyone hide in *secret places* so that *I cannot see him?*" declares the LORD. "Do not *I fill heaven and earth?*" declares the LORD.

You can find God everywhere because He is everywhere, except one place. What is it? Yes, hell, and that is the hell of it! He's gone! "Let's do this at night, when it's dark." "Let's pull the shades so no one sees." Is there really such a thing as a secret sin? No. God sees. That's a warning to us when we sin and a comfort to us when we are in need .

PSALM 139:1-4 O LORD, You have *searched me* and You *know me.* **[6]** *You know* when I sit and when I rise; *You perceive my thoughts* from afar. *You discern* my going out and my lying down; *You are familiar* with all my ways. Before a word is on my tongue *You know it completely,* O LORD.

Would you want the class tonight to know all about you, every thought, every deed? No! Your life is an open book to God. He is much more important than this class. Be honest with God tonight. There is no secret sin. Before you go to sleep tonight know that every sin you have committed is known fully by God, even those sins which you do not know are sin, but He does. You cannot hide anything from Him. Tonight be very honest with God. Tell Him the truth. He will love you anyway.

ISAIAH 6:3 *Holy, holy, holy* is the LORD Almighty.

This was the antiphonal singing of the seraphim that Isaiah saw and heard as he looked at God on His Throne in heaven. Holy means sinless, pure, perfect, to hit the mark or bull's eye. It describes the absolute ethical purity of God. He never misses the mark. How different He is from us. The seraphim looked at God and sang holy, holy, holy! So should you. God is perfect in His love for you. He deserves your holy praise. Join the seraphim daily and sing:

> *Holy, holy, holy, though the darkness hide Thee, Though the eye of sinful man*
> *Thy glory may not see; Only Thou art holy - there is none beside Thee*
> *Perfect in power, in love and purity."*

DEUTERONOMY 32:4 He is the <u>Rock</u>, His works are <u>*perfect*</u>, and all His ways are <u>*just*</u>.

Underline the three italicized words. First, God is like a huge rock, for He is **immovable**. Nothing that God does needs to be corrected. Can you think of one mistake He has made? The best of man's works are imperfect, having flaws and defects, but God's works are **perfect**. Behind the word "just" we might write the word "fair." He is **fair** in all His thoughts and deeds. How awesome He is!

EXODUS 34:6-7 The LORD, the LORD, the *compassionate* and *gracious* God, slow to anger, *abounding* in *love* and *faithfulness*, *maintaining love* to thousands, and *forgiving* wickedness, rebellion and sin.

The words "compassionate" and "gracious" mean much the same thing. Above gracious write the words, "undeserved love." How does God show His love to you? The last words tell you, "by forgiving wickedness, rebellion and sin." No greater gift can God give you than the gift of Jesus, for with Jesus He also forgives you all your sins. God would be perfectly just to condemn you and me to hell for our sin, but instead He says, "I love you." He takes His own Son, Jesus, and punishes Him for you on the cross. Truly, you tonight can get from God what you don't deserve. Please don't pray tonight, "God, give me what I deserve." You don't want it. Come and receive God's undeserved love as He forgives you every sin in your life. Little wonder we Christians love to sing, and sing it with me if you know the words:

> *"Amazing grace, how sweet the sound that saved a wretch like me.*
> *I once was lost, but now am found, Was blind, but now I see."*

Please let God love you this way tonight.

1 JOHN 4:8 God is *love*.

Behind "love" write "incomprehensible." Above "love" write the Greek word for love which is αγαπη (agape). The cross of Calvary with Jesus hanging on it for sinners is the final definition of "agape." It is the focal point of God's love which we studied in the previous verse and which will be demonstrated further in every lesson.

ISAIAH 46:8-9 <u>*Remember*</u> this, fix it in mind, take it to heart... <u>*I am God*</u>, and there is <u>*none like Me*</u>.

Underline the italicized words. Remember, mankind, don't forget, keep this ever in your mind: God is what He is, existed before all things, will exist forever, no one is like Him. Stand in awe for who

He is and what He is.

God is a SPIRIT. We cannot see Him. He is FOREVER and the SAME forever. This is wonderful for us. He is ALL-POWERFUL. He can do anything. God is PRESENT EVERYWHERE – a warning to unbelievers and a comfort to believers. He KNOWS ALL things. He knows everything about me. God is HOLY, absolutely pure and without sin. He cannot accept sin. We can come to God only because Jesus takes our sin away and makes us holy. God is PERFECT and RIGHT. God is COMPASSIONATE, GRACIOUS, and FORGIVING. He has patience with those who sin against Him. He shows mercy by forgiving all who ask for it through Jesus. God is LOVE. He loved every human being so much that He gave His only Son to be their Savior. His love for you is higher than the sky, deeper than the sea, and will last forever. There is NO ONE LIKE HIM. What a great God for us to love!

4. How did God make everything?

GENESIS 1:1 In the *beginning* God *created* the heavens and the earth.

"You were made FOR the Lord"

Above the word "beginning" write "the absolute beginning of created things." Above "created" write the Hebrew word "bara" which means to create out of nothing.

GENESIS 1:3 And God said, *"Let there be... and there was..."*

John 1:3 explains who did the creating: "Through Him (Jesus) all things were made; without Him nothing was made that was made." Here we see the divine knowledge and power of Jesus Christ. How did He make the world? Simply by His word. He simply commanded, and it was done.

EXODUS 20:11 In *six days* the LORD *made* the heavens and the earth, the sea, and *all* that is in them.

The word "all" tells us that this included the creation of angels since they are creatures. Above the word "days" write the Hebrew word "yom" which is a twenty-four hour period. Just a simple reading of the text demands the assumption that the world was created in six ordinary days. **God takes full credit for the creation and gives none to evolution.**

COLOSSIANS 1:16 By Him *all things* were created: things in *heaven* and on *earth*, *visible* and *invisible*... all things were created by Him and for Him.

Above the second word "Him" write Jesus. He created everything in heaven and earth, visible and invisible, which includes the angels (We are not told what day they were created on.) Everything was created by Jesus. For whom was everything created? For Him! Everything owes its existence to the infinitely supreme Lord Jesus. **You were made by Him. You were made for Him**. Watch that truth as we continue through this course: You were made **for** the Lord! Be aware of that truth day by day. You have Someone great to live for! That's what you were created for!

GENESIS 2:7 The LORD *God formed the man from the dust* of the ground and *breathed into his nostrils the breath of life*, and the man became a living being.

23

The Lord made man of soil or earth. This defines the beginning of man's life and his end. Man and man alone is the recipient of divine breath and becomes a living person. Divine breath also suggests that man is to live spiritually and in close fellowship with His Creator. This is an honor not bestowed on the other lesser creatures. Man has body and soul, the latter constituting the real person. Remember how Jesus emphasized this? "What shall it profit a man if he shall gain the whole world and lose his own... (what?) soul or what shall a man give in exchange for his... (what?) soul?" **This soul is the real you; your body is the house in which you live. God loves the house (He made it), but He specially loves the "ego," the real person living inside the body – you!**

GENESIS 1:26-27 Then God said, "Let us make man in *our* image, in [7] *our likeness*, and *let them rule* over the fish of the sea and the birds of the air, over the livestock, over all the earth, and over all the creatures that move along the ground." So God created man in *His own image*, in the image of God He created him; male and female He created them.

Underline "us" and "our." This informs us that the three Persons of the Trinity counselled together concerning man's creation. Four clear points are made about man: 1. He was created; he did not evolve, 2. He was made in the image or likeness of God – he was holy, 3. While God does not have sexual identity and function, it was His will that Adam and Eve possess sexuality, and 4. Man was to have sovereignty over the earth. **In verse 27 the word "create" (bara) is used three times and states that man had no previous existence, but was now being called into existence by his Creator. This does away with reincarnation and all types of evolutionary thinking.**

GENESIS 1:31 God saw *all* that He had made, and it was *very good*.

The "all" would include such things as food, drink, sex, etc. On the previous days God called every created thing good, and after the last day of creation God called every thing very good. Even the word "Eden" means pleasantness or delight. There were no imperfections.

God created the world out of nothing by His almighty Word over a period of six natural, consecutive days. This is the *creationist* view. (Two other opinions: *Atheistic evolution* says everything came about without help from a supernatural being, and *theistic evolution* says that a supernatural being aided the process of evolution.) God made everything perfect, including the angels in heaven. The crown of His creation was man. God made people like Himself – holy. He blessed them and gave them full authority to rule the earth.

"Adam and Eve had the power to be faithful to God"

5. How did man fall away from God?

GENESIS 2:16-17 And the LORD God commanded the man, "You are *free to eat* from any tree in the garden; but you *must not eat* from the *tree of the knowledge of good and evil*, for when you eat of it *you will surely die*."

Above the word "free" write the words "free will" (unhampered or uncoerced choice; freedom to choose.) God gave them permission to eat of any tree with a single exception, a single tree. This was to serve as a demonstration of their love. Remember that they had the power to be faithful to God and thereby demonstrate that love (We, today, of ourselves, do not have that power.) The penalty for disobedience was death. It would be a threefold death, and write this down on the bottom of this page: 1. Immediate **spiritual death** (loss of fellowship with God), 2. Eventual

physical death resulting in the separation of body and soul from God, and 3. **Eternal death** in hell, an everlasting separation from God.

GENESIS 3:1-7,9-10 Now the serpent was *more crafty* than any of the wild animals the LORD God had made. He said to the woman, *"Did God really say,* `You must not eat from any tree in the garden'?" The woman said to the serpent, "We may eat fruit from the trees in the garden, but *God did say,* `You must not eat fruit from the tree that is in the middle of the garden, and you must not touch it, or you will die.'" *"You will not surely die,"* the serpent said to the woman. "For God knows that when you eat of it *your eyes will be opened,* and *you will be like God,* knowing *good and evil."* When the woman saw that the fruit of the tree was *good for food and pleasing to the eye,* and also *desirable for gaining wisdom, she* took some and *ate* it. She also gave some to her husband, who was with her, and *he ate* it. Then the *eyes* of both of them *were opened,* and they *realized they were naked*; so they sewed fig leaves together and made *coverings for themselves.* The LORD God called to the man, "Where are you?" He answered, "I heard You in the garden, and *I was afraid* because *I was naked; so I hid."*

The serpent was not a snake, but an upright creature, most cunning and beautiful. Satan, who had sinned and had been cast out of heaven (Revelation 12:9), entered this animal. He said to Eve, "Is it really possible that Someone as good and kind as God would have said you can't eat of the fruit of this tree? You must have misunderstood." Eve repeated what God said, but then added to the command, "You must not touch it or you will die." Satan, whom Jesus called the father of all lies, then brazenly lied, "You will not die... Instead, your eyes will be opened and you will be like God." Eve looked at the tree and saw three things: 1. Fruit **good for food**, 2. Fruit **pleasant to the eye**, and 3. A tree that could **make one wise**. Adam and Eve bit the apple. Some time later Adam and Eve bit the dust. They also knew evil with all of its guilt and shame. How sad that our first parents would rather believe a lie of the devil than the truth of God. When God came into the garden to walk and talk with them they both hid, and man has been hiding from God ever since. Adam confessed that he was afraid. Did he eat of the forbidden tree? Yes. Then he had the audacity to blame God. God should never have given him the woman. God did not even reply to that. Eve tried to blame the devil for her disobedience. What would God do now? We'll see in just a moment.

Adam and Eve had the choice of obeying God or disobeying (free will). God commanded them not to eat from the tree of the knowledge of good and evil. God wanted to see if they loved Him. But they disobeyed God, and they plunged the human race into sin. This is called original sin (Romans 5:12; Psalm 51:5). Sin is rebellion against a loving God and brings sad results: a guilty conscience, a spiritual **[8]** void, and death as God promised. (For information on evil angels read 2 Peter 2:4 and Jude 6.)

"If you want to go to heaven, He is the way. He is the only way!"

6. **How did God plan to win man back again?**

GENESIS 3:15 I will put *enmity* between you and the woman, and between your offspring (or seed, plural) and hers (one great Seed); *He will crush* your head, and *you will strike* His heel.

Here we have the first promise of a Savior who would come to save the fallen human race. Man would be eternally lost unless God intervened. The scene is the Garden of Eden. Adam, Eve, Satan, and God who is speaking to all three and telling what He will do. Above the word "enmity" write the word "warfare." Above the first "you" write "Satan." God is saying that He will bring about a warfare between Satan and the woman, between those who follow Satan and the woman's Seed. By the word "He" write the word "Messiah." The Messiah will crush your head, namely, Satan's head (like a heel grinding the head of a snake into the ground), and you, Satan, will strike His heel. The battle will come to a head when the Messiah wins the victory over Satan on the rugged cross of Calvary. In that great battle on Calvary Satan would mortally wound the Savior. **This promise of a Savior who will rescue the fallen human race will be repeated many times during the next four thousand years.**

• JOHN 3:16 For God *so loved* the world that *He gave* His one and only Son, that whoever *believes* in Him shall *not perish* but *have eternal life.*

Jesus here speaks to Nicodemus. **Above the word "loved" write the word αγαπη (agape). This agape of God is the highest form of love; it is loving the unlovable. It is unconditional love in contrast to our love which is usually very conditional.** For example, how could you sacrifice the life of your own son to save the life of some criminal who just murdered your spouse? But Jesus is the eternal Son of God, His only begotten from all eternity. How could God love sinful and wicked mankind and sacrifice that Son to save them? He could, and He did! No human intelligence can comprehend how God could do this. Notice that God loved the **world**, every single sinner, no matter how bad. Whoever believes in this Son as his Savior from sin will not perish, but will have everlasting life. Notice that the people in the Old Testament had to believe in a Savior to come. We, however, in the New Testament, believe in a Savior who has come. It is just a matter of tense. **Jesus saves! Period.** If you want to go to heaven, He is the way. He is the only way!

God provided a way for mankind to escape the penalty for sin. He promised man a Savior, the woman's Seed, who would pay the penalty for man's sins and crush Satan. Through His sacrifice on the cross Christ saved all people from Satan's tyranny. We know that God loves us. He sent Jesus to suffer and die for us. When we truly believe in Jesus, we will not die but will live with Him forever. This is God's promise to us.

7. How does God care for us today?

JOB 33:4 The Spirit of *God has made me*; the breath of the *Almighty gives me life.*

We must confess with Job that Almighty God has made us. Jean, how old are you? She replies 36. Jean, where were you 37 years ago? She says she didn't exist. Right. Jean, can you take any credit for your creation? No. You were nothing. You were not even a kind thought. You were a zero. You were nothing until God said, "I will make Jean, and I will give her life." Job comforted himself with this thought, and you should, too. God did not make you to be a freak, a failure or a loser. When He finished making you He broke the mold into a thousand pieces and threw it away because He didn't want a duplicate. You are unique and precious. Don't let the devil or anyone else put you down or insult you. **God made you to be a winner and through Jesus you are!** Please think in those terms even when things are not going well.

MATTHEW 10:29-31 Are not two sparrows sold for a penny? Yet not one of them will fall to the ground apart from the will of your Father. And even the *very hairs of your head are all numbered.* So *don't be afraid*; you are *worth more* than many sparrows.

Two sparrows for a penny? That's dirt cheap. But so vast is God's providence that it even includes little creatures like sparrows. Are you not worth more to your heavenly Father than many sparrows? Sure you are. How many hairs do you have on your head tonight? You don't know, but God does. That's how much your heavenly Father cares about you. One of our biggest problems in life is that we put ourselves down or we permit others to put us down. Know tonight that God cares more about you than you care about yourself! **You are SOMEBODY very important to Him. Who says so? Jesus says so.**

1 JOHN 3:1-2 How great is the *love the Father has lavished on us*, that we should be called *children of God*! And that is what we are! The reason the world does not know us is that it did not know Him. Dear friends, <u>*now*</u> *we are children of God.*

Look at the fifth word. What do you think that word is in Greek? Right, agape! There was nothing in us to deserve it. John doesn't say that we're Methodists, or Baptists, or even Lutherans. What does He say God calls us? His children! The world has no conception of what we are. Why is that? Because the world does not know the Father. John does not say that when we get to heaven we'll be God's children. What does he say? Now. Underline that word. Now I'm a child of God! Say that right now out loud with me: **Now I'm a child of God!** Hallelujah! What does hallelujah mean? Praise God! A suggestion: Think less of denominationalism and more of God's family. This is so important. Stop saying you are nothing or a nobody. That's ungodly. **You are a member of God's family by faith in Jesus. Start thinking that way now. Start acting that way now.**

God demonstrates His great love for us today, too. He made us and gives us life. He cares for us daily and gives us only those things which will bless us. His greatest act of love is this – He forgives us all our sins for Jesus' sake, calls us His very own, and will continue to do this in the future.

8.   What can we give God for all His love?

GENESIS 32:10 *I am unworthy* of all the kindness and faithfulness You have shown Your servant.

Have you ever asked yourself: "Why was I born in the United States and not some poor third world country?" Was there anything in and of yourself that merited the favor of God that He should, of the billions of people on earth, place you here? Are you worthy of all the good things God has given you? No. You are not worthy. Jacob prayed the words of Genesis 32:10 only after all of his own schemes and plans were exhausted. Tonight you must confess with Jacob: "God, I am unworthy. I have not been faithful to You, but You have always been faithful to me!" Would You honor God with that confession before you go to sleep tonight? Would you repeat it again to Him tomorrow?

PSALM 118:1 *Give thanks to the LORD*, for He is good; His love **[9]** endures forever.

Every day should be Thanksgiving Day. Why? Because God is so good. For example, every meal should begin by asking God's blessing on what you are about to eat. And when you are finished, you ought to say, "Thank You, Lord. Thank You for this food." Before you go to sleep at night: "Thank You for my life and health and family and friends. Thank You not only for my glad days, but thank You even for my 'bad' days. God, You are so good to me."

1 CORINTHIANS 10:31 So whether you eat or drink or whatever you do, *do it all for the glory of God*.

Why? Because everything is His. A little rule of thumb: "If it can't be done to God's glory, don't do it!" This would include all the big and little things in life. **This week try to be more aware that God made you and everything else so that you would bring glory to Him.**

GALATIANS 6:10 Therefore, as we have opportunity, let us *do good to all people, especially* to those who belong to *the family of believers.*

Pay close attention to this truth: We believers here and all over the world make up one divine family. We are joined together. And we are to demonstrate our Christian faith by doing good to everyone, especially to fellow believers.

MARK 16:15-16 Jesus said to them, *"Go* into all the world and *preach the good news* to all creation. Whoever believes and is baptized will be saved, but whoever does not believe will be condemned."

Not to tell others about God's love in Christ is cold and selfish. On the other hand, one of the nicest ways to show my thankfulness to God is by sharing the Good News of Jesus with others.

We do not deserve to get any of God's blessings. And so we thank God. We live, work, and play to the glory of His name. We tell other people the Good News that God loves them, too. Then, those people can live with Him forever also.

"The demons believe but do not have saving faith"

9. What does it mean to believe in God?

I am going to put on the board three words. I am going to suggest that saving faith has three aspects. Please jot them down on the bottom of this page. 1. **Knowledge**. 2. **Assen**t. 3. **Trust** or the Latin word *fiducia.* The heart of saving faith is *fiducia* or trust. Usually a necessary prelude to trust is knowledge and assent. The Holy Spirit works trust or *fiducia* in our hearts. Let's see how this is demonstrated in the following verses.

JAMES 2:19 You *believe* that there is one God. Good! Even *the demons believe* that – and shudder.

The demons know about God and Jesus' victory over Satan on the cross, but they do not have saving faith. Some people have this kind of faith. It consists of knowledge about Calvary and even intellectual assent to that knowledge. We might call that "head faith." **Saving faith is not simply the assent of the intellect to religious knowledge. It is a personal trust or faith in Jesus as Savior which occurs within man's heart and is the work of the Holy Spirit.**

JOHN 17:3 Now this is eternal life: that they may *know You*, the only *true God*, and *Jesus Christ*, whom You have sent.

To have eternal life you must know the true God, and the way to know that true God is by faith in Jesus Christ as your Savior – know Jesus not only intellectually, but know Him in your heart.

• JOHN 3:36 Whoever *believes in the Son has eternal life*, but whoever rejects the Son will not see life, for God's wrath remains on him.

> Everything depends on each person's relationship to Jesus Christ. Saving faith in Jesus as Savior produces the free gift of eternal life. Unbelief brings God's wrath and everlasting death. God does not know of another way for you to be saved. This verse is suggested for memoriation.

ISAIAH 12:2 Surely *God is my salvation*; I will *trust* (Latin *fiducia*) and not be afraid. The LORD, the LORD, is my strength and my song; He has become my salvation.

> God not only brings salvation, He is salvation! He is Savior! He sent Jesus without any prior commitment on man's part to believe. He just did it. Notice the words, "I will trust." No one can do this for you. Your response to God's gift of Jesus is trust or *fiducia*. It is a simple, child-like trust that says, "Lord Jesus, I believe you."

To believe in God means to KNOW Him and the Son whom He sent. It does not mean to believe in God intellectually, but to ACCEPT in your heart God's Son as Savior for all your sins. And it means to TRUST God completely to save you, for strength, and for everything.

Let's pray together

Almighty and Triune God, Father, Son, and Holy Spirit, we thank You for letting us study these Scripture verses together. You have told us that You are a caring and loving God. If we did not know You we would be worshiping some false god. Thank You for all You've done. You've poured out a thousand blessings upon us. Thank You for sending Jesus to save us from our sins. We are so happy to know that You are eager to forgive us. Thank You for our food, clothing, and shelter. Thank You for this Bible study. Help us tell our friends all about You. Bless us as we study the Bible at home. Bring us all safely together again a week from now. Assist us in bringing a friend along with us. Hear us for Jesus' sake. Amen. **[10]**

Let's sing together

O Lord my God! When I in awesome wonder Consider all the worlds Thy hands have made. I see the stars, I hear the rolling thunder, Thy pow'r throughout the universe displayed. *Refrain:*
Then sings my soul, my Savior God to Thee; How great Thou art, how great Thou art!
Then sings my soul, my Savior God to Thee; How great Thou art, how great Thou art!

And when I think that God, His Son not sparing, Sent Him to die, I scarce can take it in;
That on the Cross, my burden gladly bearing, He bled and died to take away my sin. *Refrain*

Bible reading schedule for the next seven days

❑ 1st day – John 1   ❑ 5th day – John 5
❑ 2nd day – John 2   ❑ 6th day – John 6
❑ 3rd day – John 3   ❑ 7th day – John 7
❑ 4th day – John 4

Worksheet no. 1

1. From what two sources can all men know that there is a God? *Nature* and *conscience*

2. True or *False*: The true God is three Gods: Father, Son, and Holy Spirit.

3. True or *False*: The Father was first, then Jesus, then the Holy Spirit.

4. God is a *Spirit* and no human eye has seen Him. God never had a *beginning* and will have no *end*. God is always the *same*. All things are *possible* with God. He is present everywhere and no one can *hide* from Him. God knows when I *sit* down and *rise* up. My life is an open *book* to Him. He is also holy which means He is *pure, sinless*. He always keeps the *promises* He makes. The greatest way in which He shows His mercy is when **[11]** He *forgives* those who *sin* against Him. God truly *loves* me and sent His *Son* to be my *Savior* .

5. a. The Bible says God made the world. Evolution says *it developed by itself*

   _____

   b. The Bible says God created all things in six days. Evolution says *it took millions of years*

   _____

   c. The Bible says God made man and gave him a rational soul. Evolution says *man is a highly developed animal without a soul*

6. Mention three ways in which God cares for you. List the best way last.

   a. *Gives me food, clothes, shelter*

   b. *Gives me health, family, friends*

   c. *Forgives me my sins for the sake of Jesus, my Savior*

7. What is sin? *The transgression of God's Law, rebellion against Him*

8. Write the Bible reference containing the first promise of a Savior. *Genesis 3:15*

9. How did God plan to win men back to Himself? *He would send His only Son to die on the cross for the sins of all men*

10. True or *False*: God cares for us because He feels sorry for us.

11. True or *False*: The way to be saved is to believe in God.

12. What can you give God for all His love for you? *Myself, body and soul, everything I am and everything I hope to be*

[12]

et's bow our heads for prayer: Almighty God, You have given us divine Law which we call the Ten Commandments. Give us grace tonight as we study these Commandments and as they describe our duties to You and to our fellow men. Please send the Holy Spirit into our minds and hearts so that we may better understand these Commandments and how You want us to live. Give us grace to tell You that we are sorry where we have sinned. Help us understand that we cannot be saved by the Law. Forgive us our many sins because of Jesus' suffering and death upon the cross. Fill us all with true love for You and true love for our fellow man. Give us such a love for You that we will hold these Commandments before our eyes in the days ahead so that we will, out of love, try to be more obedient. We ask this in the name of Jesus, our Savior. Amen.

A minister had just assumed his duties as new pastor at a certain church. The first Sunday morning He decided he would visit some of the Sunday School classes. He entered the first room while the lesson was in progress and heard the teacher ask one boy, "Who broke down the walls of Jericho?" "Not me, sir," said the boy. The minister turned to the teacher and asked in unbelief, "Did you hear what he said?" The teacher answered, "Yes, and if he said he didn't do it, I believe him. I really don't think he did it."

Distressed, the minister sought out the chairman of the Board of Education and explained what had happened. "I'm appalled," said the pastor. "Why, I've known both the teacher and the boy for years," said the chairman, "and I believe that if the boy said he didn't do it, he really didn't do it." By this time the minister was heartsick. At the next congregational meeting he reported this experience to those present, explaining that he thought they really had a serious problem. Thereupon the Chairman of the Board of Maintenance arose and said, "Mr. President, I make a motion that we simply pay for the damages and charge it to upkeep!"

That is the kind of Bible knowledge that we have in too many congregations today by members and even by official boards and chairpersons. If they were to take a test on the very basics of Christian doctrine they would fail miserably. This is not only true of all denominations in general, it would even include many Lutheran congregations.

The Lesson tonight is going shake us up. It's a rough and difficult Lesson. All the other lessons that follow are predicated on this particular Lesson. About 90 percent of this Lesson will be divine Law. We will have a bit of Gospel at the end so that you still know that God loves you. Next week we'll reverse it – most of that Lesson will be Gospel.

Lesson 2

I HAVE GOOD NEWS FOR YOU

About A Bible Which Guides and Frees You

1. What is the Bible?

1 PETER 1:10 Concerning this salvation, the _prophets_, who *spoke of the grace that was to come* to you, searched intently and with the greatest care.

> **The Old Testament covers about 4,000 years. The New Testament era covers about 2,000 years. Now let's establish the time frame of the prophets' writing. To the left of 1 Peter 1:10 write: "O.T. 1,500 B.C. to 400 B.C."** Underline "prophets" and "grace." Above the word "prophet" write "announcer" or "declarer." These men were divinely inspired to communicate God's will and many times disclosed future events, although sometimes they spoke about present and even past events. They were men chosen by God to be His mouthpiece. They announced or declared the "grace" that was to come. In just one word, what do you think that "grace" was? Yes, Jesus or as

He was called in the Old Testament, the Messiah! Here we learn an important truth: In the Old Testament the prophets' primary message was Jesus.

When I was a child I thought that the Old Testament was Law and the New Testament was Gospel. This is what the average church member would think. But now Peter says, "Wrong!" The Old Testament prophets talked primarily of the grace of God, the undeserved love of God which would be manifested in the giving of His Son. And folks, **when you go from Genesis 3:15 to the end of Malachi the common thread and subject is Jesus, Jesus, Jesus.** It's fantastic! And one more important thought: In the Old Testament there was only one way to be saved and that was to believe in the Jesus to come. They were not saved by keeping the Ten Commandments. We in the New Testament believe in a Savior who HAS come. It's just a matter of tenses. They looked forward. We look backward. Only Jesus saves!

2 PETER 1:21 For prophecy never had its origin in the will of man, but *men spoke* from God *as they were carried along* by the Holy Spirit.*

The Bible was written by ordinary men like Moses, Isaiah, Job, Malachi, but they were men who were "carried along" by the Holy Spirit. This Greek verb for "carried" was used in Bible times with reference to ships carried along on the sea by the wind. We believe that the holy writers were moved by the Holy Spirit to write what they put down. Moses, for example, was not present at the creation of the world, so the Holy Spirit had to tell him what to write. And so with Isaiah and all the Old Testament writers; the Holy Spirit moved them to write what they wrote. That means a great deal to me. When I open my Bible to Proverbs, Psalms, Isaiah, or any Old Testament book, I have the assurance that the Holy Spirit is the true author. He wrote through the pens of these men. I can believe every word.

2 TIMOTHY 3:16 *All* Scripture is *God-breathed*.

Underline "all" and "God-breathed." We believe that all of the Bible is God-breathed. It is absolutely incomparable – there is no other book in the world like it. Nothing in the Bible was put there by the will of man. God was the author, the writers were only His instruments. **We believe that the Bible is God's inerrant and infallible Word historically and prophetically.** Most churches and pastors do not subscribe to this. Over 70% of American clergy deny that this Book is God-breathed.

One day Jesus said that the Bible is inspired even to the smallest letter in the Greek alphabet, the letter "I" or iota. Jesus teaches that everything in the Bible is God-breathed, even this small Greek letter iota. I believe "The Bible **is** God's Word." If you asked clergymen in America over 70% of them would say, "No, the Bible only **contains** the Word of God." Class, if the Bible only contains God's Word, then what does it also contain? Other things, myths, untruths. Frequently these pastors speak of demythologizing the Bible, that is, taking the myths out. They say, for example, that the story of Jonah and the whale is a myth and so is the story of creation or the virgin birth. They say it was only made up. I say, "Oh, no! This is true; it was written by the Holy Spirit." God says so!

JOHN 17:17 Sanctify them by the truth; Your *word is truth*.

Jesus prayed this prayer to His Father the night before His death. He was praying for all believers who were to come down through time. "Father, sanctify them." That means, "make them holy by the truth, Your Word is truth." **I believe that the Bible is the veritable truth of God.** Truth is, among other things, the total absence of error. Is our local newspaper the total absence of error? Hardly. Believe Jesus tonight and the prayer He prayed, "Father, make My followers holy not by the church, not by the clergy, but by the truth of Your holy Word." Jesus also told us that if we continue in His Word we would know the truth and the truth would set us free.

PSALM 119:105 Your word is a *lamp* to my feet and a *light* for my path.

The picture here is one of total darkness and you are trying to walk. What is going to happen? Sooner or later you will run into something and maybe get hurt. That is a picture of man by nature as he walks through life. Take a few steps, fall down. Get up, a few more steps, get hurt again. This is a picture of our lives at times. We need a light, and the kind in this ceiling won't work. The psalmist says that God's Word is like a lamp. The perfect spiritual lamp for you is the Bible. One of the things we're going to learn in this course is how to better use the Bible for our daily living so we don't get hurt so much.

JOHN 20:30-31 Jesus did *many other miraculous signs* in the presence of His disciples, which are not recorded in this book. But *these are* **[13]** *written that <u>you may believe</u>* that Jesus is the Christ, the Son of God, and that *by believing <u>you may have life</u>* in His name.

Underline "you may believe" and "you may have life." John says that the Bible was written so that you may learn how to live a good moral life. Do you buy that? A lot of people do. They say, "This Book is here to show me how to live." Wrong! Some people say this Book is basically a history book. Wrong! It is partially history and tells you how to live, but that is not its primary purpose. The primary purpose of your Bible is that you may come to saving faith in Jesus and have eternal life. Some day you're going to die. God doesn't want you to die eternally. He wants you to have life, and that is the purpose of this Book – that you have eternal life through Jesus.

REVELATION 22:18-19 I warn everyone who hears the words of the prophecy of this book: If anyone *adds anything* to them, God will add to him the plagues described in this book. And if anyone *takes words away* from this book of prophecy, God will take away from him his share in the tree of life and in the holy city, which are described in this book.

While this warning by Jesus applies particularly to Revelation, it applies to all the Bible. If anyone adds to Revelation, Jesus promises that God will give to him some of the plagues described in this Book. If anyone takes away from Revelation, God will take his name out of the book of life. **In effect God is saying, "Don't play; don't tamper. You can tamper with your newspaper, you can play with your magazines, but leave Revelation (or for that matter all the Bible) as it is."**

The Greek words for "the Bible" (Το βιβλιον – write this on marker board and have students write it in their books) mean "the Book; it's above all others. Testament means will or agreement. Men called prophets wrote the 39 books of the Old Testament in Hebrew at the direction of the Holy Spirit. Their message centered on God's grace, the promise of a Messiah. The 27 books of the New Testament were written by the apostles and evangelists after Christ's death. All of the Bible is inspired or "God-breathed." It is wholly true. It is like a brilliant light to light up the path that leads to heaven. Not everything Jesus did is in the Bible, but what is there is there so you may have life in His name. God warns people not to add anything to or take anything away from it.

Before we take question 2, I want to make a bold statement: **The vast majority of clergy do not know the difference between Law and Gospel.** Let me illustrate. When you attend a funeral you will discover if the preacher knows the Biblical difference between the Law and the Gospel. Have you ever attended a funeral like this: The pastor is in the pulpit and aunt Mildred is lying in a casket there in the church? The pastor says, "We know that aunt Mildred is now in heaven. She was a kind and gracious woman." Everyone nods their heads yes, she surely was. He says, "She was loving, merciful, and kind hearted. She couldn't even kill a fly without breaking down in tears." And the congregation says, "Yes, yes." He continues, "She lived a good life, lived according to the Golden Rule." The people say, "Oh, yes, yes." And he says, "Now she is in heaven." And they say, "Yes." Anyone here ever hear a funeral sermon something like that? Sure. Now I am going to say that preacher does not know the difference between Law and Gospel. We're going to learn tonight that man is confused about the two, and the results will be devastating for him and those who agree with him. **He is telling the people a lie, and the people are believing a lie on the most important issue of all – life and death.**

All of the Bible can be divided into one of two categories: Law or Gospel. Martin Luther once said that the person who can differentiate between Law and Gospel and apply the same to life deserves the degree: Doctor of Divinity. His point is well taken. Not many people know the difference. Tonight you will learn and understand and you will be happy because of it. It will have a profound effect on your life even tonight.

2. What are the two great messages of the Bible?

LEVITICUS 19:2 _Be holy_ because I, the LORD your God, am holy.

Underline "Be holy." This is a Law passage. God is not saying, "Please be holy. If you are in the mood. If the sun is out." What is He saying? "BE holy!" He is telling you what to be, namely, holy like Him. **Law passages tell you what to do or not do or how to be, holy. But there is another distinguishing feature about a Law verse: The activity is always on the part of man.**

EXODUS 20:3FF You _shall..._ You _shall not..._

The Greek word for Law is νομοσ. It even sounds like a hard, difficult word. And it is. Each Commandment begins with a solemn "You shall" or "You shall not." The commandments do not begin with "please." God does not say that there will be some exceptions to Commandments 3, 5, and 8 on sunny days. Instead you are subject to the Law on sunny and cloudy days, whether you like it or don't like it. That's why they are called Commandments, not Suggestions.

1 JOHN 4:9 This is how _God showed His love_ among us: _He sent_ His one and only Son into the world that we might _live_ through Him.

Underline "God showed His love" and "He sent" and "live." This is Gospel. It is just the opposite of what the Law is. In the Law the activity is on the part of man. In the Gospel the activity is on the part of God. What did God do? He showed His love. He doesn't tell us to do a thing. The Gospel tells how God showed His love. He sent His only Son that we might what? Live through Him. The Law says that if we do not obey, we will die. Is that good news or bad? That's bad. We will die now and forever in hell. That is horrible news. But when the Gospel gets through with us we have good news. We do not end up in hell, but if we believe we end up in heaven. The Law will always finally bring sinful man death. Do this or else! In the Gospel God says, "I give you life."

JOHN 3:16 For _God so loved the world_ that _He gave_ _His one and only Son_, that whoever _believes in Him_ shall not perish but _have eternal life._

Jesus is speaking here to Nicodemus. He was a Pharisee who thought that to get to heaven you had to keep the Law. What great news Jesus has for him. Underline "God so loved the world" and "He gave" and "have eternal life." Do you think this is a Law or Gospel passage? Yes, it is Gospel. Is it good news or bad? Good news. Is the activity on the part of God or man? God. If you believe in Jesus as your Savior, does it end up with bad news for you or good news? Good. Does it end with you being in hell or in heaven? Heaven. Most pastors and church people do not understand these simple differences between Law and Gospel.

ROMANS 1:16 I am not ashamed of the Gospel, because it is the _power of God for the salvation_ of everyone who believes.

Above the word "power" write the word "dynamite." This comes from the Greek word δυναμισ from which we get the English word dynamite. The Gospel is the dynamite of God to salvation. Is this Law or Gospel? Gospel! Good news or bad? Good!

The Law and Gospel are the two great messages of the Bible. The Law is the holy will of God in which He tells us how to be, holy, and what we are to do and not to do. In the Law the activity is on the part of man. In the Gospel the activity is on the part of God. It is the Good News that Jesus is our Savior. The Law shows us our sins, condemns us, and pronounces death. The Gospel shows us a Savior and gives us life.

Can you see how the preacher who said aunt Mildred was in heaven because of the good life she lived did not understand Law and Gospel? He was really preaching a Law sermon, and people don't get to heaven by the Law. He preached an untruth to the people, and sadly, the people were more than ready to believe it. How very sad. We'll now take a peak at each of the Commandments. Note that not all churches number the Commandments the same way. I like the way they are numbered here. **The first three Commandments will deal with you and your relationship to God. The last seven Commandments will deal with you and your relationship to your fellow men.**

3. How does the Law guide us? First Commandment [14]

EXODUS 20:3 **You shall have no other gods before Me.**

MATTHEW 22:37-38 Jesus replied: "'_Love the Lord_ your God with _all your heart_ and with _all your soul_ and with _all your mind.'_ This is the first and greatest commandment."

Is this passage Law or Gospel? Law. Is there anyone here who believes they have loved God perfectly? I'm glad no hands went up. Every once in awhile a nice little old lady will put her hand up and in a pious way say, "Well, I think I have." Really, Matilda, have you really loved God (αγαπη, a perfect love) with **all your heart** (the seat of your personality) and **all your soul** (your very being itself) and **all your mind** (your thinking and activity)?" You say, who puts it that way? Only God. Unless there is perfect loving obedience there is sin. Here we've taken just the first verse which explains the First Commandment and we find that we've broken it.

ISAIAH 42:8 _I am the LORD_; that is My name! I will not give _My glory to another_ or _My praise to idols._

God is a jealous God. He will not share the glory that belongs to Him with anyone else. He will not share His glory with the Virgin Mary, with a spouse, with children, with money, with yourself or whatever it may be. Before we become Christians, who do you think gets most of the glory and praise and honor? The individual. This command counteracts the propensity of people everywhere to attribute to man that which belongs to God alone.

JOHN 5:22-23 The Father has entrusted all judgment to the Son, *that all may honor the Son just as they honor the Father*. He who *does not honor the Son does not honor the Father*, who sent Him.

To disregard or in any way ignore the Son is fatal. I know that some of you here sometime in your life did not give honor to Jesus as you did the Father. **There are a lot of religious people today who speak of the "loving Father in heaven" or "the Supreme Architect of the Universe" or whatever other name they use and who never mention the name of Jesus. That is sin. That is idolatry.**

EPHESIANS 5:5 For of this you can be sure: *No immoral, impure or greedy* person – *such a man is an idolater* – has any inheritance in the Kingdom of Christ and of God.

Have you ever been immoral, impure, or greedy? Yes. What does God call immoral, impure, or greedy people? Idolaters. This passage condemns all of us. If we have to get into heaven by being perfect we'll never make it. Obviously this is a Law passage.

PSALM 33:8 Let all the earth *fear the LORD*; let all the people of the world *revere Him*.

"Fear the Lord" means stand in awe of Him for who He is and what He has done. Have you always stood in awe of God and revered Him as you should? No. This is sin.

PROVERBS 23:26 My son, *give Me your heart* and let your eyes *keep to My ways*.

"My son, give me your money." "Give me your car." "Give me your brain." "Give me an hour on Sunday morning." Is that what God wants from you? No, keep those things for now. God says that He wants your heart. He wants you. Does He have your heart right now?

This is the foremost commandment. God forbids worship of any idols, money, job, home, family, saints or statues. God insists that He occupy first place in our lives and that we make a full commitment to Him. We are to love, trust, and believe in Him more than anyone or anything else.

Second Commandment

EXODUS 20:7 **You shall not misuse the name of the LORD your God**.

This Commandment was taken so seriously by Israel at one time that the scribes wouldn't even write the name *Yahweh (Jehovah)* until they had first taken a bath and changed their clothes. Then after they had written it, they would take another bath and change their clothes again. It's a different story today. Today we misuse God's name by hypocrisy, by making a profession of His name but not living up to the profession, by breaking promises to God, by cursing and swearing, by using

God's name lightly or carelessly. Where does this profane impulse come from? Why say, "Jesus," "God," "damn," and "hell." Why not the names of politicians, entertainers, or athletes? You say, "Big deal. Why should God mind so much?" Let me ask you something: Do you mind if someone misuses your name? Sure you do. To misuse your name is to misuse you. Your name stands for you. You take on your name. Likewise with God. I met a man not long ago, and he was swearing, and I said, "Oh, you know the Lord, too, don't you?" He gave me that look like, "I can't believe this."

EXODUS 20:7 The Lord will not hold anyone *guiltless* who *misuses His name.*

If you misuse God's name, He is going to hold you guilty. How many of us have used God's name in vain? All of us. You can see that by the Law we are doomed, because we're not perfect. Judges and courts will not put you on trial and find you guilty for misusing God's name. **The sinner himself may think that to misuse God's name will bring no harm, but God here promises that He will be the avenger of those that take His name in vain.** In the Old Testament using God's name in vain was punishable by death. If this command were still in force, how many of you would be alive tonight? I'm afraid we would have mass funerals. That is how serious God is about this whole matter.

JAMES 3:9-10 With the tongue *we praise our Lord* and Father, and with it *we curse men*, who have been made in God's likeness. Out of the same mouth come *praise and cursing*. My brothers, this should not be.

"To praise God is the exalted function of the human tongue"

To praise God is the exalted function of the human tongue. **The tongue blesses God and then curses man and imagines it can do both. What is the brain behind the tongue thinking? It's not!** God is deeply offended and we should be, too. We curse human beings who were made in God's likeness. This is not right! This simply should not be! Some time ago I had a boy mow my lawn. Before he started I pointed out five nice tomato plants near the house, suggesting that he be careful. I love tomatoes. After he finished mowing and had left I happened to walk around the house, and he had mowed all five plants down to the level of the grass. I confess that I had to really work at saying, "God bless that little rascal!" Do you work at controlling your tongue?

LEVITICUS 19:12 *Do not swear falsely* by My name and so *profane* the name of your God.

Taking an oath is not forbidden, such as in court, but taking a false oath is. When I was ordained into the ministry I took an oath that I would teach and proclaim the Bible and only the Bible. A false oath, however, profanes the name of God and we sin.

LEVITICUS 19:31 Do not turn to *mediums* or seek out *spiritists*, for you will be *defiled* by them. I am the LORD your God.

Above "mediums" write "fortune tellers" and above "spiritists" write "those who talk to the dead." You will be defiled by them. Fortune telling and people who say they can talk to the dead are still big business in the world today, including our own country.

PSALM 50:15 *Call upon Me* in the day of trouble; I will deliver you, and *you will honor Me.*

The first time I drove on the Dan Ryan Freeway in Chicago I prayed, "Oh, God, You better help me or else I'm coming Home to meet You real soon!" What is the first thing you should do when you have trouble? Why not cry to the Lord? Pray! God promises to answer, and God asks you to then honor Him for it. I think we fail in this last part. How many times hasn't God delivered us, but we then failed to honor Him? Remember the ten lepers who were cleansed? What a terrible disease. Only one of the ten came back to thank Jesus. Let's be like that one man on a daily basis.

PSALM 103:1 *Praise the LORD*, O my soul; *all my inmost being*, praise [15] His holy name.

To bless the Lord is to delight Him with genuine heartfelt praise and thanksgiving. Underline "all my inmost being." That means to praise God with all our being, totally, with all our heart, with our emotions, our will, and our understanding.

God's name is holy. He forbids using it carelessly. Cursing is asking for God's wrath on some person or object. Swearing is using His name to assert truthfulness to something you said or did. Thoughtless expressions such as "oh, my god," "good heavens," "by gosh," etc., are also sinful. Witchcraft, lying, or deceiving by His name are forbidden. We should believe, confess, and spread His name and call on Him in prayer and praise.

Third Commandment

EXODUS 20:8 **Remember the Sabbath day by keeping it holy**.

Above "sabbath" write "rest." This was the seventh day in the Old Testament. It began on Friday night at 6:00 and went to 6:00 Saturday night. No work was to be done by the men or the women during this period. All work for the next day had to be completed beforehand. This command was imposed only on Israel. This is the only one of the Ten Commandments that has been abrogated or set aside. In the following passages we'll see what God tells us to do.

COLOSSIANS 2:16-17 *Do not let anyone judge* you by what you eat or drink, or with regard to a religious festival, a New Moon celebration or a Sabbath day. *These are a* *shadow* of the *things* that were *to come; the reality,* however, *is* found in *Christ*.

Underline all the italicized words. Look at the first words. Don't let your preacher judge you, your church judge you, other people judge you about what you eat or drink. I know of churches that say you can't wear this and you can't drink that and you can't eat this and you can't use makeup on your face and on and on. Paul says don't let anyone judge you. In the Old Testament God made judgments. He gave many rules and set many parameters, all kinds of ceremonial laws. But those Old Testament laws were pointing forward to Someone to come. They were a shadow of things to come. Who was it? Christ! Let's imagine that this noon it is sunny. I'm standing outside on the lawn facing south, and I'm looking straight down at my feet. John, here, is south of me about twenty feet. Slowly he walks up to me. What do I see creeping up on the grass? John's shadow. As he gets closer his shadow gets bigger and bigger and finally, what do I see? I see John. What has happened to his shadow? It's gone. Why? Because John has arrived. **Paul says, "Can't you see that all of these Old Testament laws were only shadows of that great God-Man, Jesus? When He comes these shadows are gone, done away with. Let no man say that you have to keep these laws anymore."** Our friends who are Seventh Day Adventists, and God bless you if there are any of you here, say, "Oh, no, we have to keep the Sabbath!" Paul says no. Jesus has come. The shadow is gone. Christian friend, don't let anyone judge you.

ACTS 2:42 They (the 3,000 new believers) *devoted* themselves to the *apostles' teaching* and to the *fellowship*, to the *breaking of bread* and to *prayer*.

This is a brief description of the religious life of the first Christian congregation in Jerusalem following Pentecost. They did not "play" church. They did not simply attend church for one hour a week. They devoted themselves to the daily teaching of the apostles. Tonight in this class we are endeavoring to do this very same thing. The new believers and the apostles were in close fellowship. There was no fighting, no division of any kind. They broke bread together which means they ate together and the meal was concluded with the celebration of the Lord's Supper. And to "prayer." This word was usually used to designate a worship service and not merely praying. They studied together, they fellow shipped together, they ate together, they worshiped together, and they took Communion together! We must be devoted to this today.

JOHN 8:47 He who *belongs* to God *hears* what God says. The reason you *do not hear* is that you *do not belong* to God.

Underline the italicized words. Here is a simple observation by the Lord. He directed these words to some unbelieving Jews. **The Greek verb for "hears" is used in reference to an inward hearing in the heart, hearing which perceives and believes.** Think back to a time in your life when you didn't really listen to God, you really didn't hear God. What does Jesus say of you at that time? You didn't really belong to God. You can go to church every Sunday and sit in that pew and go through all the right motions and you could just as well have been back home in bed sleeping. Tonight may be the first time that some of us have really listened to God's Word in a long time.

LUKE 11:28 Jesus replied, *"Blessed* rather are those who *hear* the word of God and *obey* it."

Let's underline three words: "Blessed," "hear," and "obey." Above blessed write happy. We're going to be happy if we hear the Word and then do what it tells us.

HEBREWS 13:17 *Obey* your leaders and *submit* to their authority. They keep watch over you as men who must give an account. Obey them so that *their work will be a joy, not a burden*, for that would be of no advantage to you.

Above the word "leaders" write "spiritual." For those of you without a pastor, be sure that you exercise great care in whom you select. If you choose a poor doctor, at worst, you might die. If you choose a poor pastor, you might die eternally. The first key word is **obey.** You can see why it is so important to have a pastor who teaches only what God says. Then you are to **submit** to their authority. How blessed it is if we have a preacher we can obey and submit to. Underline the word **joy** and **not a burden**. Do you make your pastor's work joy or grief?

The early Christians chose Sunday as their special day of worship because Jesus rose from the dead on this day and because God began the creation of the world on Sunday. We break this commandment by not coming to church at all, by coming irregularly, by not listening, by not believing, or not doing what the Word tells us to do. God promises a special joy to all who study and obey His Word and to those who obey and follow their spiritual leader, their pastor.

Fourth Commandment

EXODUS 20:12 **Honor your father and your mother, so that you may live long in the land the LORD your God is giving you.**

EPHESIANS 6:1-4 Children, obey your parents in the Lord, (Why? Well, here's the answer!) for *this is* **[16]** *right. "Honor your father and mother"* – which is the first commandment with a promise – "that it may go well with you and that you may enjoy long life on the earth." Fathers, *do not exasperate* your children; instead, bring them up in the *training and instruction of the Lord.*

Above the word "obey" write: "Teach them." **Children need to be taught obedience**. They frequently need to be "deprogrammed." You as parents are stand-ins for God. "Honor your father and mother." How long? Till you're eighteen? No, as long as you live. Parents are not to exasperate their children, but train them and bring them up in the Lord. Listen – boys and girls need to be taught what the Lord expects of them. If you don't teach them the devil will.

ROMANS 13:1-2 Everyone must *submit himself to the governing authorities*, for there is no authority except that which God has established. The authorities that exist have been established by God. Consequently, *he who rebels against the authority is rebelling against what God has instituted*, and those who do so will bring judgment on themselves.

The Fourth Commandment applies to anyone over us, at home, in school, at work, and, in this case, the government. It matters not what form of government is in authority. Anarchy is not God's will. An example: Pharaoh in Egypt was as hardened a ruler as any, yet God expected obedience.

1 PETER 2:18-19 Slaves, *submit yourselves to your masters* with all respect, not only to those who are good and considerate, but also to those who are harsh. For it is commendable if a man *bears up under the pain of unjust suffering because he is conscious of God.*

Today we might write "employees" above the word "slaves." Whether our employers are good and considerate or whether they are harsh, submit and be obedient. This is God's will.

ACTS 5:29 We *must obey God* rather than men!

The Sanhedrin, the Jewish high court, had commanded the apostles not to teach about Jesus, adding that they would be killed if they did. This is Peter's response. There is one situation in which we are to disobey parents, a boss, the government, a pastor – and that is when they tell us to do something contrary to God's will.

God puts people over us in the home, school, state, and church. We are to honor them by obeying, serving, and loving them. This is pleasing to God. This is the only commandment with a special promise of blessing such as long life.

Fifth Commandment

EXODUS 20:13 **You shall not murder.**

GENESIS 9:6 Whoever sheds the blood of man, *by man shall his blood be shed;* for in the image of God has God made man.

> **What is God's observation and conclusion on capital punishment? He commands it.** A man's life is the most precious earthly thing he has. In our country we've made human life cheap, and that is a sin!

ROMANS 13:4 He (the government) is *God's servant* to do you good. But if you do wrong, be afraid, for he does not bear the sword for nothing. *He is God's servant*, an agent of wrath *to bring punishment on the wrongdoer.*

> Twice Paul calls the government a servant of God. One of the functions of government is to punish those who do wrong. As Christians in a free country, we should encourage our government to punish those who do evil, in fact, we should insist on it.

ROMANS 12:19 *Do not take revenge*, my friends, but *leave room for God's wrath*, for it is written: *"It is Mine to avenge; I will repay,"* says the Lord.

> One problem with our giving out vengeance is that we either give too much or not enough. Another problem is that it is not our responsibility. We are incompetent. A hand more perfect than ours will mete out full vengeance and that is the hand of God. Let God take care of vengeance.

1 JOHN 3:15 Anyone who *hates his brother is a murderer*, and you know that no murderer has eternal life in him.

> John here speaks of murder just by hating. This is not a crime in the eyes of the world, but it is murder in the eyes of God. Such a person is without eternal life and will be damned by God. A Tokyo company recently began offering a mail order curse kit, featuring a straw doll to represent the hexee, along with eight accessories, including nails, a curse manual and a curse blocking doll to ward off return curses. The company at first marketed it to boys and girls bullied at school, but discovered the major market is women who hope to put spells on neighbors, in-laws and husbands. Among the hints in the manual is this: "It is important to specify the kind of misfortune you wish upon the victim... It is important to imagine the unhappy scenes." God says that they, too, are murderers and will be lost eternally. Now let's learn what we should do instead.

EPHESIANS 4:32 Be _kind_ and _compassionate_ to one another, _forgiving_ each other, just as in Christ God forgave you.

> Underline "kind," "compassionate," and "forgiving." Paul here shows what Christian forgiveness is. Christian forgiveness simply forgives immediately. If I hold the wrong against the person I sin against God. **I must forgive whether the person repents or not, whether he asks my forgiveness or not.** I instantly forgive him. He must face God with the wrong he has done. And what is my motivation? Well, how often must God forgive me in just one day? Many, many times.

God is the giver of life and reserves the right to take it. A person's most valuable earthly possession is his life. God forbids us to hurt our neighbor in any way – physically or emotionally. We should never take **[17]** revenge. We should take care of our minds and bodies and do the same for others.

Sixth Commandment

EXODUS 20:14 **You shall not commit adultery**.

I remember a couple of years ago I was teaching this Lesson. There was a nice little Baptist girl sitting in front of me in this class. She was finally convinced that she had committed murder in having hatred toward others, and she looked at me in an odd way when we read Exodus 20:14 on adultery. I ask her what she was thinking, and she replied, "Well at least I haven't committed adultery." I said, "Ma'am, hang on. You are in for a big surprise." At that her friend who was sitting next to her poked her in the ribs and laughed. Let's find out how we fare here. Marriage usually begins with engagement and too often ends in divorce. I remind you of Mary and Joseph who were engaged, and they were already called husband and wife. They were already married in God's sight, but the marriage had not yet been consummated.

MATTHEW 19:6 So they are no longer *two*, but *one*. Therefore what *God has joined* together, *let man not separate*.

We believe that marriage is a divine institution, that it is holy, and that it was designed and devised by our Creator. When two people come together they are no longer two but one; it is to be for life.

MATTHEW 19:9 I tell you that anyone who *divorces his wife*, except for marital unfaithfulness, and marries another woman *commits adultery*.

The reasons given for divorce today are almost without number. Many reasons are simply put under the umbrella of incompatibility, but this is not Scriptural. Unfaithfulness is one Biblical reason for divorce. Invariably when there is divorce sin has been involved. Let me say a word to any of you who have been divorced and feel guilty. Tell God about your sin. You contributed to the breakdown of your marriage to a greater or lesser extent. There is hope for you, and that hope is found in Jesus who died on the cross for this sin. You might want to write down a Bible reference: 2 Corinthians 5:17. This is a beautiful word for the person who has gone through divorce and still feels guilt. This verse reads: "Therefore, if anyone is in Christ, he is a **new creation**; the **old has gone**, the new has come!" With the sin of divorce there is only one thing to do and that is to come to Jesus for forgiveness. Won't you come to Jesus with any sin that has caused discord in your marriage and let Jesus make you clean and new?

1 CORINTHIANS 7:15 If the *unbeliever leaves*, let him do so. A *believing* man or woman *is not bound* in such circumstances.

This verse speaks of malicious desertion. The marriage is ended in this case, and the believing spouse who did not leave is no longer bound. There are, then, two grounds for divorce: adultery and malicious desertion. Death can also bring a marriage to an end.

EPHESIANS 5:24-25 As the *church submits* to Christ, so also *wives* should *submit to their husbands* in everything. *Husbands, love your wives*, just *as Christ loved the church* and gave Himself up for her.

The Church subjects herself to Jesus voluntarily and joyfully. That is how Christian wives are to submit to their husbands, not because of law, but because of love. Now for the men. How much did Christ love the church? So much that He came down from heaven and served us and died for us. That is the kind of love husbands are to have for their wives. They would even die for their wives, so complete is their love. Just as the Church is not fearful in submitting to Jesus, so a wife is not to be fearful in submitting to such a husband. Just as Christ tenderly loves the church and takes care of it, so the husband who loves the Lord will love and take care of his wife. This is a beautiful, loving relationship. This is God's prescription for happiness in a marriage. If you follow it, you'll have it, and if you don't follow it, you won't have it. You'll have a lot of sadness and tears.

MATTHEW 15:19 *Out of the heart come* evil thoughts, murder, adultery, sexual immorality, theft, false testimony, slander.

By nature you have a bad heart. By nature you are in need of a heart transplant. Your need is for a new spiritual heart. You know your old heart is bad. Ever so often you stop and ask yourself, "How could I possibly think or say or do some of the things that I think, say, or do?" Have you ever asked that? You have a bad heart, a sinful heart. You ask, "How long will I have to put up with this?" Only till the day you die. Until then, the struggle will continue.

MATTHEW 5:28 I tell you that *anyone who looks at a woman lustfully* has *already committed adultery with her in his heart.*

The same is true of a woman who has lust for another man. I have known of some people who said to themselves, "I have already thought it my heart so now I may as well go ahead and commit the sin." Wrong. Just the lust in the heart is sin. To act on that thought is the second sin. It would be best to stop at the thought.

1 CORINTHIANS 6:18-20 He who *sins sexually sins against his own body.* Do you not know that your <u>body</u> *is a* <u>temple</u> of the Holy Spirit, who is in you, whom you have received from God? <u>You are not your own</u>; you were bought at a price. Therefore *honor God with your body.*

Underline "body" and "temple." Also underline "You are not your own." I hear people say, "I can do whatever I want to do. It's my body!" Wrong. You cannot do whatever you want. You never have, you never will. If you are an unbeliever you belong to the devil, and you do what he wants. And if you belong to God you'll do what He wants. In either case you are not your own. We all have a master. As a Christian you were bought at a very high price, the death of Jesus Christ on the cross.

Marriage is an ordinance of God for the happiness, procreation, and morality of the human family. Marriage is for life and is entered into by engagement. Adultery and malicious desertion are the only Biblical grounds for divorce. God wants our lives and actions to be pure. Bible study, prayer, hard work and play, avoiding certain people and places help us stay pure.

Seventh Commandment

EXODUS 20:15 **You shall not steal.**

LEVITICUS 19:35 Do not use *dishonest standards* when measuring *length, weight* or *quantity.*

"Imagine what would happen to lazy people if we no longer gave them food"

Above "dishonest standards" write "cheating is a sin." We are to be honest in our business dealings.

JEREMIAH 22:13 Woe to him (King Jehoiachin) who builds his palace *by unrighteousness,* his upper rooms *by injustice*, making his countrymen *work for nothing*, not paying them for their labor.

This simply means woe be to the employer who does not pay a decent and fair salary to his employees. Failure to do so is stealing in God's sight.

2 THESSALONIANS 3:10 If a man *will not work*, he *shall not eat*.

This is God's prescription for the lazy person. **Imagine what would happen to lazy people if we no longer gave them food. How long do you think it would take before they would change?** It would take me only a few hours. This also means that parents ought to teach their children to work at home.

1 PETER 4:10 Each one should use whatever *gift he has received to* [18] *serve others,* faithfully administering *God's grace* in its various forms.

Above "Each one" write your first name. Above the words "serve others" write the word "steward." In Peter's day the steward was often a slave. He was responsible for managing the household business and property and provided for the needs of all members of the family. God has given to each of you various gifts that you are to use to serve the members of His family.

Owning property is a God-given right; to some He gives more and to others less. But man does not really own – God owns and man owes. Man is a steward (manager) of God's possessions loaned to him. Employers are to pay their employees good salaries. Employees are to do their best work in return. We should use our possessions for our own, our neighbor's, and God's good.

Eighth Commandment

EXODUS 20:16 **You shall not give false testimony against your neighbor.**

PROVERBS 19:5 A *false witness* will not go unpunished, and he who pours out *lies* will not go free.

God forbids all lying, whether it be in a court of law or not. Lying is a despicable sin. God promises to punish the liar.

PROVERBS 11:13 A *gossip betrays a confidence,* but a *trustworthy* man *keeps a secret.*

A gossip reveals secrets. A trustworthy person can keep a secret. Which are you? Aren't you grateful that God doesn't tell others all that He knows about you? **If you want to be godly, try to be as discreet as He is.**

ZECHARIAH 8:17 *"Do not plot evil* against your neighbor, and do not love to *swear falsely.* I hate all this," declares the LORD.

Just thinking evil about someone is sin and so is false swearing. God is blunt in saying that He hates it; you should, too.

44

PROVERBS 31:8-9 *Speak up for those who cannot speak* for themselves, for the rights of all who are destitute. *Speak up* and *judge fairly; defend the rights* of the poor and needy.

> Underline "speak up," "judge fairly," and "defend the rights." Many people need your help in these areas. This might take place at work or in your neighborhood or concerning the unborn and abortion.

A person's name and reputation are very important and can quickly be destroyed by lies and gossip. Once hurtful words are spoken, they cannot be retracted. Three tests for speaking about someone might be: 1. Is it true? 2. Is it needful? 3. Is it kind?

Ninth and Tenth Commandments

"Lusting will not get you what you want"

EXODUS 20:17 **You shall not covet your neighbor's house. You shall not covet your neighbor's wife, or his manservant or maidservant, his ox or donkey, or anything that belongs to your neighbor**.

> Above the word "covet" write "to desire or long after," usually something not lawfully yours. It's basis lies in discontentment with what one has.

JAMES 4:2 You *want something* but don't get it. You *kill and covet*, but you cannot have *what you want*. You *quarrel and fight*. You do not have, because *you do not ask God*.

> James says that coveting will not get you what you want. Turmoil exists inside you because of it. Try to be content. If you want something, ask God in prayer.

PSALM 37:4 *Delight yourself in the LORD* and *He will give you the desires of your heart*.

> What a marvelous promise from God. We like to sing about that in this little song:
>
> *Seek ye first the Kingdom of God, And His righteousness.*
> *And all these things shall be added unto you! Allelu, alleluia!*

It is not wrong to want to get ahead, but it is sin to wish to have something at some one else's expense. Covetousness is the base desire for what one does not have and which has its basis in discontentment with what one has. **[19]**

4. How does the Law condemn us?

• MATTHEW 5:48 *Be perfect*, therefore, *as* your heavenly Father is perfect.

> One big problem we have is that people compare themselves to people. How often have you not compared yourself to people who are inferior to you. This makes you look good. Jesus does not compare you to another person, but to your heavenly Father. Perfect means completely, pure, holy. Sons of God must be like their Father. Unfortunately, we cannot reach the goal, only strive.

JAMES 2:10 For whoever keeps the whole law and yet *stumbles at just one point* is *guilty of breaking all of it*.

What does this verse say to the most pious person on earth? You are still a sinner! Let's imagine that Diana here would keep all of the Ten Commandments, but would break one only one little bit. What has she done? Broken them all. Why? Because the Ten Commandments are not really ten, but what? One! Please know that no one could possibly keep any of the Commandments perfectly.

• PSALM 14:3 *All have turned aside*, they have *together become corrupt*; there is *no one who does good*, not even one.

Human depravity is stated here in the most emphatic terms. Everyone has left the path of righteousness. Everyone is filled with spiritual corruption. There is no one who does good in the sight of a holy God, not even one! This, by nature, is your true spiritual condition this evening.

ROMANS 3:20 No one will be *declared righteous* in His sight by *observing the law*; rather, through the law we become *conscious of sin*.

No one, no matter how pious and good they may be, will be declared holy by their actions before the bar of divine justice. Instead, as we stand in front of the Law we stand condemned. Yet, there is a benefit coming from the Law. What is it? We become conscious of our sin. The Law is like a mirror. In the morning Joe here gets up and stands in front of his bathroom mirror. The sight is not a pretty one. He says, "Mirror, mirror on the wall. Who is the fairest of them all?" And then it shatters into a million pieces. The Law, like a mirror, shows us our sin.

• ROMANS 6:23 For the *wages of sin* is *death*.

After death write three words: Physical, spiritual, and eternal. When you go to your doctor, you want to know the truth. Let me, as your spiritual doctor, tell you the truth about your condition this evening. You are contaminated with sin. Your sin pays wages. What are the wages? Death! You are going to die physically, and you will be eternally separated from God. Not good news, is it?

How many of God's laws must we obey to get into heaven? Not 65%, not 99%, but 100% – perfection! We have failed the entrance exam! Only a brief look at the commandments quickly shows that we have broken each of them (this is actual sin in contrast to original sin which we inherit). Beside sins of commission, we also sin when we should have done something and did nothing (sins of omission). As the bathroom mirror reveals how we look when rising early in the morning, so the perfect mirror of God's Law shows us as we are spiritually, sinners, with the sentence of physical and eternal death upon us.

Would you like to hear some really Good News before you go home tonight? Okay!

5. How does the Gospel free us?

ROMANS 10:4   Christ is the *end of the law* so that there may be *righteousness* for everyone who *believes*.

Above the word "end" write "termination." Now let's put the word "man" on the marker board. Above man we'll write the word "Law." Above Law we'll write the word "God." Man is under God's Law and condemned. Now we'll put a cross under man. God sent Jesus down from heaven as the God-Man.

> God placed all our sins on Jesus and sent Him to the cross. There He was charged with all our sin. He died in our place. He went to hell in our place. So that we could be what, class? Free. We are free from the condemnation of the Law because Jesus took the condemnation for us. You are free from your sins right now even if you don't believe it, but it won't do you any good because you have refused it. You will never get the benefit until you believe.

GALATIANS 3:13 Christ *redeemed us from the curse* of the law by becoming a curse for us.

> Above "redeemed" write the words "bought back." It means to pay a price, like the payment of a ransom. The price Jesus paid was His life, blood, and death. On the cross He was cursed as you should have been cursed forever in hell. The curse would have crushed you forever in hell; instead, it crushed Jesus. Class, is this verse good news or bad? Good! Is the activity on the part of God or of man? God! Is your final destination heaven or hell. Heaven!

GALATIANS 3:21-22 Is the Law, therefore, opposed to the promises of God? Absolutely not! For if a law had been given that could impart life, then righteousness would certainly have come by the law. But the Scripture declares that the whole world is a prisoner of sin, so that *what was promised*, being *given* through *faith* in Jesus Christ, might be *given* to those who *believe.*

> Underline the italicized words. Notice that righteousness was promised, then **GIVEN**, through faith, and again **GIVEN** to those who believe. Do these words in any way suggest that we can earn our way to heaven? Absolutely not! Salvation is given to the sinner; it's a **GIFT**; and it's received by faith. Do you really believe in Jesus as your Savior tonight? He is waiting. Please don't put this off. If you are having any kind of a problem about believing in Jesus as your Savior, please see me so that we can take care of it.

The Good News is that Jesus took our place under the curse of the Law and has freed us from our sins and from eternal death. He paid the penalty for our sins. He kept all the demands of the Law which were upon us. Now we are free, forgiven, and redeemed. You may receive this GIFT right now. Confess your sins to Him. Believe in Jesus in your heart right now, just as you are. Jesus will come into your heart and life and the promised gift WILL be your very own. This [20] is His promise.

Let's pray together

Lord God, our Father, we praise You for the gift of Your holy Word, the Bible! Surely it is the Book of books in which we find an honest description of our utter depravity, our inability to save ourselves, and the marvelous message of the sacrifice of Your only Son, Jesus Christ, on the Cross. Bless our study of the Book in this study group, in church, and in our homes. Help us to erect the family altar in our homes so that we may feed daily upon this satisfying bread of life and may live. For Jesus' sake hear our prayer, forgive us our sins and short-comings, help us to bring our friends to You, and lead us on a closer walk with You this week. Amen.

Let's sing together

Break Thou the bread of life, Dear Lord, to me, As Thou dids't break the loaves Beside the sea; Beyond the sacred page I seek Thee, Lord, My spirit pants for Thee, O living Word.

Bless Thou the truth, dear Lord, To me, to me, As Thou dids't bless the bread By Galilee; Then shall all bondage cease, All fetters fall; And I shall find my peace, My all in all.

O send Thy Spirit, Lord, Now unto me That He may touch my eyes, And make me see:
Show me the truth concealed Within Thy Word, And in Thy Book revealed I see the Lord.

Bible reading schedule for the next seven days

❏ 1st day – John 8   ❏ 3rd day – John 10   ❏ 5th day – John 12
❏ 2nd day – John 9   ❏ 4th day – John 11   ❏ 6th day – John 13
                                                            ❏ 7th day – John 14

Worksheet no. 2

1. The Bible (   ) contains the Word of God, (   ) is the Word of God and men, (✖) is the Word of God.

2. True or _False_: The main reason why the Bible was written is that it may show us how to live.

3. True or _False_: The main theme of the Bible is that God is kind, gentle, and good. **[21]**

4. The _Law_ brings us to a knowledge of our sins. The _Gospel_ brings us to a knowledge of our Savior.

5. There are _39_ books in the Old Testament and _27_ books in the New Testament for a total of _66_ books. The Old Testament was written in the _Hebrew_ language by men called

   prophets, and the New Testament was written in the _Greek_ language by men called _apostles_ and _evangelists_. In the original the words, "The Bible," really mean _The Book_. The word "testament" means _will or agreement_.

6. True or _False_: We can prove to anyone that the Bible is true.

7. Name several religious groups which sin against the message of John 5:23 and state why: _Unitarians, Mormans, Christian Scientist – because they remove Jesus as their Savior._

8. The early Christians chose Sunday as their special day of worship because (   ) it was usually a sunny day, (   ) God commanded it, (✖) Christ rose from the dead on this day.

9. True or _False_: I have never committed adultery or murder.

10. "Mirror, mirror on the wall. Who is the fairest of them all?" What does the mirror of God's Law tell you? _That I am a sinner and have broken God's Law._

11. _True_ or False: God's Law says that all have sinned and that the wages of sin is death, physical and eternal.

12. What must you do to become a Christian? _Confess my sins to the Lord Jesus and believe in Him as my personal Savior._

13. _True_ or False: Even after one becomes a Christian, he can and will sin.

14. What two messages should you share to bring a person to Christ? _The Law and the Gospel._

15. _True_ or False: From the Gospel I know for certain that I am forgiven of all my sin. If I die tonight, I will go to heaven for sure. **[22]**

As we begin Lesson 3 let's fold our hands for prayer: Dear Lord Jesus, You are the blessed Savior of all men. I believe that I am a sinner. If I had to get to heaven on the basis of my good living I would never make it. You came to save sinners like me. Thank You Lord! For the sake of your suffering, death, and resurrection forgive me all my sins. You have promised that where two or three are gathered in Your name, You are present. Help me and my friends who are here with me to understand more precisely who You are, why You came to earth, and what You accomplished. Above all, bless my faith in You that it will be real, genuine, sweet, and strong. I want You as my Savior. I want to go to heaven some day to live there with You forever. I ask this in Your wonderful name. Amen.

The Lesson this evening is the most important one in this course. The heart and core of Biblical Christianity is Jesus Christ. Everything centers on Jesus. I am sure that all of you have some knowledge of Jesus. You know some things about Jesus. And that is fine. This, however, is not my major concern – how much you know. There is something more critical than your knowledge and that is your personal faith in Jesus as your Savior.

There was a time in my life when I knew quite a bit about Jesus, but I didn't really know Jesus. It is like knowing a lot about some person and yet not knowing them. One night, as a senior in high school, about three months before graduation, I really got to know Jesus as my personal Savior.

Some of you this evening have saving faith in Christ. Some of you may think you have saving faith in Christ, but you will discover tonight or at the next lesson that you didn't really have the genuine article. You will have to make that discovery – I can't make it for you. Some of you may have a strong faith in Jesus, and some of you may have a very weak faith – either way you have a faith that saves.

If you do not have saving faith, you are in need of a second birthday. You had your first birth, but in John 3 **Jesus clearly says that you need a second birth.** He says, "You must be born again. Unless you are born again, You will never see the Kingdom of God." You can take all your confirmation classes, all your Methodism, all your Presbyterianism, all your Lutheranism, or whatever it is that you have, and you can go straight to hell with it. I believe that there will be plenty of people in hell because they hung on to their denomination and played church. The devil delights in that. It is imperative that you have a second birth. Perhaps you already have it. Then it will be good for you to really know that. If you have never really had the second birth, then it's vital that you discover that.

Everything that we are going to study in Lessons 4 - 10 and everything that has to do with your life in this world and in the world to come hangs in the balance on what you do with this Lesson and with Jesus. You must know that nothing can be more important than this. Now we're ready to start.

Lesson 3

I HAVE GOOD NEWS FOR YOU

About A Savior Who Saves You

1. **What are some important promises of a coming Savior?**

You remember that last week we spoke about the prophets who wrote the Old Testament. Their central message was the Messiah who **would** come. The New Testament speaks about a Messiah who **has** come. Question 1 is asking, "What are some of the promises given by the prophets in the Old Testament concerning the Savior who was to come?" We're going to look at just a few of them.

MICAH 5:2 But you, _Bethlehem_ Ephrathah, though you are small among the clans of Judah, out of you will come for Me One who will be _Ruler_ over Israel.

Underline "Bethlehem" and "Ruler." Micah wrote between 750 to 700 B.C., about same time as Isaiah. Micah foretells which town the Messiah will be born in over 700 years before the birth. It will be the tiny town of Bethlehem. Bethlehem had nothing going for itself; it was small, insignificant. It would be the last place you would expect God's Son would be born. Its only reputation was that it was David's town. That is all the notoriety it had. The Messiah would come from David's seed, yet He would be David's Lord. It is interesting to see how God picks such an insignificant town for Jesus' birth. If the choice were ours, we would say, "Let the Child be born in Jerusalem, the capital of Judah, the royal city." God is not impressed with the grandeur of this world. He is not impressed with false pride. **Above Bethlehem write "house of bread." This is interesting because Jesus said that He was the Bread of Life**. Ephrathah was a broad region around Jerusalem, but this name was applied to the town itself. **Ephrathah means fruit region**. Under "Ruler" you can note that Jesus will be the Head of spiritual Israel or the one true Church.

This verse helps us test others who claim to be the Messiah. Down through time people have claimed to be the promised Messiah. There is only one problem: they do not meet the very first test; they haven't been born where? In Bethlehem. Oh, yes, I want to ask you: Is this a Law verse or a Gospel verse? Gospel. Why is it Gospel? Because it's good news. Because the activity is on the part of God. Because it brings us life and heaven.

ISAIAH 7:14 The _virgin_ will be with Child and will give birth to a Son, and will call Him _Immanuel_.

Underline "virgin" and "Immanuel." In Isaiah's day the word "virgin" meant a girl, unmarried, and a virgin. Isaiah wrote these words over 700 years before Jesus' birth. He foretold that God's Son would not come normally, but abnormally. He would be conceived and born of a virgin. You should know that over 70% of American clergy deny the virgin birth of Jesus. What do you suppose Pastor Ginkel (use your name) believes? The virgin birth. God here gave the Messiah a beautiful name, Immanuel. Next to Immanuel write this three word definition: "God with us." When the shepherds came and saw the Baby Jesus on Christmas night they could look at Him and say, "He is God with us." **When, in your mind's eye, you see Jesus dying on the cross you can say, "Yes, there is Immanuel. There is God for us, for me!"**

Last week we studied the Law and God said do this, and this, and this, and you didn't do it. Tonight God tells you that He is still for you. Last week you saw the justice side of God. Now you see the other side of God, a side full of mercy and love. In Jesus God is on your side. Some time after His birth some wise men came and found Jesus and knelt down to worship Him. I'll let you in on a secret: wise people still find Jesus and bow down before Him. Fools don't. If you will be a wise man or a wise woman you will seek until you find Him and then adore Him as your Savior. The Lord promises, "If you seek Me, you will find Me." The very fact that you are here this evening seeking tells me that you are going to find Him. That is a promise from the Lord. I commend you for being here tonight and being a wise person. I'm happy for you.

ISAIAH 9:6 For to us a _Child_ is born, to us a _Son_ is given, and the government will be on His shoulders. And He will be called _Wonderful_ Counselor, Mighty God, Everlasting Father, Prince of Peace.

50

Underline "Child" and "Son." **"The government will be on His shoulders"** means that Jesus will bear on His shoulders the burden of ruling the Church and the world. Underline "Wonderful." He comes as a little Child. He will be a **Wonderful Counselor**. When is a counselor needed? A counselor is needed when there is conflict, such as in a marriage or with labor and management. He brings two warring factions back together. Who are the warring parties that Jesus has come to bring back together? Man and God. We have been separated from God because of sin and He from us. Try as He may, God knew of no other way to bring peace between us and Himself. He would send His own Son down to the cross to hang between heaven and earth to bring earth and heaven back together. Jesus came to bring you back to the Father. He is that Counselor. He says, "Please let me bring the Father to you and you to the Father." You would have to be insane to say, "Oh, no, I don't want to be with my heavenly Father in this world. I don't want to be with Him when I die. I want to be away from God." Jesus is also called **mighty God**. He is **Everlasting Father** which means He is like a Father to us. He is **Prince of Peace** – not between nations but between God and man. All these names describe the Messiah and His work.

As we read the next verse, underline all the italicized words.

ISAIAH 53:5-6 But He *was pierced* for our transgressions, He *was crushed* for our iniquities; the *punishment* that brought us peace was upon Him, and by *His wounds* we are healed. We all, like sheep, have gone astray, each of us has turned to his own way; and the *LORD has laid on Him the iniquity of us all*. [23]

Look at the third word. What is the tense of the verb? Past tense. Go back to Isaiah 9:6 and look at the sixth word. What is the tense of the verb? Present tense. And in Isaiah 7:14 what is the tense of the verb? Future tense. So Isaiah goes from future, to present, to past tense. As far as Isaiah is concerned in Chapter 53, the Messiah has already come, suffered, and died for our sins. You must understand that when a prophecy is given by God, even though it will take place in the future, it is as good as done; it is history. Notice that Jesus was our substitute, He for us.

How many sins have you committed so far in your life? Thousands upon thousands. How many people have lived so far in human history? Over twenty billion people have lived so far. Take these thousands upon thousands of sins which each person has committed and multiply that by twenty billion. It was this huge, unbelievable number of sins which we cannot even calculate in our minds which our Father picked up and placed upon Jesus. That is why no mere man could be our savior. The Bible says that if you go to hell to be punished for your sins, it will take – how long? Forever and ever and ever! There was only one Person who could do this impossible thing – Jesus, the Son of God. **I don't know of many people who would lay down their lives physically to save your life. I don't know of anyone who would be willing to go to hell for you – except Jesus.**

From Genesis 3:15 on through the Old Testament the single, common thread is the infinite love of God for mankind in Christ. Over 300 Old Testament verses clearly promise that the Savior is coming and His task: the redemption of the whole human race from sin. Even the names given Him, such as Immanuel, meaning "God with us," show His mission and purpose.

"But you, O Bethlehem... from you shall come forth for me, one who is to rule..." Micah 5:2

2. **What is significant about Jesus' birth and early life?**

LUKE 1:28,31,32,34,35,37   The angel went to Mary and said, "Greetings, you who are highly favored! The Lord is with you... *You will be with Child* and give birth to a Son, and you are to give Him the name *Jesus*. He will be great and will be called the Son of the Most High..." *"How will this be,"* Mary asked the angel, *"since I am a virgin?"* The angel answered, "The *Holy Spirit will come upon you* and the power of the Most High will overshadow you. So the *holy One* to be born will be *called the Son of God...* For *nothing is impossible* with God."

Look at the fifth word, Mary. She was about fifteen or sixteen years old. Girls in that day were really young ladies for their age. They were usually quite mature. It becomes obvious that Mary was very mature spiritually. She must have been beautiful inside and out. It is this woman that God chooses to be the earthly mother of Jesus. "You are highly favored," says the angel. Bewildered, she asks, "How can this be?" You can tell that she was not promiscuous. She knows the facts of life and so the question. The angel tells her that the Holy Spirit will cause her to have the Child. He will be the Son of God.

Then notice the last words, "For nothing is impossible with God." I just wonder what our clergy friends in America who deny the virgin birth of Jesus do with a verse like this. All I can say is that if you do not believe in the virgin birth, you have got to have a very tiny, dismal, dinky God. I confess that the God I have is not dinky. He is omnipotent and omniscient. He occupies all things. He is all in all. He is the God of miracles. Do you want a God of miracles in your life or some small God that you can look at and comprehend with your little mind? You need a God you can stand in awe of, a God whom you can worship and bow down before. This is what Mary did.

Can you imagine Joseph stopping by to visit Mary, and she says, "Joseph, sit down. I have to tell you something. I am expecting a baby. Now don't get upset. It's not what you think, because it was God who made me pregnant." Can you imagine Joseph's reaction? What do you suppose Joseph would think? He wouldn't buy it. Here you can see again how much God cares about little human beings like Joseph and you and me. God appreciates the "predicament" Mary is in. He appreciates the predicament Joseph is in. In His love He sends one of the thousands of holy angels who await His beck-and-call to Joseph. And so we read the following words. Please underline the italicized words as we come to them.

MATTHEW 1:20-23 An angel of the Lord appeared to him in a dream and said, "Joseph son of David, do not be afraid to take Mary home as your wife, because what is conceived in her is *from the Holy Spirit*. She will give birth to a Son, and you are to give Him the name *Jesus,* because He will *save His people from their sins.*" All this took place to *fulfill what the Lord had said* through the prophet: "The *virgin* will be with Child and will give birth to a Son, and they will call Him *Immanuel*" – which means, "God with us."

We assume that this angel was Gabriel, the same one that appeared to Mary. Like Mary, Joseph was also a descendant of David. The choice of the Child's name is not left to Joseph. Joseph is under a far higher Father. God the Father attends to the important task of giving the name. God names His Son Iησουσ, Jesus. Look at the last words of that sentence and tell me what Jesus means. Savior from sin. What does that mean? Listen closely. **To save people from their sins is to separate the sinner from his sins.** They can no longer damn him. Only Jesus can save you from your sins. You can sense God's love for Joseph, for all people, for you this evening. Jesus has separated you from your sins!

LUKE 2:6,7,10-12,16,21,40,49,52 While they were in *Bethlehem*, the time came for the Baby to be born, and she gave birth to her firstborn, a Son. She wrapped Him in cloths and placed Him in a manger, because there was no room for them in the inn... The angel said to the shepherds, "Do not be afraid. I bring you *good news of*

"Why did they name the Baby a swear word?"

great joy that will be *for all the people*. Today in the *town of David* a Savior has been born to you; He is *Christ the Lord*. This will be a *sign* to you: You will find a Baby *wrapped in cloths* and *lying in a manger*"... So *they hurried off* and *found* Mary and Joseph, and *the Baby*, who was lying in the manger... On the eighth day, when it was time to circumcise Him, *He was named Jesus* (The giving of the name was connected to circumcision. Circumcision was a part of Ceremonial Law. Jesus put Himself under the Law so that He might keep all the requirements of the Law in order to redeem us who are under the Law and cannot fulfill it.)... And the Child *grew* and became *strong*; He was *filled with wisdom* (The Savior grew up physically in a normal way except for sin. He grew physically and mentally and in wisdom. As God He knew all things. As Man He grew and acquired wisdom. We cannot fathom the mystery of this development in Jesus.), and the *grace of God was upon Him*... "Why were you searching for Me?" He asked. "Didn't you know I had to be in My Father's house?" (Jesus is twelve years old. Mary and Joseph thought Jesus was returning home with friends and relatives, but a search shows He was missing. They return to Jerusalem and look everywhere. Finally, exhausted and perhaps frustrated, they find their Son in the Temple listening to and asking questions of the teachers. Jesus cannot understand the action of Mary and Joseph. He does not scold them, but He is surprised. "Why were you searching for Me?" This question implies surprise at finding His parents so ignorant. So at twelve Jesus knew that God was His Father in a very unique way.)... And Jesus *grew* in *wisdom* and *stature*, **[24]** and in *favor with God* and *men* (At twelve years of age He KEPT GROWING in wisdom. He must have grown into a rather strong and impressive figure. He was not the pale and anemic Christ some people think. The last words say He grew in favor with God and men, standing in high favor with both.)

A woman had the opportunity to tell the Christmas story to a little boy who had never heard it before. She told how Jesus was conceived in Mary, the journey to Jerusalem, the birth of Jesus in a stable, and of how the angels sang and the shepherds came and found the Baby Jesus lying in the manger. The boy listened to her with wide-eyed amazement. When she finished he said, "That is a beautiful story, but I have a question. Why did they name the Baby a swear word?" How sad.

But listen to this little poem that says there still may be hope. It's entitled "A Christmas Thought" by Madeline Welch:

I used to tell my children A great big fairy tale About a guy named Santa Claus
Who came through snow and hail. He had a velvet red suit And a sleigh with 8 reindeer,
And brought us lots of presents At Christmas every year.

Then I became a Christian And found a better way. I told them the true story
Of our glorious Christmas Day: There was a little Baby Born to be our King,
They named the Baby Jesus, And He gives us everything.

We celebrate His Birthday Now each Christmas Day,
And we have no need for fairy tales For He is the True Way!

Jesus will change your Christmases. He'll change your Mondays and your Fridays and your mornings and your evenings. He is everything. That first Christmas Eve God was wrapping up His Gift, His Son, with special wrappings. The wrappings were the manger, the shepherds, the animals, the inn, the town, and Mary and Joseph. But too many times I see people on Christmas Eve getting all wrapped up in the wrappings and not really getting to the Gift – the Lord Jesus!

When my four sons were at home as children, I never saw them at Christmas time take off the wrappings, keep the wrappings, and throw away the gift. It would be a weird kid who did that. But I see people doing that in the church. They come to a beautiful Christmas Eve Candlelight Service. They look at the wrappings, and it moves them to tears. Every Christmas Eve the entire world, even unbelievers, stop and ask, "What's going on?" Do you know? You'll never know until you believe in Christ Jesus as your personal Savior. Then the Gift will be yours.

MATTHEW 2:13-15 An angel of the Lord appeared to Joseph in a dream. "Get up," he said, "take the Child and His mother and escape to Egypt. Stay there until I tell you, for Herod is going to *search for the Child to kill Him.*" So he got up, took the Child and His mother during the night and left for Egypt, where he stayed until the death of Herod. And so was *fulfilled what the Lord had said through the prophet:* "Out of Egypt I called My Son."

God honors Joseph as the foster father of Jesus. The care of the Child Jesus is in Joseph's hands. Joseph is to move his little family to a distant, foreign land for safety. While Bethlehem is asleep, in the dark of night, Joseph quickly leaves with Mary and the Child. We doubt that he told anyone they were leaving or where they were going. Herod could have found out and followed. Joseph is to stay in Egypt with the Child until the angel himself tells him when to come back. The Baby Jesus is barely born and what are His enemies trying to do? Kill Him. And class, they keep it up, until they finally succeed. Many hundreds of male babies were ruthlessly slaughtered by Herod in order to get Jesus. Why did Herod do it? Because he was threatened by Jesus. Herod wanted to kill Him. What will you do with Jesus tonight? Right now you have the power, as God gives you the Holy Spirit, to believe in Jesus as your Savior. I pray that you will do that.

By a miracle of the Holy Spirit the eternal Son of God received a body in the virgin Mary. His name, Jesus, means "Savior." Christ means "the Anointed One." He was anointed to be our Prophet (Teacher – Matthew 17:5), our Priest (who would sacrifice Himself on the Cross – Hebrews 7:26-27), and our King (who would rule His Church and the world – Philippians 2:10-11). Everything about Jesus clearly points to His role as man's Savior from sin, Satan, and eternal death. Following His appearance in the Temple at age twelve nothing is said of our Lord until He is thirty. He goes to the Jordan river where John is preaching and baptizing. He is baptized, chooses twelve disciples, lives a life of poverty, travels and preaches constantly, performs innumerable miracles, and proves Himself to be God's Son and the Savior of the world. Some believe in Him, but many others reject Him, and his enemies plot His death.

3. **What two natures are united in Christ?**

I am going to put on the marker board a circle and let that represent Christ. Let's draw a horizontal line through it at the middle. In the top half we'll put a "D" and let that stand for His divinity. In the bottom half we'll put an "H" and let that stand for His humanity. We have only one Lord, but there are two natures within.

1 TIMOTHY 2:5-6 There is one God and one *Mediator between* God and men, the *man* Christ Jesus, who gave Himself as a ransom for all men.

We said a few moments ago that God and man were at war. A mediator is a middleman or go-between. God sent His Son down on Christmas night when He took on humanity. **Jesus was both God and Man. He had to be God in order to be able to affect so great a salvation. He had to be Man in order to take our place under the Law and suffer and die in our stead.**

We want to be careful, however, that we do not divide Jesus as I have done in this circle. He cannot be divided. I like to use the illustration of taking a piece of iron and placing it in hot coals so that the iron is red hot. Now there are two properties. We have the iron and throughout the iron we have the intense heat intimately intermingled. So **Jesus' divinity was intimately intermingled with His humanity.** Jesus frequently covered or hid His divinity while on earth except on certain occasions such as on the Mount of Transfiguration. There He let Peter, James, and John take a peek at how glorious and beautiful He really was. The next verse tells what they heard.

MATTHEW 17:5 A voice from the cloud said, *"This is My Son*, whom I love; with Him I am well pleased. Listen to Him!"

> Underline "This is My Son." There are people in and out of the church who do not believe that Jesus is truly the divine Son of God. Who are they in disagreement with? God the Father. Jesus was always God's Son. He had no beginning. He is still God's Son after the incarnation. If God the Father says this about Jesus, isn't it time that we say it, too?

1 JOHN 5:20 We know also that the *Son of God* has come... Jesus Christ. He is the *true God* and eternal life.

> Here the divinity of Jesus is ascertained again. Jesus is God. We, today, confess and believe that.

Christ was both God and Man. He had to be man so that He might take our place under the Law and that He might be able to suffer and die in our stead. He had to be true God so that He could keep the Law perfectly and that His suffering and death would be sufficient and complete.

"I give myself to Jesus because nobody has loved me like that. No one else can – but Jesus!"

4. How did Christ suffer and die?

JOHN 10:18 No one takes My life from Me, but *I lay it down of My own accord.*

> Those last italicized words are critical. There are some people who say that Jesus died because He could not escape His enemies. Wrong! Some say that Jesus just got caught up in a terrible trap. Wrong! Look at those last words again, and you tell me why He died. Because He wanted to. And He wanted to die for who? You! It was a willing death. He wasn't forced to do this by His Father.
>
> **When this was discussed in eternity by the Trinity, the Lord willingly said, "I will go."** That's how much Jesus loves you. With such a love for you tonight, how can you possible say, "But, Lord, I just don't want to trust You. I just don't want to honor You. I just don't want to glorify You." Such a love, you see, demands a quick and positive response. We sing about that in one hymn: *"Love so amazing, so divine, demands my soul, my life, my all."* And in another hymn:
>
> > *"Oh, the height of Jesus' love, Higher than the heavens above,*
> > *Deeper than the depths of sea, Lasting to eternity.*
> > *Love that found me – wondrous thought – Found me when I sought Him not."*
>
> **I give myself to Jesus because nobody has loved me like that. No one else will ever love me like that. No one else can – but Jesus!**

MATTHEW 26:38-39 Jesus said to them, "My *soul is overwhelmed with* **[25]** *sorrow to the point of death.* Stay here and keep watch with Me." Going a little farther, He fell with His face to the ground and prayed, "My Father, if it is possible, *may this <u>cup</u> be taken from Me.* Yet not as I will, but as You will."

> Jesus tells how overwhelmed He is – to the point of death. In fact, we are told that if the Father had not sent holy angels to strengthen Him, He would have expired right there in the Garden. He would never have made it to the cross. Another verse tells how His sweat fell to the ground like drops of blood. We cannot imagine what it was like to have all the sin of all sinners come down upon Him

in one terrible curse. Usually, when Jesus prayed, He would simply say, "Father." On the verge of death He cries, "MY Father," reaching out intimately and desperately. From Hebrews 5:7 we learn that He prayed "with loud cries and tears" to His Father.

Underline the word "cup." This word is frequently used to represent that which we are experiencing. Here the word "cup" refers to all the agony, suffering, and dying that He is beginning to experience. We have no conception of what this suffering and dying for all sinners meant for the holy Jesus. As He starts to drink this cup, it is so horrible, so horrendous, that He asks His Father: "If there is any other way for mankind to be saved other than my drinking this cup, take it from Me." How happy we should be that He adds, "But not My will, but Your will be done." He proceeds to drink it. By the time He is through drinking, He has experienced hell for every sinner, and He is dead. **Who else would drink the cup of hell for you? Only Jesus.** He did it for you. We will now see more of what was in that cup in Matthew 27.

MATTHEW 27:28-30,33-35,39,44-46 They stripped Him and put a *scarlet robe* on Him (This was undoubtedly an old, faded cloak they had found.), and then wove a *crown of thorns* and set it on His head (The crown was a circle of twigs that were full of thorns.) They put a *staff* in His right hand (This was simply a reed they found. The "King" was now properly dressed.) and *knelt* in front of Him and *mocked* Him. "Hail, King of the Jews!" they said (This sarcasm was intended to humiliate Jesus as much as possible.) They *spit* on Him (This is one of the most disgusting insults one human being can give another.), and took the staff and *struck* Him on the head *again and again* (They also beat His head with their hands.)... They came to a place called Golgotha (which means The Place of the Skull) (The hill had the shape of the round top of a skull.) There they offered Him wine to drink, mixed with gall (This was doped wine. It was intended to make their work of crucifying a bit easier.); but after tasting it, He *refused to drink it* (Why? Because He wanted to suffer fully for our sins.) When they had *crucified* Him, they *divided up His clothes* by casting lots (The soldiers gambled for His robe. You should know that one of the prophets in the Old Testament plainly foretold that when the Messiah is come and when He hangs between heaven and earth, men will gamble for His robe. Here we see again that every prophecy by the prophets had to literally be fulfilled. How was the victim crucified? A block of wood was fastened to the cross. The victim would then sit on this block. Jesus' body, arms, and legs were tied to the cross with ropes. Large nails were driven through each hand. Each foot was nailed with a separate nail.)... Those who passed by *hurled insults* at Him, *shaking their heads* (This was a gesture of indignation and mockery. You should know that these folks were the "good church people" of their day. Many times some of the worst enemies of Jesus are not people outside the church, but people in the church.)... In the same way the robbers who were crucified with Him also *heaped insults* on Him (Luke tells us that, later, one of the robbers came to repentance and faith. Now come the signs.) From the sixth hour until the ninth hour *darkness* came over all the land (Even though it is noon with the sun at its zenith, a strange darkness covers the land until three o'clock.) About the ninth hour Jesus cried out in a loud voice, "Eloi, Eloi, lama sabachthani?" – which means, *"My God, My God, why have You forsaken Me?"*

What does that last sentence mean? God had turned away and left. Jesus thirsts for God, but God is gone. The Son has not left God, but God has left the Son. To be forsaken by God is to taste the full wrath of God. It is to go through hell. A number of years ago a little three year old girl in California was thrown away by her mother. She drove down a freeway, stopped by the median strip, opened the door, set the girl down, and drove off. A little while later state highway patrolmen saw the girl and pulled up. They plucked her off the freeway and took her to a police station. They said that they had never seen anything like it in their lives because on the face of the little girl was written fear and abandonment in bold letters. She knew that her mother had abandoned her.

Jesus, on the cross, knew that His Father had abandoned Him. And He cried, "Father, Father, why have You left Me?" The Father would not answer Him. He was left there in hell alone. Hell is a place where God isn't around anymore. The worst part of hell isn't the fire, isn't the loneliness, isn't the guilty conscience, isn't the anguish, nor any of the other things that Scripture uses to describe hell. The hell of hell is being without God. I would like you to think about that tonight before you go to sleep. Don't even take a gamble on going to a place like that. **It was black Friday for Jesus. It was Good Friday for us. Is it a Good Friday for you or just another day, another church day? It all depends on what you do with Jesus.**

JOHN 19:28,30 Later, knowing that *all* was now *completed*... Jesus said, *"It is finished."* With that, He bowed His head and *gave up His spirit*.

Underline "all" and "completed" and "It is finished." The time is 3:00. Jesus knew that His redemptive work was complete. He cried out in a loud voice to His Father and to all mankind: Τεστελεσται, which means finished, done, paid for in full! Everyone of your sins are completely paid for! When you even try to pay for one of your sins you're insulting Him. Now, like a very tired child, He lays His head to rest in His Father's arms. He gives up His spirit and goes to heaven.

MATTHEW 27:51,52,54,59,60,65,66 At that moment the curtain of the temple was *torn in two* from top to bottom. The *earth shook* and the *rocks split*. The *tombs broke open* and the *bodies* of many holy people who had died were *raised to life*... When the centurion and those with Him who were guarding Jesus saw the earthquake and all that had happened, they were terrified, and exclaimed, *"Surely He was the Son of God!"*... Joseph took the body, wrapped it in a *clean linen cloth*, and placed it in his own *new tomb* that he had cut out of the rock. He rolled a *big stone* in front of the entrance to the tomb... "Take a guard," Pilate answered. "Go, *make the tomb* as *secure* as you know how." So they went and made the tomb secure by putting a *seal* on the stone and *posting the guard*.

Jesus is dead, and now God speaks loudly giving awesome signs. These signs all occur simultaneously the moment Jesus died. Each sign is emphatic.

Sign # 1: The inner curtain, about four inches thick and measuring 60 x 30 feet, which hung between the Holy and Holy of Holies in the temple, was suddenly torn in two. As if by an unseen hand it is ripped starting at the top. Suddenly the Holy of Holies is exposed. Absolute consternation must have occurred. This happened at 3:00, at about the time when the priests were preparing the evening sacrifice. Only once a year the high priest alone could go behind this curtain on the Great Day of Atonement when he sprinkled blood on the mercy seat for the forgiveness of sins of the people. Once, in the Old Testament, two young men went into the Holy of Holies. They were not authorized to do so. Do you know what happened to them? They were killed on the spot, instantly, right there in the Holy of Holies, by God. When the curtain was ripped and the priests could look right into the Holy of Holies, what do you suppose they thought? "We're going to die!" What was God saying? He was saying that all these Old Testament functions were through because Jesus, the great High Priest, had come and entered the Holy of Holies with His atoning blood.

Sign # 2: The earthquake and the breaking of huge stones indicate the presence and power of God, a God of grace for those who believe and a God of judgment for unbelievers.

Sign # 3: The tombs broke open and the bodies of many believers arose and appeared in Jerusalem. Matthew leaves the impression that they were raised the moment Jesus died. This sign said that Jesus' death conquered death. Those raised from the dead offered proof of that victory.

The centurion and his soldiers saw all this and immediately offered this conclusion: "Surely He was the Son of God!" The Jewish church leaders said Jesus was a devil. Here we have pagan Roman soldiers with no religious learning and what do they say of Jesus? "SURELY He was the Son of God."

How strange that many within the church were going straight to hell, and some outside the church were going straight to heaven. If the soldiers with as little as they knew about Scripture could come to this conclusion, then tonight after all we've been through so far in these first three lessons, there is no reason in heaven or on earth why you cannot say in your heart of hearts, "Jesus, You are God's Son. You are MY Savior." Won't you please say that tonight? It is not enough to call Him God's Son. You must truly call Him your Savior. You will be without excuse if you do not believe in Christ. What would your excuse be? Can you say, "Oh, I don't know." My friend, you know! You've been told – in the clearest of terms. You know much more than the centurion ever knew. What will be your excuse in the hour of your death and in the day of judgment if you do not confess Him as Your Savior and honor Him? My friend, you will have none.

Legend says that the Roman army officer became a believer and powerful worker for the Lord. Joseph, a believer, took charge of burial plans. He wrapped Jesus' body in fine linen cloth. It was torn into long strips. The body was wrapped with these strips of linen, and spices were placed in between the layers. Joseph's new tomb was near Golgotha. It was a rich man's tomb. The big stone was really a flat, upright, circular slab like a wheel. It was placed into a grove by the entrance either to open or close the tomb. Pilate gives the Jews some Roman soldiers. A seal is affixed and connects the slab with the rock wall at the door. If there was any tampering the seal would be broken.

Of His own free will our Lord suffered unimaginable agony of body and soul. At 9:00 He was nailed to the cross. At 12:00 darkness covered the land. The Father completely forsook Jesus. Jesus experienced hell. Finally, at 3:00, He had endured the suffering for every sin and every sinner. He cried from the cross for the sixth time, "It is finished!" Hell, death, and the devil were conquered. We have all been redeemed. This is the Good News. It is the greatest news we can hear and believe. **[26]**

This finishes Christ's **state of humiliation** which began at the incarnation and concluded with His death on the cross. In this period He covered His divine majesty and did not always display His divine attributes. His **state of exaltation** consists in this, that even according to His human nature Christ always and fully uses the divine attributes given to His human nature. The Man Jesus is Lord over all things in heaven and on earth. He will exercise this Lordship now and forever.

5. What does the Bible say about Jesus' resurrection and ascension?

1 PETER 3:18-19 He was put to death in the body but made alive by the Spirit, through whom also *He went and preached to the spirits in prison.*

Christ who had gone to heaven now returned to the body in the tomb. The linen wrappings around the body suddenly lay there flat. Before Christ came out of the tomb He descended, in both His human nature and His divine nature, into hell or prison, the place where spirits are locked up eternally. Did Jesus go there to give lost souls another chance? No. This was proclamation time.

The Greek verb suggests that Jesus didn't just go and preach, but it means: "speaking as a herald." He heralded proof to the condemned spirits of His victory over sin, death, and hell. They could see in His exalted body the print of the nails. We speak of His descent in the Apostles' Creed with the words: "He descended into hell." Let me give you one more Scripture reference to His descent. Write down Colossians 2:15.

MATTHEW 28:1-2,5-7,9 After the Sabbath, *at dawn* on the first day of the week, Mary Magdalene and the other Mary went to look at the tomb. There was a *violent earthquake*, for an angel of the Lord came down from heaven and, going to the tomb, *rolled back the stone* and sat on it... The angel said to the women, "Do not be afraid, for I know that you are looking for Jesus, who was crucified. *He is not here; He has risen, just as He said. Come and see* the place where He lay. Then *go quickly and tell* His disciples: 'He has risen from the dead and is going ahead of you into Galilee. There *you will see Him...*'" Suddenly Jesus met them. *"Greetings,"* He said. They came to Him, clasped His feet and *worshiped* Him.

Early Sunday morning Jesus' body is suddenly filled with life. Instantly and silently He passes right through the walls of the tomb. An angel then appears and jars the earth with a violent earthquake. The two Marys were on their way to the tomb at dawn with spices to complete the burial. They had to feel the earthquake. They continue to the tomb and see the entrance wide open. They look inside and see the angel and are filled with fear. The angel knows why they are there. He invites them to come closer to see where the body had been placed, but there is no body. They see only the linen wrappings lying there undisturbed. The angel tells them the great news: "He has risen, just as He said... Go quickly and tell His disciples." On their way Jesus makes His first appearance to them. **"Greetings" He says. This word in Greek conveys the wish of happiness and well-being.** The women are overcome with joy. They come up to Him and fall prostrate at His feet in happy adoration and worship Him. What will we do when we see Jesus in heaven? Much the same thing.

ACTS 1:3 After His suffering, He showed himself to these men and gave *many convincing proofs* that He was alive. He appeared to them over a period of *forty days* and spoke about the Kingdom of God.

Jesus used forty days to let the apostles and others see Him, hear Him, touch Him, and eat with Him. There was to be no doubt that He was indeed alive. The resurrection of Jesus is mentioned in the New Testament a total of 104 times. It is interesting, then, to hear our Mormon friends say that Jesus' body is still lying in that Palestinian grave. From this time on the apostles mentioned Jesus' resurrection every time they preached. You must remember that the resurrection of Jesus was to them a most important event. With the resurrection all the pieces of the Messiah puzzle fell into place for them. Today He does not give us His visible presence to look at; He gives us His Word to look at and believe. Forty days later Jesus goes Home as we see in the next verse.

LUKE 24:50-52 When He had led them out to the vicinity of Bethany, He lifted up His hands and *blessed* them. While He was blessing them, *He left them and was taken up into heaven.* Then they *worshiped* Him and returned to Jerusalem with *great joy.*

"Jesus' arrival in Bethlehem was utterly unique – so was His departure near Bethany"

These were not just the apostles. Jesus led His followers out to the hill of ascension. He gave them last minute instructions, and then He lifted up His hands and spoke a divine benediction. As the words came from His lips He slowly separated from them, rising visibly. Their eyes followed Him. Jesus' **arrival** at Bethlehem was utterly unique – so was His **departure** near Bethany. What an impression it must have had on them. They were honored to see His final going to the Father. Finally a cloud enveloped Him, and they saw Him no more. The disciples were absolutely overcome with joy at what they had just seen, and they bowed down and worshiped. Even though His body was in heaven, they remembered His promise that He would be with them in spirit for all time. He is here tonight in this room with us. The disciples return to Jerusalem with great joy. No longer would they be afraid and hide behind locked doors. Their hearts sang with joy.

ROMANS 8:34 Christ Jesus, who _died_ – more than that, who was _raised_ to life – is at the right hand of God and is also _interceding for us_.

Underline "died," "raised," and "interceding for us." Have you ever wondered if you are truly safe from the judgment of a Holy God when you think of your sin? There are three reasons why you should know tonight that you are safe and secure. **1. Jesus died for you. 2. Jesus was raised to life for you. 3. Jesus is now invested with all power and authority in heaven and there pleads your cause before the Father.** What does He do for you when you sin? He intercedes for you. Have you ever asked the question: What would happen to me if I should commit a sin and would not have a chance to confess it before I died? What is the answer? Would you go to heaven or to hell? To heaven. Jesus says, "Father, You must forgive My child because I died and rose again for him or her. Father, You have promised forgiveness for My child, and You must honor that." One of the things you should do tonight is to thank the Lord that He daily intercedes for you.

He bore the sin of many & made intercession & for the transgressors.

Isaiah 53:12

Being made alive spiritually, Christ descended into hell, not to suffer, but to proclaim His victory over Satan and his followers. No power on earth could keep Him in the grave. When the women came to the grave, they were greeted by a holy angel, an empty tomb, and a message of joy. Soon Jesus showed Himself to the women and the rest of the disciples and offered insurmountable proof of His resurrection. He instructed His disciples, commissioned them to make disciples of all people, promised the power of the Holy Spirit, and then ascended into heaven. Now we know God has accepted Jesus' sacrifice on our behalf as satisfactory for our redemption. We have been brought back to God, and because He lives and intercedes for us we, too, shall live with Him soon in unending glory.

6. What did Christ really accomplish?

GALATIANS 4:4-5 When the time had fully come, God sent His Son, [27] born of a woman, born under law, to _redeem_ those under _Law_, that we might receive the _full rights of sons_.

Underline the word "redeem." Above it write "to buy out of" and "free from." Christ bought out of and freed everyone under the Law. He paid the price. Who did Christ redeem? Everyone in the world. Someone has put it this way: If Christ would have redeemed everyone but one person, I might well be that person. Our status is that of full-grown sons no longer under guardians like the Jews were under the Law in the Old Testament. We are free from the demands and curse of the Law. He didn't redeem us to become Lutherans or Catholics but to become God's sons and daughters with full rights. When God adopts you and gives you full rights everything that the Father has belongs to you, including heaven itself. You own it all tonight.

• 1 JOHN 4:9 This is how God showed His love among us: He sent His one and only Son into the world that we might _live through Him_.

Is this Law or Gospel, class? Gospel. Good news or bad? Good. Does it bring us life or death? Life.

Heaven or hell? Heaven. What did Jesus accomplish? I now have life through Him. Without Jesus I am a walking dead man who is going straight to hell. I am a walking dead man and don't know it. The dead don't know they are dead. It is only when I become alive that I realize that I was dead.

1 JOHN 3:8 He who does what is sinful is of the devil, because the devil has been sinning from the beginning. The reason the Son of God appeared was to *destroy the devil's work.*

Jesus destroyed the grip that Satan had upon all men and this includes everlasting death in hell.

JOHN 8:34,36 Jesus replied, "I tell you the truth, everyone who sins is a slave to sin... So if the Son *sets you free*, you will be *free indeed.*"

Is the first part of the passage Law or Gospel? Law. Good news or bad? Bad. Bring you to heaven or hell? Hell. Is the last part Law or Gospel. Gospel. Good news or bad? Good. Bring you to heaven or hell? Heaven. If the Son sets you free from your sin, you are free indeed. Free also from the grip Satan had on you. If just your pastor said it, you might wonder. If just your mommy said: "Oh, come on. Your sin isn't that bad, honey. Don't you worry." I don't think you would buy into that at all. When Jesus says you are free from your sin and free from hell, are you free? Yes, yes, yes! Who is it who says this? No one less than the Son of God. Don't let the devil or your neighbors or anyone tell you that you are lost in your sin and going to hell. You are not. Christ has freed you. You are free! That is the greatest news you can hear.

Corrie Ten Boom once said, "When God forgives you your sins, He throws them in the deepest part of the ocean. Then He puts a sign up on the surface: No fishing allowed!" What a beautiful statement. Sometimes you want to bring up your past sins. You want to bring up the guilt and go on a miserable guilt trip. "Oh, I can think of this one sin. That was horrible. And yes, I remember the time when I did such and such. That was bad. Oh, yes, here is some more sin." When Jesus frees you from your sin, where are they? They are gone. You are free. That is good news, isn't it? It's so good there are times when it is even hard to believe. But believe it – Jesus says so!

2 TIMOTHY 1:10 Christ Jesus has *destroyed death* and has *brought life* and *immortality to light* through the Gospel.

Underline the italicized words. Above "destroyed" write "put out of commission" and "abolished." Death's grip has been destroyed, and Jesus has brought everlasting life to the world by the Gospel. We naturally fear death. And immortality. Isn't it the dream of man to have immortality? Man does not want to grow old. Man does not want to die. Man would give anything to escape that. But what we could never do, Christ has done for us. When you read that Don Ginkel has died, don't believe a word of it. I will be very much alive. If there will be tears, let them be tears of joy.

By His suffering, death, and resurrection Jesus not only defeated the devil, but conquered sin and hell and restored peace between God and man. When Christ Jesus frees a sinner from his enemies, he is really free, and he has fellowship in God's family. Lidie Edmunds wrote –

> *The great Physician heals the sick, The Lost He came to save;*
> *For me His precious blood He shed, For me His life He gave.*
> *I need no other evidence, I need no other plea;*
> *It is enough that Jesus died And rose again for me.*

7. Who receives these wonderful blessings?

- LUKE 19:10 The Son of Man came to seek and to *save what was lost.*

> This verse is for suggested memorization. Who are these blessings for? Everyone who is lost. You, too, were lost. It is a sad thing to be lost, in this case, lost, far from God. Jesus came to save you.

1 JOHN 2:2 Jesus Christ is the *atoning sacrifice* for our sins, and not only for ours but also for the *sins of the whole world.*

> When Jesus atoned for sin on the cross, He did this not only for those of us who believe, but also for those who do not believe, even for those in hell tonight. He made atonement for everyone who has lived or will live in the future. Don't you think that every human being should hear that Good News at least once before they die? Yes! True or False: People go to hell because of their sin. False. People perish, not because Jesus did not save them, but because they do not believe it.

2 PETER 2:1 They *deny* the sovereign Lord who bought them – *bringing swift destruction on themselves.*

> People who reject the Savior who bought them with His precious blood and saved them bring what on themselves? Swift destruction. Swift in the hour of death. Destruction in the lake of fire. Not because the Lord did not buy them back from Satan with His blood, but because they refuse Jesus as their Savior.
>
> A man by the name of John Parker had been in a New Jersey prison for forty years because he murdered someone. The parole board ordered his release, but Parker doesn't want to go. He has no money, no family, and no friends. Prison life is all he has known for much of his 65 years. He doesn't want to leave. We can, perhaps, understand that. We can more easily understand that than we can understand people, imprisoned by sin, who do not want to be set free. That spiritual freedom and heaven should be refused and that men should wish to remain in unbelief is amazing. It is amazing but true. Thousands upon thousands have been offered their freedom, but have refused to accept it. Someone has appropriately said, "There is no greater sin then unbelief!" And, we might add, "There is nothing sadder."

JOHN 3:16 For God so loved the *world* that He gave His one and only Son, that *whoever believes in Him* shall not perish but *have eternal life.*

> Jesus is talking to the Pharisee Nicodemus, and He sums the entire Gospel message up in this one lovely sentence. What a revelation this must have been for poor Nicodemus who all his life had trusted his good works for entrance into heaven. The love of God is αγαπη, the highest form of love there is. How could God, who is absolutely holy, love sinful and rebellious mankind? He didn't **like** the world. He **loved** it with this unfathomable love, **agape.**
>
> Try this analogy: Could you love someone who killed your spouse? Could you love that person so much that you would give your only child to die in the murderer's place? God did that and much, much more. He loved the world, no one excepted. He loved, and He gave. Jesus is God's gift to you. **This love of God separates the Christian religion from all other religions.** Christianity is filled with agape and is divine; all other religions are human and not divine. Anyone who simply believes in Jesus Christ as his Savior will never perish (that is what we were headed for), but have eternal life.

> Today you had to eat for yourself. Today you had to breathe for yourself. Tonight you have to sleep for yourself. And there is something else you must do as the Holy Spirit works in your heart: you must believe for yourself. Your parent's faith in Jesus will not save you. Your pastor's faith in Jesus will not save you. Be sure that right here and now you believe in Jesus as your personal Savior, and the gift of eternal life is yours now and forever.

The benefits of salvation are for everyone. All have been redeemed. All sins are forgiven. Only those who deny their Lord deny also these blessings and receive in their place destruction. God's love, however, goes out to all. He invites everyone to come. He promises that whoever believes in Jesus has, in place of death, everlasting life. What Good **[28]** News this is – to believe and to share!

Let's pray together

Lord Jesus, we thank You for all You have done to be our Savior. When we see You on the cross, we realize what a terrible thing sin is. People beat You, crowned You with thorns, spit on You, and killed you – for us. Forgive us for having made Your cross so heavy by our sins. Because You came out of the grave alive we know that we, too, shall be raised from the dead on the last day. Strengthen our faith. Help us love and trust You more. Help us share this Good News with others. We dedicate ourselves to You, dear Lord. We praise You and love You. Amen.

Let's sing together

> When I survey the wondrous cross On which the Prince of glory died,
> My richest gain I count but loss And pour contempt on all my pride.
>
> See, from His head, His hands, His feet, Sorrow and love flow mingled down,
> Did e'er such love and sorrow meet Or thorns compose so rich a crown.
>
> Were the whole realm of nature mine, That were a tribute far too small;
> Love so amazing, so divine, Demands my soul, my life, my all!

Bible reading schedule for the next seven days

- ❏ 1st day – John 15
- ❏ 2nd day – John 16
- ❏ 3rd day – John 17
- ❏ 4th day – John 18
- ❏ 5th day – John 19
- ❏ 6th day – John 20
- ❏ 7th day – John 21

Worksheet no. 3

1. (✖) Most, ( ) Many, ( ) Few of the Old Testament people could understand the Messianic prophecies.

2. The name JESUS means *Savior from sin.*

3. The name CHRIST means *the anointed One.*

4. The name EMMANUEL means *God with us.*

[29]

5. Jesus was both true *God* and true *Man.*

6. *True* or False: Jesus had to be true man so He could take man's place under the Law and

suffer and die in his stead.

7. The virgin birth of Jesus is so important because *it was prophesied by God and so that He could be born without sin.*

8. *True* or False: Jesus never hesitated or flinched in dying for us (Unless one wishes to consider the incident in Gethsemane).

9. Jesus was anointed to a threefold office, namely, to be our *Prophet*, *Priest*, and *King* (You may want to check to see that everyone understands the function of each office).

10. When Jesus said "It is finished!" He meant *that the suffering for the sins of the entire human race was finished and the plan of redemption completed.*

11. True or *False*: Jesus descended into hell to suffer.

12. *True* or False: Jesus redeemed everyone, even those who finally perish.

13. True or *False*: Jesus came to show us a loving God and that God has nothing against us.

14. True or *False*: Most ministers and churches do a pretty good job of getting the Good News of Jesus out to their communities (On the basis of their experience some students might mark this true).

15. Why did Jesus' enemies seem to repeatedly attack the doctrine of His deity? *If He was not truly God they would not have to listen to Him or believe Him (There were also other less but obvious reasons, too).*

16. What reason did Jesus have for loving you and saving you? *Really no reason other than his great love (agape) (Emphasize the meaning of the word "grace" here).*

[30]

O Holy Spirit, Comforter and Teacher of all spiritual truth, I am here tonight seated before the Holy Scriptures. I seek to be enlightened on the way of salvation and the will of God for my daily living. I want to better understand You, who You are, and what You do. Please come to me. Please dwell in me. Remove the shades from my spiritual eyes so that I may understand and when I cannot understand enable me simply to believe. Comfort me with the Good News of Jesus as my Savior. Give me an even stronger faith in the Lord in the days ahead. Give me the joy and peace that comes with saving faith. Fill me with Your love, zeal, and power so that I may be a better worker in the Kingdom of my Savior here on earth. Give this to me and to everyone in this room. I ask this in the name of Jesus. Amen.

Let us suppose that the CIA has chosen you to be an agent for them in China. You would be trained to talk, act, look, and think Chinese. You would attend school and learn the Chinese language so that you could speak it fluently. You would learn their mannerisms. You would have plastic surgery so that you would look Chinese. The CIA would then smuggle you into China. The people would accept you. As far as anyone is concerned in China you are Chinese.

Now let me ask you a question: Would you really be Chinese? No, not if you did not have Chinese parents. Nothing you do can change your race.

It's the same way spiritually. **You may talk and dress like a Christian. You may join a Christian congregation and sing Christian hymns and in all ways act like a Christian. However, none of these things will make you a Christian. Your saying you are a Christian does not make you a Christian.** I could spend tonight in my garage – that would not make me a car. Yet somehow we think if we do all these Christian things we are Christian. Tonight's Lesson is going to dispel a lot of false concepts that we have and restore them with beautiful truths from God.

This very moment some of you may have no faith in Christ as your Savior. You may have knowledge, but you do not have saving faith in the Lord. Others of you have what might be called a small or immature faith in Jesus. Because of your little faith you are struggling spiritually, and you go through a lot of valleys. I know for a fact that some of you are tired of staying in spiritual valleys. You really want to get up on the mountain top.

A few of you tonight have a rather healthy and vibrant faith in Jesus; it shows in the way you think, the way you speak, and the way you act. You show your mature faith in your Christian joy and the other fruits of faith. For everyone of us tonight the paramount need is for a meeting with the third Person of the Trinity – God, the Holy Spirit.

I am going to put one of you on the spot. Jolene, tell us everything you know about the Holy Spirit – how many hours do you want? How about two hours? No? A half hour? No. Ten minutes? No. How about five minutes? Yes? Now she is being very honest. Many of us, however, are like Jolene. Isn't it sad that some of us this evening could share all our knowledge on the Holy Spirit and we wouldn't need any more than five minutes? We have more knowledge of the Father and much more of Jesus. Many of us do not know much about the Holy Spirit.

Think about last week's Lesson on Jesus. He came, He suffered, He died, and He rose again, but were it not for the work of the Holy Spirit, you and I would still go straight to hell despite the fact that Jesus has saved us. Listen to this: **Were it not for the Holy Spirit we would never ever see the pearly gates of heaven.** That's how critical this Lesson is.

Now we're ready for a most important study.

Lesson 4

About A Spirit Who Converts You

> The Lesson last week was the most important one in this course because Jesus Christ is the Cornerstone of Christianity. He is the heart, the core of God's love. Tonight's Lesson will be the most critical Lesson in this course and will be more difficult. Some of us may not grasp everything. Try to understand what you can and when you can't understand, just rejoice over what you do comprehend.

1. Who is the Holy Spirit?

MATTHEW 28:19 Go and make disciples of all nations, baptizing them in the name of the Father and of the Son *and of the Holy Spirit.*

> In the first Lesson I put on the board a triangle like this. We wrote God on the inside and then put "F" on one side, "S" on another, and an "HS" on the third. We confess that each Person is equal with the other. We do not worship three Gods but one God made up of three distinct and separate Persons. Here Jesus speaks clearly of the Holy Spirit. Just as you worship the Father and the Son so tonight you will learn that you should worship and pray to the Holy Spirit. There are reasons why, before I go to sleep tonight, I will want to say some things just to the Father, others things to the Son, and yet other things to the Spirit. All three Persons have special areas of activity. To the Father is ascribed the work of creation. The Son is known for the work of redemption. The Holy Spirit has the work of sanctification. The Spirit has entity like the Father and the Son. I heard one person say, "I think the Holy Spirit represents God." No, no, no! We cannot say that Diana here represents her family, can we? Diana is Diana. The Spirit is the Spirit who has power. He has feelings. You can make Him happy, and you can make Him grieve.

ACTS 2:1-4 When the day of Pentecost came, they were all together in one place. Suddenly a sound like the *blowing of a violent wind* came from heaven and filled the whole house where they were sitting. They saw what seemed to be *tongues of fire* that separated and came to rest on each of them. All of them were *filled with the Holy Spirit* and began to speak in *other tongues* as the *Spirit enabled them.*

> The Greek word for Pentecost means fiftieth. It was the fiftieth day after the Jewish Passover. Later on Christians retained the name, Pentecost, for the giving of the Holy Spirit, but the count was made from Easter. The place is Jerusalem. All the believers, 120 in number, are together in an upper room. At Jesus' ascension He had told them to wait in Jerusalem until He sent the Holy Spirit. As believers they already had the Holy Spirit, but now something very special was going to happen. The New Testament Church is about to be born. There will be three phenomena.
>
> **Phenomenon # 1:** About 9:00 in the morning there was the sound of a furious wind coming down from the sky. There was no wind, just the sound of violent wind. Undoubtedly this symbolized the supernatural power of the Holy Spirit. The loud sound made its way to where the disciples were. It focused on that building and went inside it. The noise attracted thousands of people to the location of the building.
>
> **Phenomenon # 2:** Fire like tongues of fire suddenly appeared in the room, and one flame then sat on the head of each of them. Twice Luke uses the word "all." All the men and women, the young and old were touched. Fire symbolizes purification.

Phenomenon # 3: They all began to speak in different tongues or languages. These were known languages. The disciples could suddenly speak languages they did not know and had never studied. Verse 6 tells us that people from many foreign countries were present in the enormous crowd. They heard the disciples speak in every language represented there. What a miracle! On that first day 3,000 people were converted to the Lord Jesus. The number of converts continued growing each day at such a rate that they finally stopped counting.

This speaking in known tongues differs sharply from some today who speak in unknown tongues (called glossolalia). To learn more about the various gifts (charismatic gifts) of the Holy Spirit you may write down a reference: 1 Corinthians 12, 13, and 14. I would suggest that you read these chapters at home. I believe that some of the gifts listed there are **abiding gifts** like the first gift mentioned, that of prophecy which means the gift of teaching. I believe that other gifts were **authenticating gifts** like the gift of miracles. These were present for very brief periods of time in the Old Testament and a brief period in the New Testament. While the gift of healing has generally been removed, I believe that God can cause any person to be healed of disease either directly or by medical means. I do not have the gift of glossolalia, that is, speaking in unknown tongues. I remain a bit skeptical of glossolalia today, but I will not deny that if the Holy Spirit wishes to bring this gift to a believer, He certainly can. I agree with St. Paul who said: "I would rather speak five intelligible words to instruct others than ten thousand words in a tongue."

ACTS 5:3-4 Peter said, "Ananias, how is it that Satan has so filled your heart that you have lied to the *Holy Spirit*... You have not lied to men but to *God."*

Ananias had deliberately and in a mocking way lied to the Holy Spirit about a gift of money that was brought to the apostles. The lie was not to the apostles but to the Holy Spirit who is God. Peter makes a clear expression of the Holy Spirit as a member of the Godhead. **Two tragedies are occurring today. First, many churches are not preaching Jesus. Second, the Holy Spirit is even more absent than Jesus.** How much instruction have you heard in your church life on the Holy Spirit? How many prayers in the church are directed to the Holy Spirit? It has been said the Holy Spirit is the forgotten Person of the Holy Trinity. I know of people who go to church for an entire year and never hear a word on the Holy Spirit. This is tragic. It is little wonder that many congregations lack power when they omit the "Power House," the Holy Spirit. He is literally the "Power House" in our Christian lives making impossible things possible.

JOHN 14:16-17 The Father will give you another *Counselor* to be *with you* forever – the *Spirit of truth*... He *lives with you* and will be *in you*. **[31]**

Last week we learned that Jesus is our Advocate and Counselor. But Jesus is about to return to heaven. He promises the disciples Someone who will take His place – the Holy Spirit. **The Greek word for Counselor means** (write these above "Counselor) **a teacher, an assistant, a helper, a comforter, and a friend, especially a legal friend.** This is what Jesus is promising the Holy Spirit will be to His followers after He leaves earth. In and of myself I do not know the truth. I get things all messed up. But Jesus says the Holy Spirit will keep me from error and lead me only to the truth. He will live in all believers, in their very bodies, in a very intimate and personal way. I truly believe that every Christian has the Holy Spirit residing in his body as a special Guest.

The Holy Spirit is the third Person of the God-Head. He has other names: Spirit of Truth, Spirit of God, Counselor, and Comforter. He is holy, builds Christ's Church by making people holy (called sanctification), and lives with and in God's people.

PENTECOST

I want to make a quick comment on what is called the sin against the Holy Ghost. Has anyone here ever asked, "Have I committed the sin against the Holy Ghost?" It is the only sin which Jesus says will not be forgiven a man. I would suggest that you answer this question: "Do you have any spiritual desire left in your soul?" If you do, you have not committed this sin. The very fact that you are here in this Bible study is powerful proof that you have not committed this sin. You may want to jot down two references on this subject: Mark 3:29 and Matthew 12:31-32.

2. Why is it necessary that the Holy Spirit work saving faith in you?

Diana, "Do you have saving faith in Jesus as your Savior this evening?" Okay, you do. Question 2 is asking: "Diana, why was it necessary for the Holy Spirit to work or give you saving faith in Jesus?" For all of you who believe in Jesus, why was it necessary that the Holy Spirit work faith in your soul? For those who do not have saving faith, why must the Holy Spirit do His work in your heart? Let's find out.

EPHESIANS 2:1 As for you, *you were dead* in your transgressions and sins.

Underline the italicized words. Paul is writing to the Christians at Ephesus. At this time they are Christians. Paul is saying, "Before you became alive in Jesus you were dead people." We can look at Diana or any of you who have saving faith and say, "Before you became alive in Jesus you were spiritually dead." How dead? Almost dead? No, completely dead. You were dead as a result of your sins. In fact the Bible says that this deadness is inherited from our parents and they from their parents all the way back to Adam and Eve. It's called original sin.

Quite a few years ago I took my family to a cabin in Arkansas. We had lunch one day and then walked to the car to go for a ride. I put the key in, turned it, and nothing happened. The battery was so dead it didn't even go, "Rrr!" I opened up the hood and looked at the dead battery. Then I picked up a 2 x 4 lying nearby and said, "Battery, I'm going to give you three seconds to start this car or I'm clubbing you." What did the battery do next? Nothing. What was it capable of doing? Nothing. At that moment a fellow pulled up in his pickup truck and offered to jump start the battery. The engine started and then my dead car battery boasted about what it had just done to start the car. You think it could make that boast? No. The battery was totally passive. It was dead. It was incapable of doing anything.

That is exactly the way you were spiritually. You were dead! A dead man cannot do anything. A dead man doesn't decide to become alive. A dead man doesn't decide to get up out of his casket and walk away. A dead man remains dead. Everything must be done for him. **There isn't a thing you could do to make yourself alive spiritually or even help in the process. This is the Holy Spirit's work, His task.** Until that happens, I wouldn't give a plug nickel for your life. How much is a plug nickel worth? Zippo! You say, "Reverend, you're being blunt!" Yes, but that is the way it is. **Unless the Holy Spirit comes down and makes you alive you are going to live and die and go to hell.** In my opinion, that's not worth much. I don't want that, and I trust you don't want that either or you wouldn't be here. So it is the Holy Spirit's work to do this in your life. Isn't that wonderful? Is this not sufficient reason to praise the Spirit every day?

ROMANS 8:7 The *sinful mind is hostile to God. It does not submit to God's Law, nor can it do so.*

Before conversion your sinful mind was hostile toward God. He did not deserve such hostility. Furthermore, your sinful mind does not submit to God's Law, in fact, by nature it is incapable of doing so. This flies in the face of those who today teach that man is morally good by nature. Then there are those church people who somehow think that God grades on the curve – just do the best you can and you will get into heaven. Nothing could be farther from the truth. According to the Bible God does not grade on the curve. A person who is truly a believer knows that by his very nature he is sinFULL – full of sin. **Think of St. Paul. What did he call himself? The chief of sinners. By nature you and I are like Paul. Oh, how desperate we are, how lost we are.** A comedian told the story of a man who took Carter's Little Liver Pills all his life. He said that when the fellow died, they had to take a big stick and beat his liver to death. We can identify with that illustration when we think of our corrupt nature within us. The only trouble is that we are so full of sin that we can't find a stick big enough to get rid of it all. Left to ourselves, the picture is very bleak.

Underline the italicized words as we come to them.

1 CORINTHIANS 2:14 The man without the Spirit _does not accept_ the things that come from the Spirit of God, for they are _foolishness_ to him, and he _cannot understand_ them, because they are spiritually _discerned_.

Man without the Holy Spirit cannot do three things. **Put a number 1 above "does not accept."** People who do not have the Spirit cannot accept the things that come from the Spirit. It is an impossibility. **Put a 2 above "foolishness."** The things of the Spirit are silliness, simply myths that you might tell little children. **Put a 3 above "cannot understand."** This means he is unable to understand or perceive or grasp spiritual truth. Just as a person who is blind cannot see the sun, so is that person spiritually without the Holy Spirit – he is blind, blind as blind can be. Is it possible, then, for anyone to come to faith in Jesus on his own. No!

1 CORINTHIANS 12:3 Therefore I tell you... _no one can say_, "Jesus is Lord," _except by the Holy Spirit_.

One night I went out making evangelism visits. When I returned home one of my sons asked, "Dad, did you save anybody tonight?" It's a sensible question, but evangelists don't save anybody. Someone came up to me one time after I had received an invitation to become the pastor of another congregation, and he said, "Oh, pastor, you can't leave. You got me saved." We should know that pastors don't save anybody. Tonight Diana here says that Jesus is her Savior. Do you believe that in your heart, Diana? She can say that by the power of the Holy Spirit who has worked in her heart. And so with each of you who believes in Jesus as your Savior. It is by the Holy Spirit that is taking place. Every believer has the Holy Spirit in his heart working this miracle. John Newton wrote a hymn that believers love to sing.

> _Amazing grace! How sweet the sound - That saved a wretch like me!_
> _I once was lost but now am found, Was blind but now I see._

By nature we are totally blind to spiritual things. We cannot understand them. We are spiritually dead. We are at war with God. We refuse to do His will. Only the Holy Spirit can restore spiritual life and sight so that we can look at Jesus and honestly say, "He's my Savior!"

3. **How does the Holy Spirit bring you to faith in Christ?**

2 THESSALONIANS 2:13-14 God chose you to be saved _through the sanctifying work of the Spirit_ and through belief in the truth. _He called you_ to this _through our Gospel_.

"Faith in Christ does not come by watching a NFL football game on Monday night"

Here Paul is writing to the Christians at Thessalonica. God sanctified them, that is, set them aside for a holy purpose for Himself by the work of the Holy Spirit. How did the Holy Spirit do this? By the Gospel of Jesus Christ. What does the Holy Spirit use to regenerate sinners? The Good News of Jesus. If you know someone who is not a true believer, it is vital that he or she hears the Gospel.

I recently explained some of these concepts to a person, and he said, "You make me feel as if I don't really have anything to say about being a Christian." He said, "I want to make my own decision when I am ready." According to this verse we don't make a decision. Look at the first three words of both sentences in this verse. Who decides? God decides.

ROMANS 10:17 _Faith_ comes from _hearing the message_, and the message is heard through the _word of Christ_.

Underline "Faith" and "hearing" and "Christ." Saving faith in Christ does not come by watching a NFL football game on Monday night. It does not come at the end of a fishing pole in northern Minnesota. It does not even come just by sitting in a pew in church. How does saving faith come? From a message that centers in Jesus. Class, I want to tell you something. When you go church shopping be sure you look for a church which clearly teaches Jesus. When you look for a minister look for one who preaches Christ. No matter what the text, no matter what the occasion, Jesus must be the center and core of our teaching and our hearing. Let me ask those of you who have been around me for awhile – have you ever heard me preach a sermon or teach a Bible class that did not clearly speak of Jesus as Savior? No!

ROMANS 1:16 I am not ashamed of the _Gospel,_ because it is the _power of God_ for the _salvation of everyone who believes._

Above the word "power" write the word "dynamite." This Gospel is the dynamite of God for salvation which the Holy Spirit uses to bring people to saving faith.

REVELATION 22:17 The _Spirit_ and the Bride say, _"Come!"_

Above "Spirit" write "Holy." Above "Bride" write "Church," that is, the Church of Jesus here on earth. Their united invitation to the sinner is "Come, come to the Savior, and live." When Harry Truman was President years ago there was a little saying that was popular: "Give 'em hell, Harry!" You really don't have to give that to people. They already have hell. The message of the Holy Spirit and of the Church on earth is "Give 'em heaven! Come to Jesus!" My invitation to you tonight is come, come to Jesus. That is the message God wants you to convey this week to people you know and will meet. "Come to Jesus and live." That is the primary message of our congregation. Our primary mission is to invite the sinner to come to Jesus. Our entire ministry can be summarized in this. The very purpose of this Class is that we may come to Jesus and be converted by the miracle of the second birth. We look at a little baby that has been conceived and born and we say, "What a miracle." But I know of an even greater miracle – when I was born a second time. I hope the same for each of you can say the same thing.

Underline the italicized words as we come to them.

2 CORINTHIANS 4:6 God... _made His light shine_ in our _hearts_ to give us the light of the _knowledge_ of the _glory of God_ in the _face of Christ_.

70

Class, you can't see Jesus as your Savior before you're converted. Your heart is dark; it is totally black. What does God do? Paul says, if you will, that God takes His special "Flashlight," the Holy Spirit, and shines the light of Jesus whom the Bible calls the Light of the world into your heart. The Spirit of God drives back the darkness so that one day you "see Jesus by faith." "There He is! He's my Savior!" That's why one time I knew a lot about Jesus, but I never saw Jesus by faith. Your need is not for Lutheranism or Methodism but for God to shine in your heart the light of Jesus. And it is God's will not only to do that tonight, but every night and every day until some day you step into the eternal light of heaven and see Jesus face to face.

Even though this Lesson is on the Holy Spirit, Jesus is and must be the focal point of the Lesson. Christ is the focal point of Christianity, not the Holy Spirit. It is in Christ that we have new life. It is in Christ that we are born again. It is in Christ that we are made sons and daughters of God. It is with Christ that we walk through the valley of death. **The Holy Spirit is present to help us focus every amount of energy in the direction of Jesus Christ.**

The Holy Spirit calls people to saving faith by the teaching and preaching of the Good News about Jesus. The Holy Spirit uses the Gospel to convert people from spiritual deadness to spiritual life. The Holy Spirit invites and urges the sinner to come. He shines the bright [31] beam of God's love in Jesus into a person's heart where the miracle of new birth or conversion takes place.

"Why is 7:55 the time to believe?"

4. When should you believe in Jesus Christ as Your Savior?

What a critical question this is for some of us tonight who have been putting the Savior off. Let's see what the Bible says, and let's underline the italicized words.

• 2 CORINTHIANS 6:2 I tell you, *now is the time* of God's favor, *now is the day* of salvation.

Class, what time is it? What do your watches say? 7:55 p.m. What is the time to believe in Jesus? 7:55! Why is 7:55 the time to believe? Right – there may not be a 7:56. This is the time to believe. What is the day and date today? Sunday, June 23. Why is this day and date the day of salvation? There is a possibility that we'll never see June 24. A more acceptable day and hour will never be found. Let me ask you a question. If God offered you a brand new $200,000 house out on the edge of town free, all taxes paid, no upkeep – would you take it? Yes, yes. But tonight God is not merely offering a $200,000 home out in some prestigious part of town. He is offering you a mansion in heaven where the streets are paved with gold. And a few of you may want to sit here and say, "I don't know if I want that." What is your problem? No sane, thinking person would turn down an offer like that. For anyone here tonight who has been turning this offer down, I'm talking about you. I love you. You can't do that. It won't be long and you'll say good-bye to Kansas and to this earth. Where are you going to move? I know where I'm going. In the words of the old spiritual –

> *I've got a home in gloryland that outshines the sun,*
> *I've got a home in gloryland that outshines the sun,*
> *I've got a home in gloryland that outshines the sun - 'Way beyond the blue.*

The second stanza:

> *I took Jesus as my Savior, you take Him too - While He's calling you.*

Underline the italicized words as we come to them in this verse.

ISAIAH 55:6 Seek the LORD *while He may be found*; call on Him *while He is near.*

The day of grace will not abide forever. I sometimes tell people, when making evangelism visits, I'll ring the doorbell once. If there is no response I'll ring it again. If it's not raining I may ring it three times, but after the third time I'm getting in my car and leaving. I can imagine a few of you saying, "Well, no big loss. He's gone." But tonight it's not the pastor who is standing before you. Tonight the Holy Spirit presents Jesus to you as your Savior. What are you going to do with Him? I made the Lord stand outside my heart for a long time. I'm very grateful that He stood there and stood there and stood there. But the Lord can remove His presence. Don't take that chance. He says in Revelation 3:19-20, "Those whom I love I rebuke and discipline. So be earnest, and repent. Here I am! I stand at the door and knock. If anyone hears My voice and opens the door, I will go in and eat with him, and he with Me." Please believe in Jesus as your Savior tonight. Not long ago I heard a radio preacher say that hell is full of people who had good intentions. How true that must be. If you want to stop smoking, the time to quit is now, not tomorrow. If you want to believe in Jesus and be saved, the time to do that is now, not tomorrow.

Hell has many citizens who, while on earth, had good intentions. The right time to believe in Jesus is right now while there is time and while the Holy Spirit is working on a person's heart.

5. How can you know for sure whether you are converted?

Is there anyone here tonight who would like to know for sure if they are converted? Raise your hand. Before we take the first verse I want you to know that something awesome is going to take place on Judgment Day. Jesus says, "Many will say to me in that day, Lord, Lord, have we not prophesied in Thy name? and in Thy name have we cast out devils? and in Thy name done many wonderful works? And then will I profess unto them, **I never knew you**: depart from Me, ye that work iniquity" *(Matthew 7:22-23)*. Notice that on Judgment Day many people are going to say, "Lord, we knew You. We did great things in Your name." But Jesus will say, "I never knew you." Just because you say you belong to Jesus does not mean that Jesus will say you belong to Him. Tonight we want to find out not only if you can honestly say you belong to Jesus, but as Jesus looks at you, can He say, "Yes, you belong to Me."? This is what really counts – if Jesus says it. Underline the italicized words as we come to them in Ephesians 2.

EPHESIANS 2:8-9 It is by _grace_ you have been saved, through _faith_ – and this not from yourselves, it is the _gift_ of God – _not by works_, so that no one can boast.

Below "not by works" write "not by synergism." Synergism is the belief that man must help God to a lesser or greater degree in the matter of conversion. Earlier in this Lesson we learned that man is spiritually dead and incapable of doing anything; in fact, he is an enemy of God and the things of the Holy Spirit make no sense to him. How, then, can man be converted? Above "grace" write "undeserved love." Above "faith" write "in Christ." This faith in Jesus did not come from the person. Diana said a while ago that she has saving faith in Christ as her personal Savior. According to this verse can she make any boast about doing anything to get that faith? No. How did she get it? God **gave** her this faith; it is a **gift**. If she had to do anything, it could no longer be called a gift. God has done two big things for her. First, God made Diana; He created her. Secondly, He has made her alive spiritually. He gave her first birth and second birth. When you get to heaven you will not find a single person boasting about what they did to get there. Instead, all the people in heaven this evening are lifting up their arms and giving all honor and glory to the Lamb seated upon the Throne for their being there. Tonight the believer alive in Jesus on earth also gives all credit to Jesus and to Jesus alone; he takes none for himself. If a person believes he can do anything to help Jesus concerning his salvation we say that person is involved in work righteousness – he is trying to help save himself. It's just like we sing in one hymn:

> *Not the labors of my hands Can fulfill Thy Law's demands;*
> *Could my zeal no respite know, Could my tears forever flow,*
> *All for sin could not atone; Thou must save, and Thou alone.*

Someone put this grace of God in the form of an acrostic. I'll it put on the marker board. Please write it on the bottom of this page.
G - od's
R - iches
A - t
C - hrist's
E - xpense

ACTS 16:29-31 The jailer called for lights, rushed in and *fell trembling* before Paul and Silas. He then brought them out and asked, "Sirs, what must I do to be saved?" They replied, *"Believe in the Lord Jesus*, and *you will be saved."*

The jailor had arrested and beaten Paul and Silas for preaching the Gospel and then put them in chains in prison. That night God caused a great earthquake, the doors to the prison flew open, and the prisoners chains fell off. The jailor woke up, stood in the courtyard and saw the opened doors but no prisoners' (they were still there, in the jail). Assuming that they had escaped, he drew his sword to kill himself rather than face punishment. Paul is inside, sees the jailor, and says, "Don't harm yourself. We are all here." And in that moment the Holy Spirit touched the jailor's heart. He asked for a light, came in where Paul and Silas had been confined, and asked, "Sirs, what must I do to be saved?" He doesn't ask which church he should join. That and a hundred other religious questions are not the issue. The issue is: "What must I do to be saved?" This is the most important question a person can ask. Paul and Silas said, "You know, if you shape up and live a good life and believe in God and live according to the Golden Rule you'll get into heaven." Is that what they said? No. They said nothing about living a good life. The man was a sinner just like everyone else. "You believe in Jesus as your Savior and you'll be saved." We're told that he and his household believed that very night. He then took Paul and Silas to his house and attended to their wounds. And for the rest of the night Paul and Silas shared the Gospel with them. They all believed and they were baptized. Who caused this transformation? The Holy Spirit. The Holy Spirit must come to you and show you your sins and your Savior. The Spirit of God must then work saving faith in your heart. How should you come to Jesus? Come like the jailor. Come just as you are.

> *Just as I am, without one plea, But that Thy blood was shed for me,*
> *And that Thou biddest me come to Thee - O Lamb of God, I come, I come!*

JOHN 6:47 I tell you the truth, he who *believes has everlasting life*.

Underline "believes has everlasting life." When I believe in Jesus, I don't have to wait to have eternal life. As I believe in Jesus tonight, I have eternal life. It is mine. And it's also yours tonight by faith in Christ.

A person is converted if he is truly sorry for his sins, trusts not in himself or his good living, but trusts wholly and solely on Jesus Christ for his redemption. He may then know beyond a shadow of a doubt that he is converted, for God has plainly said so in His Word.

How can you know for sure you are converted? Question 1: Do you believe that in the sight of a holy God you are a sinner and deserve His wrath and condemnation? Question 2: Do you believe that God took His only Son, brought Him to earth, put Him on the cross, and there punished Him for all of your sins? Do you believe these two points? If you honestly answer yes you have the promise from God that you are converted and heaven is your home. God wants you to have this assurance. He wants you to know that if you die tonight you will wake up in heaven.

6. What else does the Holy Spirit do for you through the Gospel?

ROMANS 15:13 May the God of hope *fill you with all <u>joy and peace</u>* as you trust in Him, so that you may *overflow with hope* by the *power of the Holy Spirit.*

Underline "joy and peace." God wants you to have these fruits of faith. Just as a fruit tree produces fruit, so saving faith produces the fruit of joy and peace on a daily basis. This is an inner joy and peace which the world cannot give, not even our family and friends can give this. God wants your hope to overflow by the power of the Holy Spirit. Before closing my eyes in sleep tonight I will pray to the Holy Spirit: May my faith grow in Jesus, and may my joy and peace grow in Christ. The Spirit is the Person who will bring that to me.

EPHESIANS 2:10 We are God's *workmanship, created* in Christ Jesus to *do good works*, which God *prepared* in advance *for us to do.*

What role do good works play in the life of the Christian? We do not do good works to be saved by them. We are already saved. Just as the sun was created to shine, the flowers to bloom, so the believer is created to do good works to glorify God. Why do we do good works? Because God created us for this purpose and because we love the Lord. These works are a manifestation or demonstration of that saving faith which exists within us.

The Holy Spirit gives a believer the fruits of faith, namely: joy, peace, strength to resist sin and power to live a Christian life filled with good works.

7. What is a good work in God's sight?

The question is not what is a good work in man's sight, but **in God's sight**. There is a huge difference between the two.

JOHN 15:5 I am the Vine; you are the branches. If a man *remains in Me* and *I in him*, he will <u>*bear much fruit*</u>; apart from Me *you can do nothing.* **[33]**

Underline "bear much fruit." The secret to bearing fruit or doing good works to God's glory is that we must abide in Jesus and Jesus in us. He is the one who makes it possible. Let's state it another way. When Jesus came into my life He not only made me acceptable to God, He also made my works acceptable to God. Let's say we have two people, Jim here and Pastor Ginkel. Let's say that we both do the same good works day by day. I'm a Christian and Jim is an unbeliever (sorry about that Jim). He gives to the cancer fund and helps little old ladies across the street even if they don't want to go across the street, on and on, and I do the same thing. We both do the same kind of works. According to this verse my good works are acceptable to God because I am in Jesus. Jim's good works are not acceptable because he is not in Jesus.

You say, "Pastor, what makes your works acceptable?" Jesus. What makes you acceptable? Jesus. What makes Jim unacceptable? No Jesus. You see, you will never be accepted by God if you come to Him outside of Jesus. He cannot accept you, but in Christ He accepts you totally. The neat thing is that God not only accepts you, but He also accepts the good works you do, even the so-called small good works. I remind you of what Jesus said to His disciples: "Whoever gives a cup of water to a little one in My name shall in no way lose his reward." Wouldn't you agree that giving a glass of water to a little child and doing it as a Christian would appear to be a small good work? But Jesus promises, "You will be rewarded in heaven for that good work." What does that teach me? It says that everything that I do as a Christian, day by day, that is part of my Christian duty, is a good work in God's sight – when I go to work, when I earn a living, when I prepare dinner, etc., etc., this is pleasing and acceptable to God. Listen to Isaiah 64:6 – "But we are all as an unclean [thing], and all our righteousnesses (or good works) [are] as filthy rags (that is, in the sight of God)." Christ Jesus not only makes you good and holy, He also makes your works good and holy to God.

JOHN 14:15 If you love Me, you will *obey what I command.*

You say, "Pastor Ginkel, why do you try to obey the commands of the Lord Jesus? You have to do that, don't you?" If I were an unbeliever I would have to obey, but I am a believer. I do good works because I want to, because I love Him. Have you ever noticed the difference between **having** to do something and **wanting** to? We believers try to obey the Lord because we love Him. The Lord looks us dead center when we are converted, dead center as He daily washes us clean of all sin, He looks us right in the eye and says, "My child, if you love Me, please try to obey My commands." You say, "What do you do, then, when you disobey Him, when you sin?" Well, what then? We have to come to the Lord and say, "Please forgive me my sin, Lord." Will He forgive? Yes.

HEBREWS 11:6 *Without faith* it is *impossible* to please God.

Above "faith" write "in Jesus." This is the well known "faith chapter." This verse simply says that without saving faith in Jesus we can't please God. **Jesus makes me pleasing to God, and He makes my life pleasing to God.**

A good work is whatever God commands people to think, say, or do. This is done out of love for Jesus and by the power of the Holy Spirit.

8. Will you stay in your Christian faith? How can you be sure?

Tonight I rejoice that most of you, if not all of you, have saving faith in Christ. But I have a big concern for you and that is: Will you live all your life in Christ and finally die in Him? In a way I wish that the Lord would come in the sky tonight to take us all Home. That way we could be sure that we won't fall away from the Lord. Can you have the assurance that you will stay in your Christian faith to the end? Let's find out.

1 PETER 1:5 You who through faith are *shielded by God's power.*

The picture here is one of doing battle with the enemy, with Satan and the forces of this world. Left to ourselves we are very vulnerable, we will never make it through enemy lines to safety. But God offers to shield us, to guide and protect us as we move through enemy territory toward the friendly lines of heaven.

1 THESSALONIANS 2:13 God *is at work in you* who believe.

The Greek verb for "work" used here and in the New Testament usually means some form of **"supernatural activity"** (Write those two words above the word "work"). So Paul is saying of you who believe: "God is working in your life in a supernatural way. Rely on Him. Stay close to Him. You are working in God's power and strength." Would you think about that in the days ahead as you forge forward to the goal of heaven? "I will live and work in the power of God."

ISAIAH 43:1 Now, this is what the LORD says... "Fear not, for *I have redeemed you; I have summoned you by name*; *you are Mine.*"

These words were originally addressed to Israel. Though they were held captive by the Babylonians and had suffered long, they should not fear. God declares that He has redeemed them. Redeem means something was given in the place of that which was redeemed. God would deliver them. In a real sense we are all held captive by sin. But God has redeemed us. He put His own Son to death. He says, "I have called you by name" which suggests an intimacy of friendship. What's your name? Peggy, Ruth, Dottie, Jean, Joe. I've called each of you by name. You are Mine." Not only was Israel of old God's, but the same is true of all believers today who make up spiritual Israel or the one true Church of Jesus. We belong to God. That is first. That is foremost. We belong to a certain denomination only in a very remote sense compared to this. What a comforting promise, and God makes it to you tonight. Maybe we should print His promise out and post it on our bathroom mirror as a daily reminder. **Now write your first name under the words "by name." Let's read the quote again together, with your name inserted, out loud: "Fear not, for I have redeemed you; I have summoned you (Don Ginkel); you are Mine."**

God the Holy Spirit promises to keep the believer in saving faith through the Gospel.

9. Does the Holy Spirit desire to do these things for everyone?

EZEKIEL 33:11 *As surely as I live*, declares the Sovereign LORD, I take *no pleasure* in the death of the wicked, but rather that *they turn from their ways and live. Turn! Turn from your evil ways! Why will you die?*

Originally God spoke these words through Ezekiel to Israel, and He speaks them again to us tonight. God begins by taking an oath. Since He cannot swear by someone greater, God swears by Himself. There is absolutely no way the promise can be broken, because God is giving it and making it a sworn statement. He has no pleasure in the death of the sinner. Then comes the earnest call: "Turn! Turn from your evil ways!" Turn is stated twice for emphasis. The word turn might also be translated, "Be converted." It means to do an about face, a 180 degree turn. And then comes the grieving, sorrowful question: "Why will you die?" **This is astounding. Men insist on dying forever and God begs them to live.** You must know that it grieves God greatly when just one sinner perishes in hell because of unbelief. A question for any here who are still putting God off: Why do you want to die? Hear God talking to you, pleading with you.

• 1 TIMOTHY 2:4 God *wants all men to be saved* and to come to a *knowledge of the truth.*

Here is a suggested verse for memorization. God wants all men to be saved and that has to include you. "Truth" is used frequently in the New Testament as another term for the Gospel, so write "Gospel" above the word "truth." Tonight you are the object of God's affection. This verse clearly says that you are included in this affection. God wants to see you in heaven some day. To this end He wants you to know the truth about Jesus and the gift of salvation.

Swearing by His very existence, God openly declares that He wants all people to turn from their sins to Jesus and be saved.

10. Why, then, are not all people converted?

"If you do not want to eat with the Lord at the banquet feast in heaven, your wish will be granted – you will be excused"

Jesus speaks these words as He overlooks the city of Jerusalem for the last time, and He cries. As He cries, He speaks these words:

MATTHEW 23:37 O Jerusalem, Jerusalem, you who kill the prophets and stone those sent to you, how *often* I have *longed to gather* your children together, as a hen gathers her chicks under her wings, but *you were not willing.*

These words are filled with tenderness, and you can tell that they come from a broken heart. Jerusalem stands for the entire nation. God sent His prophets to tell of the Messiah, and they killed them. The Messiah came, and they killed Him, too. In His ministry Jesus repeatedly called the Jews to Himself as a hen gathers her chicks under her wings for safety's sake. But there was a problem. Was God the problem? No, the people were. They perished eternally in hell. Class, whose fault was it? Theirs. Earlier we learned that when men are converted and go to heaven all the credit goes to God. Now we learn that when men perish eternally, it is not God's fault, but their own. We cannot understand this mystery. Why can two people hear the same Law – Gospel message and one will repent and believe and the other will not repent and perish? We call this the unanswerable theological problem.

MATTHEW 22:4-6 Tell those who have been invited that I have prepared my dinner: My oxen and fattened cattle have been butchered, and everything is ready. *Come to the wedding banquet.* But *they paid no attention* and went off – one to his field, another to his business. The rest seized his servants, mistreated them and killed them.

Verse 3 says that the king had already reminded the invited guests that the dinner in honor of his son's wedding was ready, but they refused to come. This is a picture of God calling the Jews to the banquet feast of salvation. Verse 4 says that the king sent another set of servants to these invited guests repeating the invitation to come to the king's palace. But they paid no attention. One man went to his land and another to his business. Each found these earthly possessions more important than accepting the invitation to the wedding dinner. **Spiritually the Jews, and for that matter, many Gentiles, prefer earthly things to heavenly things.** Most people turn down God's invitation to salvation and eternal life with Him in heaven. Whose fault is it that so many people perish eternally in hell? It is their own fault. **I want to tell everyone here tonight that if you do not want to eat with the Lord at the banquet feast in heaven, your wish will be granted – you will be excused.**

ACTS 7:51 You *stiff-necked* people, with *uncircumcised hearts and ears!* You are just like your fathers: *You always resist the Holy Spirit!*

Stephen speaks these words to the Sanhedrin, the Jewish high court, as he is put on trial for giving his witness to Jesus, their Savior. Shortly after this trial they would drag Stephen out of the city and stone him to death. He called these people "stiff-necked," which means they will not bend. Israel had this reputation in the Old Testament. "Uncircumcised hearts and ears" meant that they bear the covenant sign of circumcision physically but spiritually they had cut off their hearing of and believing

> in God's Word. They stubbornly resisted the Holy Spirit who was trying to convert their hearts to faith in the Lord Jesus. They had no one to blame but themselves for perishing eternally.

Many people in stubborn unbelief resist the Gospel and the Holy Spirit who strives for their conversion. Whenever a man is brought to saving [34] faith in Jesus it is wholly by God's grace. Whenever a person does not believe and is lost it is wholly his own fault. Those in hell have no excuse.

Let's pray together

Spirit of Power, Comforter, and Teacher of all spiritual truth, shine into our dark hearts that we may see Jesus. Left to ourselves we would perish in everlasting darkness. Shine into our hearts with the brightness of the Gospel of Christ. Spirit of God, abide with us. Work saving faith in our souls. Give us joy and peace. Keep our faith in Jesus strong, warm and alive. As You moved the early Church to action, so empower and direct us for action-filled lives in the building of Jesus' Church. May we yield ourselves to be Your instruments in bringing the lost to a knowledge of their Savior. May our entire lives be dedicated to this end. And thank You, Holy Spirit, for teaching us in this Bible study. We praise You. In Jesus' name. Amen.

Let's sing together

Holy Spirit, light divine. Dawn upon this soul of mine;
Let Your word dispel the night, Wake my spirit, clear my sight.

Holy Spirit, truth divine, Shine upon these eyes of mine;
Send Your radiance from above, Let me know my Savior's love.

Holy Spirit, all divine, Dwell within this self of mine;
I Your temple pure would be Now and for eternity.

Bible reading schedule for the next seven days

- ❑ 1st day – 1 John 1 & 2
- ❑ 2nd day – 1 John 3 & 4
- ❑ 3rd day – 1 John 5
- ❑ 4th day – Romans 1

- ❑ 5th day – Romans 2
- ❑ 6th day – Romans 3
- ❑ 7th day – Romans 4

Worksheet no. 4

1. Check the correct statement(s):
   - _____ The Holy Spirit represents God.
   - __✗__ The Holy Spirit is God.
   - _____ The Holy Spirit speaks for God.
   - _____ The Holy Spirit does the good works for Christians.
   - _____ The Father was first in time, then the Son, then the Holy Spirit.

2. Why could you not by your own reason or strength believe in Jesus Christ or come to Him?

   Because by nature I am spiritually dead and therefore am unable to do so.

   [35]

3. How many times have you been born? *Twice.*

4. *True* or False: The Holy Spirit alone can convert a person.

78

5. True or *False*: When a person is converted we can only conclude that he resisted the Holy Spirit less than those who are not converted.

6. Many people who hear the Gospel are not converted because ( ) they have not had the opportunity to attend a Lutheran Church, ( ) of the devil and his work, (✖) they resisted the Holy Spirit.

7. How long a time does a person have in which to be converted? *He has right now; he may have a lifetime. The time is known by the Holy Spirit.*

8. Why can't an unbeliever understand spiritual truth by himself? *Because he is spiritually blind, unable to see or understand.*

9. *True* or False: A person can know beyond a doubt that he is truly converted.

10. How does the Holy Spirit want to use you to build Christ's Church? *He wants me to share the Gospel with my friends and all people so they may hear, believe, and be converted.*

11. A Christian ( ) may do good works, (✖) will do good works, ( ) should do good works.

12. How can a person grieve the Holy Spirit according to Ephesians 4:30-32? *Through bitterness, rage and anger, brawling, slander and malice.*

13. *True* or False: According to Romans 8:5-11 we offend the Holy Spirit by resisting His work in us and refusing to do as He prompts us.

14. What are three things the Holy Spirit does for you after conversion?

    a. *Gives me joy and peace.*

    b. *Gives me strength to resist sin.*

    c. *Gives me strength to do good works. (And a 4th: Keeps me in saving faith.)*

15. The *Gospel* is God's power to *convert* people. Faith comes from the *message* which centers in *Christ*. To be God's *disciple or witness* I must be careful that people hear *the Good News* from me and see *Christ* in me.   **[36]**

PENTECOST:
Send the fire again

et's bow our heads for prayer: Almighty God, I thank You for the Good News of Jesus in this Bible study. Tonight I receive instruction on holy Baptism. Forgive me for not always understanding this special washing. Please correct all misconceptions I may have on this important subject. As I better understand Baptism, may my Baptism mean much more to me; therefore, instruct me in this hour. May my Baptismal joy and strength be great. In the name of Jesus. Amen.

There are a lot of misconceptions on Holy Baptism. There are a lot of people who just don't understand. Sometimes they belittle Baptism knowingly or unknowingly. A young Christian lady once brought her unbelieving mother along to Sunday morning worship. During the service a baby was baptized. When the service was over and the two women were making their way out, the unbelieving mother commented in disgust to her believing daughter: "I just don't see how putting some water on a baby's head is going to do everything that Pastor said." That unbelieving mother is obviously ignorant of what the Bible teaches on Baptism.

But she is not alone. Baptism has been in use for 2,000 years. That's a long time, and yet, there are few people even in the church who know much about it. There are many false ideas on Baptism. Last week I asked how much time you would need to tell us all you knew about the Holy Spirit. Most of you indicated that 10 seconds would suffice. Most of you would not need more than 10 seconds tonight to tell us all you know about Baptism.

We need to ask: Could my parents or my pastor have erred in what they taught me? Well obviously some of them have erred because there is so much diversity in what we believe about Baptism. One church says you have to be immersed, and another church says no, you don't have to. One church says you can be saved without Baptism, and another church says no, you have to be baptized to be saved. There is huge diversity of thought here. Who is right? Better yet, what does the Bible say? It's important that I find out what the truth really is. It's important that I set aside past input for a moment – that I concentrate totally on what the Bible says. I could be wrong. I want to be right.

I need to say with the Psalmist: "Lord, speak, your servant is listening." He placed the Word above himself and himself beneath the Word. So many of us, instead, put the Word below us and we decide what it is saying; we dictate to the Word. That's not the way to learn. To learn I must make myself subservient to the Word and become obedient to it. I want to suggest that you let the Bible teach. Jesus promises, "If you continue in My Word, you will know the truth, and the truth will set you free" – free from a lot of bad things you don't really need in your life.

Tonight *I Have Good News For You*. It's going to change your outlook on yourself, your status as a Christian, and the role Baptism plays in your life.

Lesson 5

I HAVE GOOD NEWS FOR YOU

About A Washing Which Cleanses You

1. Who commanded baptism?

• MATTHEW 28:18-20 *Jesus* came to them and said, *"All authority* in heaven and on earth has been given to Me. Therefore *go and make disciples of all nations, baptizing* them in the name of the Father and of the Son and of the Holy Spirit, and *teaching* them to obey everything I have commanded you."

It isn't the church that instituted Baptism, it is Jesus. He states that all authority in heaven and on earth has been given to Him. He has complete authority to give the command that He is about to give. What is the command from the One who has all authority? Go and make disciples of all people. He then describes two ways in which this is to be done. 1. By baptizing people (Put a # 1 above *"baptizing"*). And 2. By teaching people (Put a # 2 above *"teaching"*). These are the means we will use to disciple people for the Lord.

Jesus Himself gave us the sacrament of Holy Baptism. Scripture tells how the early Christians happily carried out His command to make disciples of everyone and to baptize them. Note: There are only two Sacraments, that of Baptism and Holy Communion. By a Sacrament we mean a sacred act (1) which was instituted by God, (2) in which there are certain externals such as water, (3) which are united with God's Word, (4) and which offers and conveys the forgiveness of sins and all other spiritual blessings earned by Jesus on the cross.

I want to contrast this to the seven sacraments in the Catholic Church; They are: Baptism, Lord's Supper, Confirmation, Penance, Matrimony, Ordination into the Priesthood, and Extreme Unction. We do not believe these seven all convey forgiveness of sins. I like to stick to this simple definition given here in your book as criteria for a sacrament.

2. What does the word "baptize" mean?

[37]

Look at the first line of the conclusion below. There you see "βαπτιζω (baptizo)" which is the Greek word for baptize. Circle these two words and **write "baptizo" above "baptize" in Question 2.** You can see from the letters how we get the English word "baptize." Baptize in Greek means to apply something, in this case, to apply water, but it could be other things. If I were painting my house I might say I'm going to baptize the house. If I was going to wash my hands under the faucet, I would say I'm going to baptize my hands. For a few moments we're going to look at several passages to get a better understanding of this word "baptize."

MARK 7:4 When they (the Pharisees and all Jews) come from the marketplace they do not eat unless they *wash* (baptize). And they observe many other traditions, such as the *washing* (baptizing) of cups, pitchers and kettles.

Who were the Pharisees? They were the religious elite among the Jews and were known for their meticulous obedience to religious law. Their influence was great and many Jews followed their legalistic teaching and practices. Jesus here says that when they came home from the marketplace they would first wash or baptize. What did they also baptize? Cups, pitchers and kettles. This washing was not done for sanitary reasons, but for religious reasons. It was assumed that Gentiles had touched these items thereby making them unclean. So this baptism was simply an application of water to their hands and whatever else was brought home from the marketplace to make them clean. Failure to cleanse themselves and these items was sin. Jesus is here using this word βαπτιζω (baptizo). It was used for the application of many things – in this case, the application of water. It could include immersion or an application of water in any manner.

A few denominations say that the word "baptize" can only mean immersion. Unless you are immersed you are not properly baptized. If you want to join their church and you've been baptized by pouring or sprinkling, they insist you must be baptized again. Your first baptism was not valid. The word "baptize" can mean immerse. The chances are, however, that immersion was not used nor is it specified. Some of my Baptist clergy friends insist that Jesus was immersed when He was baptized. They say, "Jesus went down into the water in the Jordan river." I have then asked them,

"But does it say that Jesus went under the water?" They respond "no." Could He have gone under the water? Could have. But maybe not either. As a boy I fished in many rivers, going down into them, but never under the water. So this does not prove baptize must mean immersion, but it does mean to apply something, in this case, water.

I imagine that a few of you are thinking, "Now Rev. Ginkel, you are getting all bent out of shape over one little word. Who cares?" I respond that if our Baptist friends want to insist on immersion (the Christian Church does the same) so be it. They have a right to do that. I don't think we should try to force anyone. But to give you an idea of the difference this little word can make, let me tell you a true story about how this one word was abused and the consequences.

About 25 miles away from my first congregation there is a little town called Lorimor. A man by the name of Bentley Demars lived there, a staunch Catholic. One day Bentley accepted Christ as his Savior and joined our church. He became a devout and energetic Christian. Two years later he died, and I met with his wife, Margaret, for funeral plans. When we finished Margaret asked if we could go visit her neighbor lady who was lying in her house close to death. I said fine. We went over. Here was an old rickety house with only one room. In the middle of the room was an old metal bed, and in this bed lay an old woman well into her nineties. Because of age and sickness her body had shrunk to about 85 pounds. She had lost her hearing, and so I yelled questions at her and she quietly responded. Finally I asked her (really yelled), "Are you ready to go to heaven?" She faintly responded, "No." I yelled back, "Why not?" She whispered, "Because I can't." I yelled, "Why can't you?" She said, "Because my pastor said so." I asked her what happened. She said her pastor from the Christian Church was over to visit her. She told him she had not been baptized. Her pastor said she could be baptized but she would have to be immersed. Now to immerse this dear lady was impossible. There was no way that could be done. And yet her pastor told her, "You'll go to hell unless you're baptized, and you have to be immersed, because that is what the word 'baptize' means." He left, and she resigned herself to hell. I must confess that at that moment Don Ginkel sinned grievously. If I would have gotten my hands on that pastor at that moment he would have received two black eyes and a bloody nose (Yes, I know the Lord wouldn't have approved). I don't know if I have ever been so upset with one person. I spent the next thirty minutes yelling the beautiful story of Jesus into her ear, how Jesus came to suffer and die for her sins, how He wants to give full salvation to her free by faith. We discussed the penitent thief on the cross. I told her that she was saved right now if she believed in Jesus as the thief did. I asked her if she believed she was a sinner. She said yes. Do you believe Jesus suffered and died to save you. She said yes. The penitent thief went to heaven the day he died. Where will you go when you die? She whispered: heaven. I briefly explained baptism to her and that the word "baptize" does not necessarily mean immerse. It means to apply water, but the method or mode are not spelled out (Jesus gives us freedom with the mode; let's therefore not become legalistic. It's precarious and fascicious the way some even want to *insist only* on "sprinkling" or "pouring." Let's just be obedient and apply water.). I asked her if she wanted to be baptized, and she said yes. I took an old pan from the sink, put some water in it, and placed a few drops on her hand. I left her home that day. The next day she left it, too, and moved into her Father's House! Praise God! Praise Him! He is so good!

MATTHEW 3:11 I *baptize* you with water for repentance. But after me will come one who... will *baptize* you with the Holy Spirit and with fire.

John the Baptist is speaking. The word "baptize" is used two times. John says he baptizes with water. The "one" coming after is, of course, the Lord. When Jesus finished the work of redemption and returned to heaven He baptized the 120 disciples on the day of Pentecost with what? The Holy Spirit and fire. "Baptize" here means to apply or to pour out. They were not immersed in the Spirit and fire. The Holy Spirit was poured out upon them. The fire touched their heads. It is easy to see how "baptize" here means to pour out or to apply.

ACTS 22:16 And now what are you waiting for? Get up, be *baptized* and *wash your sins away*, calling on His name.

Paul had been converted on the road to Damascus. He appears before Ananias who restores Paul's sight. Paul had a lot of guilt to deal with. He felt very guilty of his sin of persecuting Jesus. In this verse Ananias is speaking to Paul. What does he tell Paul to do? Be baptized and have all your sin (and guilt) washed away. Baptism is here described as a washing away.

MATTHEW 28:19 *Baptize* them *in the name* of the Father and of the Son and of the Holy Spirit.

Some of you in your conversation with friends about baptism may have said something like this: "Mark, are you baptized?" Mark responds, "Yes, I was baptized Catholic." And Ann here who has Lutheran background thinks quietly to herself, "Oh, that's too bad. I'm sure glad I was baptized Lutheran." And Ramona says, "I was baptized Methodist." What does this verse say? Does it say you were baptized into a denomination? No, Jesus says that when you were baptized you were baptized in the name of the true God, Father, Son, and Holy Spirit. You belong to Him.

The Greek word for "baptize" is βαπτιζω (baptizo), which means to wash, pour, or immerse. Some churches believe that a person must be immersed because they think "baptize" means only to immerse. This is incorrect as the passages above indicate. To baptize simply means to apply water whether there are only a few drops or rivers of it. We should not insist that one particular method must be used since God Himself has not done so. The Lord told us to apply water without specifying either the mode or the quantity. The important thing is to use water and God's Word.

BAPTIZED UNTO THE LORD

When we are baptized "in the name of the Father and of the Son and of the Holy Spirit," we are brought into union with the one true God. If a person is not baptized in the name of the Holy Trinity (e.g. Unitarian Church), there is no valid baptism.

Note that your baptism is not efficacious because of the denomination or the person administering it. Baptism gets its power from God. He is the One working the miracle, not man.

3. Who should administer baptism?

1 CORINTHIANS 4:1 Men ought to regard us as *servants* of Christ and as those *entrusted with the secret things of God.*

Above the word "us" write "pastors." Normally Baptism along with teaching and other duties are administered by the pastor of the flock.

Usually pastors administer baptism. You, however, can also baptize, especially in an emergency when one is in danger of death. In the case of older children and adults share the Good News of Jesus' victory over sin and death. Ask the person to confess his sins with you in prayer and embrace Christ as Savior. Then call the person by name, pour or sprinkle water on the person's head and say, "I baptize you in the name of the Father and of the Son and of the Holy Spirit. Amen." If possible, offer a payer of thanksgiving in your own words and pray the Lord's Prayer.

4. Who is to be baptized?

[38]

MATTHEW 28:19 Go and make disciples of *all nations, baptizing* them in the name of the Father and of the Son and of the Holy Spirit.

> Let me write Τα εθνη on the marker board, and now I'd like you to write that above "all nations." This word means everyone with no distinction. No distinction is to be made with regard to age or sex or color of skin. Jesus says that we're to go and make disciples of all people and that we are to baptize them. I believe we are to do just what He said, first, because He gave the command, and second, because everyone is in need of salvation.

Jesus commands us to baptize all people everywhere, without any distinction of sex or age. All people need to be born again.

5. Why should infants be baptized?

MATTHEW 28:19 Go and make disciples of *all nations, baptizing them* in the name of the Father and of the Son and of the Holy Spirit.

> This is the same verse we just looked at. All nations means everyone with no distinctions. Class, do some churches make distinctions on age? Yes. Some churches say that children must reach the "age of accountability." Well, what is that? Some churches say it's eighteen, other churches say thirteen, and others say seven or eight. There is little agreement among those who speak of this age of accountability. I don't see such a teaching here or anywhere. If this were the only verse I had on Baptism, who do you think I would want to baptize? Everyone! Why? Because Jesus says so. If He would have wanted little children to be an exception to this Great Command, do you think He would have said so? Yes. He would have said, "After they reach the age of three, baptize them" or "After they reach the age of thirteen, baptize them." There is no such comment; in fact, just the opposite, baptize everyone. These words are a command from Jesus. We shouldn't be debating the command, we should be obeying the command. These words are our Lord's last will and testament which He gave to His Church on earth before leaving for heaven. Do you listen to the last will and testament of your father and mother? Yes. Would you try to honor their words? You certainly would. We should also honor these last words of Jesus. This was the last command He gave on earth.

ROMANS 3:22-23 There is *no difference*, for *all have sinned* and *fall short* of the glory of God.

> Class, according to Paul how many human beings are infected with the terrible spiritual disease called sin? Everyone. No matter what the color of their skin, no matter if they are in the church or out of it, no matter what their age, no matter whether you believe it or not all people fall into the category of sinners. This totally shoots down the belief held by some that children are without sin and only when they get older do they sin. I once had a neighbor lady who believed that her little six year old son Jimmy was without sin. She was the only one in the neighborhood who believed that. Not only is all mankind sinful, but all people fall short of the glory of God. Obviously this verse includes little children.

PSALM 51:5 <u>Surely</u> I was *sinful at birth, sinful from the time my mother conceived me.*

> Psalm 51 is David's confession after his sin with Bathsheba and the murder of Uriah. In the opening words he asks for mercy from God as he makes confession of his sin. Here in verse 5 David,

speaking by inspiration of the Holy Spirit, is emphatic: "Surely I was sinful at birth, even from the moment my mother conceived me." Underline the word "Surely." You remember from an earlier lesson that we mentioned that **sin falls into two categories: original and actual. Here David confesses his original or inherited sin. Every human being since Adam has inherited sin.** There is only one woman who produced a holy Child. Who was it? Mary, and that happened only by divine intervention of the Holy Spirit. Some people believe that children are without sin, but sinful parents can by nature only produce one kind of offspring – sinful. And that can be seen further by observing the solemn truth that children, even infants, are subject to death. In John 6 Jesus says that the wages of sin is death. **To our sorrow little children and infants also die and so prove that they, too, were conceived and born in sin.** Every child, just like every adult, is in desperate need of the salvation earned by the Savior on the cross.

ACTS 2:38-39 Peter replied, "Repent and *be baptized, every one of you*, in the name of Jesus Christ for the *forgiveness of your sins*. And you will *receive the gift of the Holy Spirit*. The promise is for you and your *children* and for *all* who are far off – for *all* whom the Lord our God will call."

Here Peter is preaching a public sermon on the day of Pentecost in Jerusalem. He says to the huge crowd of people in front of him: "Repent and be baptized, all of you who have reached the age of accountability." How many? "Everyone of you." All are included. There were men, women, and children there, and Peter said they should all be baptized. And for what purpose? Look at the last four words of that sentence – for "the forgiveness of sins." The next sentence says they will receive the gift of the Holy Spirit who is present in Holy Baptism. The next sentence says that the promise of salvation is for you and who? **"Your children."** These words allow no restriction on age nor do they in any way suggest an age of accountability. "For all who are far off." Who are the "all?" You and me some 2,000 years later. "All whom the Lord our God will call." In Baptism God calls us to be His own. He extends the call and says, "You belong to Me." I want to emphasize that God must call little children to be His own just as He must call adults to be His own.

Let's back up for a moment in time. In the Old Testament children were presented to God at eight days of age. They received a name, and male babies were circumcised. On this occasion God really said, "You are Mine." The New Testament replacement of this activity is Holy Baptism just as the Old Testament Passover has its replacement in the New Testament sacrament of Holy Communion.

JOHN 3:5-7 Jesus answered, "I tell you the truth, *no one can enter* the Kingdom of God *unless he is born of water and the Spirit. Flesh* gives birth to *flesh*, but the *Spirit* gives birth to *spirit*. You should not be surprised at My saying, 'You *must* be born again.'"

Jesus is speaking to Nicodemus who was a Pharisee and a member of the Sanhedrin. Jesus tells him, "I tell you the truth." What you are about to hear is absolutely 100% correct. "No one." That means everyone and anyone, every human being. Rich or poor. Old or young. No age of accountability. **"No human being can enter the Kingdom of God unless he is born of water and the Holy Spirit." The earthly element in Baptism is water. The divine power, however, is the Holy Spirit.** Look at the verse now. Sinful flesh can only produce what? Sinful flesh. But what does the Holy Spirit produce? Spiritual birth or second birth. Look at the last sentence. "You should not be surprised at My saying." We can imagine astonishment written on Nicodemus' face at this just as some of you this evening may be astonished. Nicodemus had spent all his life doing good works to get into heaven, and what does Jesus tell him? You'll never make it that way. Look at the last five words: **"You must be born again."** The "You" is plural; it applies to everyone, including infants. Do you think there are any exceptions to what Jesus says here? No. Then why do some churches and people make exceptions to it and say, "This does not apply to infants."? Let me summarize the point. **No one gets into heaven unless they are born again. Normally this includes the use of Holy Baptism.** There may be an exception or two on Baptism, and we'll let Scripture speak to us about that in a few moments.

MARK 10:13-16 People were bringing *little children* to Jesus to have Him touch them, but the disciples rebuked them. When Jesus saw this, He was indignant. He said to them, *"Let the little children come to Me*, and do not hinder them, for the Kingdom of God *belongs to such as these.* I tell you the truth, anyone who will not <u>receive</u> the Kingdom of God *like a little child* will <u>never</u> enter it." And He took the children in His arms, put His hands on them and blessed them.

"Some people insist that a little child must receive the Kingdom of God like an adult, but actually the reverse is true"

Underline "receive" and "never." Parents were bringing their little children to Jesus so that He would bless them. The disciples tried to stop them. Jesus became indignant with them for their mistake. Luke 18:15 says, "People were bringing babies to Jesus." Class, I want to ask you a question. **Can little children, including babies, receive the Kingdom of God according to Jesus? Yes or no? Yes.** Next, in whose kingdom is a little child before it is in God's Kingdom? Satan's kingdom. Can a little child be received into God's Kingdom according to Jesus? Yes. Must a little child be received into God's Kingdom? Yes. This is an act of God just as it is with an adult. Instead, some church people want to insist that a little child must receive the Kingdom of God like an adult, but actually the reverse is true. Adults must receive the Kingdom like little children receive it, yes, even like babies receive it. The only way a little one can receive God's Kingdom in the New Testament, that we know of, is Holy Baptism.

MATTHEW 18:6 If anyone causes one of these <u>*little*</u> ones who *believe in Me* to sin, it would be better for him to have a large millstone hung around his neck and to be drowned in the depths of the sea.

Underline the word "little." The Greek word for little is "mikros" from which we get words like microscope or micrometer for very small measurements. There are some churches who say that their reason for not baptizing little ones is because they can't believe. Does Jesus here say that little ones can believe in Him? Yes. You say, "How can a little one do this? How can a little eight day old infant believe in Jesus?" I'll answer that question if you'll answer this one: "Tell me how an adult who is dead in sin can believe in Jesus." **How can a dead person no matter what the age come to faith in Christ? The answer: only by the Holy Spirit.** No one else can cause such a miracle. Without the Holy Spirit we cannot and will not come to faith (Lesson 4). The Bible calls this work regeneration. If Jesus says little ones can believe in Him, they can do this. If Jesus says that you as an adult can believe in Him, then you can by the almighty power of God the Holy Spirit. And here is a little after-thought. If the Holy Spirit can bring someone as dead and stubborn and obstinate as you to saving faith in Jesus, it should be no problem for Him to do that with little children. If we want to rationalize at all, it would obviously be easier for the Holy Spirit to work this miracle with a little one than an older person.

Infants are to be baptized (1) because they are a part of "all nations," (2) because Baptism is the only means by which children can <u>ordinarily</u> (underline ordinarily) be born again, (3) because children also need to receive the Kingdom of God by water and the Spirit just like adults, (4) because they, too, can believe in Jesus as their Savior.

(Underline the next sentence which is very important) <u>We note that in Baptism God is acting upon man.</u> Only God can give spiritual birth, wash away sin, and give saving faith. No one, young or old, can do this by himself or even help in the process. Many who reject infant Baptism do not understand this. They think one must be **[39]** older so that he can "understand" the Gospel. "Little children cannot make a decision for Christ," they say. Let us remember, however, that adults cannot do this either. Only God can cause a sinner to believe, and God has also plainly commanded *all* to be baptized. (Underline the next sentence) <u>God can do everything on the grand list of Baptismal blessings just as easily for a little child as He can for adults</u>.

To help the baptized person Sponsors (Godparents) have been introduced. They promise to do all they can to see that the person baptized grows in Christ and good works. They will encourage the baptized person by word, example, and prayer. Only strong Christians should be selected for this important task because only strong Christians can meaningfully promise to do these things.

There is no Biblical command for Sponsors or Godparents. They are not needed for a valid Baptism. I think it is great to have Sponsors for children, but with the understanding that the Sponsors are people who are truly alive in Jesus. Sometimes Uncle Joe and his wife Frieda are asked to be Sponsors because it's their turn or they'll be offended if they are not asked. These are poor qualifications for Godparents. **Some of the duties of Godparents are: 1. To witness the Baptism. 2. To encourage the child to grow in faith and in a closer walk with Jesus. 3. To regularly pray for the spiritual, emotional and physical needs of the God-child so that he may live and die victoriously in Jesus. 4. To remind the God-child of his adoption into the family of God and encourage him in Bible study and in regular church and Bible class attendance. 5. To communicate with the God-child on a regular basis and on his physical and spiritual birthdays with the goal that the God-child will be a faithful disciple of Jesus and someday be in heaven with the Lord.** You can see why God-parents should be fairly mature Christians. Their function is important.

6. What are the benefits of Baptism?

GALATIANS 3:26-27 You are all sons of God through faith in Christ Jesus, for all of you who were *baptized into Christ* have *clothed yourselves with Christ*.

> **"We do not believe in incremental forgiveness."**

Underline the italicized words. When we ask, "What are the benefits of Baptism?" we are also asking, "What should your Baptism mean to you?" First I'm going to ask that you find your Baptism Certificate. How many know where that Certificate is? Okay. I would like you to do this for yourself. Make a big note right now to do it. Go and buy a nice frame for your Certificate and then hang it in your bedroom. Let it remind you every day of your Baptism and what it should mean to you.

What should your Baptism mean to you? What are the benefits of Baptism in this passage? You are baptized into Christ. You have clothed or dressed yourselves up with Christ. His holiness is yours. **When you are dressed with Christ's holiness everything that Christ is, everything He did, and everything He stands for is yours.**

ACTS 2:38 Repent and *be baptized*, every one of you, in the name of Jesus Christ for the (underline the following italicized words) *forgiveness of your sins*. And you will receive the *gift of the Holy Spirit*.

What benefits are mentioned here? The forgiveness of sins and the gift of the Holy Spirit. Baptism gives and conveys forgiveness and the Holy Spirit to the individual. Baptism is not something we do for God, but something He does for us. A little note: Our friends in the Catholic Church believe that sins are forgiven, but only up to the time or point of Baptism. We do not believe in "incremental forgiveness." We believe there is total forgiveness, past, present, and future.

ACTS 22:16 And now what are you waiting for? Get up, be baptized and *wash your sins away*, calling on His name.

What is the benefit of Baptism mentioned here? Your sins are washed away. This is picturesque language for the removal or remission of your sins. They are gone!

MARK 16:16 Whoever believes and is baptized will be *saved*.

What is the benefit of Baptism mentioned here? Salvation. Underline the italicized words in the next verse as we come to them.

1 PETER 3:21 This water (flood and ark) symbolizes *baptism* that now *saves you* also – not the removal of dirt from the body but the pledge of a good conscience toward God. It (baptism) *saves you* by the resurrection of Jesus Christ.

According to 1 Peter 3:21, do you think Pastor Ginkel (use your name) believes Baptism saves and passes on salvation to sinners? Yes! Why do I believe that? Because Peter says so. He says it twice. Baptism saves you.

Let's put the following on the marker board. Please jot this down on the top of this page. Let's write God on top and draw a cross next to it so that it represents everything Christ did to save man. About an inch below that write "Man." The question is: How is God going to bring the blessings of Christ earned on the cross down to man? The answer is that He is going to do it by three particular means. We've already studied one, the Gospel of Jesus Christ. That was Lesson 3. We say that Baptism (and Holy Communion) is a means of grace. What do we mean by such an expression? We have written **God** on top and **Man** beneath. The question is this: How will God bring to man the forgiveness, life, and salvation which Jesus earned on the cross down to man? **We say that there are three means of grace or three channels which God has chosen to do this.** Let's draw three vertical channels now from God leading down to man. **On the first vertical channel write "Gospel." On the second channel write "Baptism." On the third channel write "Communion."** These are the means or channels the Holy Spirit uses to pass on to man that which Christ earned upon the cross. The Gospel, Baptism, and Holy Communion in and of themselves do not save, but they pass salvation on to man. Next Sunday morning we'll have the Lord's Supper at worship. The Lord is going to come to us and pass on to us His forgiveness in the holy meal. He is going to say, "You are forgiven. Be of good cheer. You are Mine." Can a saved sinner hear that enough? No. In each of these channels God is saying, "Yes, You belong to Me. I forgive you all your sin. It's official. Some day soon you'll be coming Home to be with Me." Can you tell how much God wants us to know that this has all taken place, and it is for real?

TITUS 3:5 He *saved us through the washing of rebirth* and *renewal by the Holy Spirit*.

Who saved us? God saved us. How? "Through the washing of rebirth" which refers to Holy Baptism. What are the benefits? **Baptism brings a rebirth. Rebirth means a new birth. Baptism is also a renewal by the Holy Spirit.** What kind of work is the Holy Spirit in? He is in the spiritual renewal business. He must take that which is old and dead and make it new and full of life. The benefits of Baptism in this verse are very pronounced, and they stand in opposition to many reformed theologians who believe that Baptism is merely a symbol or sign.

JOHN 3:5 Jesus answered, "I tell you the truth, no one can enter the Kingdom of God *unless he is born of water and the Spirit.*"

What is the benefit of Baptism here? Entrance into the Kingdom of God by rebirth.

ACTS 8:35-39 Philip... told him the good news about Jesus. As they traveled along the road, they came to some water and the eunuch said, "Look, here is water. Why shouldn't I be baptized?" Philip said, *"If you believe with all your heart,* you may." The official answered, *"I believe that Jesus Christ is the Son of God."* And he gave orders to stop the chariot. Then both Philip and the eunuch went down into the water and Philip baptized him. When they came up out of the water, the Spirit of the Lord suddenly took Philip away, and the eunuch did not see him again, but *went on his way rejoicing.* **[40]**

This man was a black man. Verse 27 says that he was an Ethiopian eunuch, an important official in charge of all the treasury of Candace, queen of the Ethiopians. He was riding in his chariot and reading the Book of Isaiah, the verses that tell of the suffering of the coming Messiah. The Holy Spirit suddenly placed Philip in the chariot with him. He asked Philip what these words meant, and Philip told him the good news about Jesus. They came to some water, and the man said, "Here is water. Why shouldn't I be baptized?" After he confessed his faith, Philip baptized him. Notice that it doesn't say they went under the water, but into it. Maybe they went under, maybe they didn't. Then the Holy Spirit suddenly took Philip away. Look at the verse and tell me: What was the benefit of Baptism for this man? Joy, joy unlike anything He had ever experienced. He went away rejoicing. Tradition says that the eunuch became an evangelist who soon baptized the queen. You who believe in Jesus as your Savior and have been baptized should have the same joy and the same desire to evangelize as he did.

Let's rehearse a couple of important points. What was the first thing the Ethiopian wanted to do after he believed in Christ? Be baptized. That's very natural. When a person becomes a Christian by faith in Jesus the first thing he wants to do is to be baptized. What's the next thing he desires? He wants to learn more, like you are doing tonight, and like we will do next Sunday morning in worship and Bible class. What's the next thing he wants to do? He wants to be around other Christians. A sure test: Someone who says he is a Christian and yet doesn't want to be around Christians has some kind of spiritual problem. Another test: If he doesn't want to be baptized he has a spiritual problem. These things are as normal as a little child going to its mother. People who have had the second birth want to be around other people who have had the second birth. People who have the second birth want to learn more. People who have had the second birth want to be baptized. And **people who are baptized and are alive in Jesus should be full of joy and should share the Good News with others!**

Write these words above the conclusion: **"The cause of conversion"** and **"A seal to their conversion."**

Baptism is more than a symbolic act. It is a real means of grace by which the Holy Spirit causes the sinner and the Savior to be joined, gives forgiveness of sins, brings salvation, new birth and new life, and fills the believer with heavenly joy. It <u>regenerates</u> infants (underline regenerates and run a line from regenerates to "The cause of conversion"), creating saving faith which accepts these blessings. It <u>seals</u> salvation (underline seals and run a line from seals to "A seal to their conversion") for adults who already believe, giving them added assurance of forgiveness and the conviction that they are children of God and heirs of everlasting life.

> You can see how Holy Baptism would be a cause of conversion for little children. But for older children and adults it is a seal to their conversion. Let's assume that the penitent thief would have come down from the cross alive. What is the first thing he would have done? Been baptized. What is the second? He would have fellowshipped with other believers and studied the Word with them. So it is to this day with people who become believers.

7.   How can water do such great things?

EPHESIANS 5:25-26   Christ loved the church and gave Himself up for her to make her holy, cleansing her by the washing with *water through the Word.*

> What is the first word? Christ. It is Christ who affects this cleansing with water and the Word. Notice that the water is connected to the Word, and the Holy Spirit is behind that Word so that we do not simply have water, but we have power, power from on high.

MARK 16:16   Whoever *believes* and is baptized will be saved

> Wherever there is a valid baptism there is also faith, faith in Jesus and in all His promises.

It is clear that just splashing water on a person will not save him. But notice that God's Word is connected to the water. God's Word is all-powerful as seen in the creation story in Genesis 1. Paul says that the Gospel is the dynamite of God to save people. This powerful Word is linked to the water and gives it energizing power. It passes forgiveness, life, and salvation on to the person. And it is faith in Jesus and these promises which accepts these great blessings so they are owned by the individual believer.

> I occasionally have the feeling that a few people think there is something magical about baptizing. You look at question 7, "How can water do such great things?" You look at the passages listed and you say, "Maybe there is a way here to really cause the Kingdom to grow." Pastor Ginkel canvasses door to door, and members go out to visit the unchurched, but maybe we can improve on this. We could form a special "God Squad," and we'll make it up of people from this class. We'll buy a little jeep and place a big empty tank in the back and fill it with water and put a little pump on it and pressurize the tank. We'll have Kim drive, Karen can man the hose, and you go up and down the streets and around playgrounds and whenever you see kids or adults, spray them with water and say, "I baptize you in the name of the Father and the Son and the Holy Spirit," and we'll get this town converted. Ethel here can throw out a few cookies to get them closer to the jeep so it will be easier to hit them with the water. I don't think this is what God has in mind. Older children and adults should first hear the Word of the Lord. And little ones should be brought to the Lord by the parents. And yet I should say that one of my members in a former congregation did take a Jewish neighbor girl who didn't believe and wasn't baptized, but because of the constant witnessing, which was unknown to the parents, the girl came to faith in Christ and then the member lovingly baptized the little girl in her swimming pool one morning. I can see how a Christian out of love would do that, but a "God Squad" with a jeep – no. That would not be appropriate or proper.

8. Can anyone be saved without being baptized?

LUKE 7:30 The Pharisees and experts in the law *rejected God's purpose* for themselves, because *they had not been baptized* by John.

Underline the italicized words. Above "law" write "O.T.," Old Testament Law. Verse 29 says that the people who came out to hear John the Baptist repented and were baptized by him. John was a hard, blunt preacher. Verse 29 says they all heard, and they were all baptized by John. Jesus here makes the observation that the Pharisees, who were leaders in the Jewish church, men who were experts in Old Testament Law, also went out to hear the Baptist preach. In this verse Jesus says they refused to be baptized by John. Look at the last italicized words: *"They had not been baptized by John."* Now look at the first italicized words. What were they doing by not being baptized? They were rejecting God's purpose for themselves. When a person rejects Baptism he is not just rejecting a doctrine, but he is rejecting God Himself. Think about that. We play church games sometimes. We play around with theology like it's nothing more than a game of dominos. We say, "I have a right to accept this" or "I have a right to reject that." I use a non-theological term and say "baloney!" We have a right to do only one thing and that is to believe and do what Scripture says. That is not hard; it's not difficult; it's not complicated.

As far as the Lord was concerned the Pharisees were not just rejecting the doctrine of Baptism, they were rejecting God Himself! When we have people today who don't want to be baptized or who do not want to have their children baptized, we ought to lovingly say, "My friend, you don't know what you are doing. Look at the huge mistake these church people made in Luke 7:30, and it is no one less than the Son of God who says they were making a colossal mistake. You are in danger of rejecting the very love and purpose of God for you, and that is a dangerous thing to do. Please don't do that. Please!" The Lord was very clear and emphatic in the Great Commission. How many people did he say we are to baptize? "All nations!" This is not difficult to grasp. Be obedient to what He says. It's a matter of life or death. When you reject the purpose of God, you're rejecting life and choosing death. In essence these Pharisees were committing spiritual suicide. Be careful. Be inclined to believe and obey God.

LUKE 23:42-43 He (the criminal) said, "Jesus, remember me when you come into Your Kingdom." Jesus answered him, "I tell you the truth, *today you will be with Me in paradise."*

This is the penitent thief on a cross next to Jesus. It would appear that this man was not brought up in the church. He had little or no Bible knowledge. Earlier in the morning he joined the other criminal and the crowd in mocking and ridiculing the Lord. That is how lost he was. He was as pagan as pagan could be. He was a robber, a murderer, and an insurrectionist. The Roman government had it with him and condemned him to death. But as time went on he heard Jesus speak. The Holy Spirit was also present on Calvary and was working on this man's heart. He came to saving faith in Jesus. His prayer: "Remember me when You come into Your Kingdom." In essence he was saying, "Lord, do not keep me out of heaven because of my sins and crimes." And yet, there on the cross, without the benefit of a class like this or a study guide like this, but with the Savior in front of him, he came to repentance and faith in Christ as his Savior. He was converted in the last hours of his life. Be sure you do not gamble with your salvation like he did.

What was Jesus' response to his prayer? Jesus said, "I tell you the truth, today you will go to purgatory and after you have suffered 500,000 years in purgatory, and after the priest prays for you as your family gives him money to do so, you can join Me in heaven." I say this for all you good old Catholics (God really loves you), if ever a man deserved to go to purgatory, this criminal deserved it. I mean he had a record of sin that was horrendous! But what does Jesus say? **"I tell you the truth. Today you are going to be with Me in heaven. Our bodies will die on these crosses,**

but we're going to Paradise." (Be careful so that no one is needlessly offended.)

Purgatory is one of the saddest teachings ever foisted upon mankind by the church in the name of God. I have Catholic friends around the country who have been faithful to the Catholic Church who still believe that before they enter heaven, they will have to spend a lot of time in the flames of purgatory. I have had Catholic neighbors who have given thousands upon thousands of dollars to the Church so that prayers would be said on behalf of a husband or wife to get them out of purgatory sooner. We will study this verse and purgatory more thoroughly in Lesson 10.

We have the three means of grace here on the marker board. Which of these three were used by the Holy Spirit on the penitent thief to convert him to the Lord? Yes, the Gospel. See how these three are a means of God's grace in Christ to lost mankind?

Suppose a baby of Christian parents dies before Baptism. Suppose a man accepts Jesus as Savior but dies immediately without being baptized. The Bible does not say that all who die without Baptism are lost. Saving faith can exist without Baptism. John the Baptist was filled with the Holy Spirit before his birth. The penitent and believing criminal, though not baptized, went to Paradise. Holy Baptism is necessary. We cannot willfully turn it down and be saved. We are bound to Baptism because God plainly commands it, yet He is not bound as the examples mentioned illustrate.

What happens when a baby is stillborn? I think of a young couple in my first parish. She was Lutheran but a weak Christian. He was Catholic and came to saving faith in Jesus. Both became active, growing members of the church. They were expecting their first baby. Everything went well until moments before delivery when the baby strangled on her umbilical cord and was born dead. She was a most beautiful baby. Perfectly formed features, hands, face, and with beautiful long black hair. She was a doll, but she was dead. It crushed the mother, Patricia, and the father. I entered the mother's room to have devotions with her and her husband, Darrell. In love I reminded them of several things. I told them of John the Baptist who was converted in his mother's womb. When Elizabeth was carrying John, Mary came to visit her, and Mary was carrying the Baby Jesus. Scripture says that when Mary walked into the room that the baby John leaped in his mother's womb being filled with the Holy Spirit. Class, the baby John was conceived in sin as all babies are conceived. And yet the Holy Spirit filled him and converted him inside his mother, making him receptive to the Baby Jesus who was present. You know, of course, that the Baptist was to have the enormous honor of announcing the arrival of Jesus and preparing people for Him. There have been a lot of great preachers, but John was the greatest. God made an exception in how the baby John would be converted, namely, prior to birth. It's the only record we have in all the Bible, but it's there. If God made an exception with John, could God also make an exception with their stillborn daughter? Pat and Darrell said, "Yes." Would it have been right for me to say: "I know for sure that your little girl is in heaven."? No. What would I use for a text to prove that? But I could hold out the hope that God made an exception as He did it with John. I also reminded them of the penitent thief on the cross who, though not baptized, went to heaven. Do you suppose that Pat and Darrell were comforted and hoped that their little girl was now in heaven? Yes, yes they did. And so did their friends, relatives, and fellow believers. I believe that we need to be baptized, but if God wants to make an exception in a certain case, He can do that, because He is God. He has bound us to Baptism, but He can make exceptions. We leave that in God's hands. I reminded Pat and Darrell of one other truth – that on the day of judgment, when their little girl stands before Jesus for judgment, as He divides the sheep from the goats, that whatever Jesus does with their little girl, mom and dad will say it was right and will say, "Amen." They both smiled and said, "Yes." On Judgment Day the Lord will make no mistakes. He will do what is right. And to what He says, every one of His children will say "Amen!"

9. What is the significance of Baptism?

GALATIANS 3:26-27 You are all sons of God (Isn't that a beautiful title?) through faith in Christ Jesus, for all of you who were *baptized into* Christ have *clothed yourselves with Christ.*

Folks, you are dressed up with the holiness of Jesus. I image Louise, here, may be saying, "But some days I don't feel very holy." That may be true, but what did Jesus do in your Baptism? He put a garment of holiness on you. Since Jesus has clothed you with His holiness, how should you feel? Very good, very reassured. That is Good News. Is this Law or Gospel? Gospel! Is this good news or bad? Good! Activity on the part of God or man? God! Does it end up with you in heaven or hell? Heaven! So know this and – be happy about it!

ROMANS 6:4 We were therefore *buried with Him through baptism* into death in order that, just as Christ was raised from the dead through the glory of the Father, *we too may live a new life.*

What amazing news! We were buried with Jesus. Through our Baptism we died with Christ. Now we are dead to sin and have a brand new life here and in eternity. Our old, sinful life is history. Our new life in Christ is fact. This is the promise that God makes to you in your Baptism. It is a contract that was signed, sealed, and delivered by Jesus' death and resurrection. What great news!

Unfortunately we do not always enjoy that new life the way we should. I share with you the story of a little boy whose cat died. He kept it in his room for a few days. After discovering the dead cat the mother said, "Please take your cat out to the garden and bury it. It smells!" So he buried it. A couple days later he was really missing his cat, so he dug it up, and dragged it back into his bedroom. It smelled like everything. The mother quickly discovered the smell and said, "Get that cat out of here! I can't stand that smell! Go bury it!" So he buried his cat again. A few days later he got lonely for his pet again, so he dug it up again, and dragged it back to his bedroom." His mother was now ready to go crazy. "Bury that cat! He stinks!"

Isn't that what you do sometimes with your "dead cats," with your sins of the past? You have a brand new life in Christ and yet I can just see some of you going back into your past and digging up some gross sin that you've committed. "God, this sin doesn't smell bad enough. Let's see if I can find one to dig up that will make me feel more guilty and miserable. Ah, yes, there is a horrendous sin. Oh, that really smells. I'll bring that back into my life." Now, folks, that's your "dead cat." What does Paul say? Your sins were buried with Christ. **Since God has buried all your sins with Jesus, don't you suppose you should just leave them there, buried? Stop digging up past sin. God doesn't do that. You shouldn't either.**

ACTS 8:39 When they came up out of the water, the Spirit of the Lord suddenly took Philip away, and the eunuch did not see him again, but *went on his way rejoicing.*

You, too, should go on your way rejoicing as you appreciate who you are and what you are because of Christ and your Baptism. You should have a celebration.

A person is born once, and Scripture says that all those so born are born to trouble and tears. A person is born a second time, but this time it is to hope, happiness, and heaven. Because Baptism forms a union between a man and his Savior, all the qualities of Christ Himself are bestowed upon the man. He shares in Jesus' burial, in His death, and in His resurrection. He is encouraged to shun sin and serve God with a Christian life. Whether Baptism is the cause of salvation such as in infants or a seal of salvation to others, there is new life and joy. Praise be to the Lord who earned it all for us by His suffering, death, and resurrection!

Let's pray together

Dear God, thank You for this instruction on Holy Baptism. Forgive us for our misconceptions and frequent lack of faith in this washing and the blessings You would bring us. Give to us and to those still in spiritual darkness new birth through water and the Holy Spirit. Take away our sins for Jesus' sake. Keep us ever mindful of how our blessed Lord suffered and died on the Cross for our redemption. Help us remember our own Baptism and the blessings which are ours through it. May our Baptismal joy and strength be great. And finally, may we do all in our power to make disciples of all people by witnessing and baptizing. In Jesus' name. Amen.

Let's sing together

> Rock of Ages, cleft for me, Let me hide myself in Thee;
> Let the water and the blood From Thy riven side which flowed
> Be of sin the double cure, Cleanse me from its guilt and pow'r.
>
> Not the labors of my hands Can fulfill Thy Law's demands;
> Could my zeal no respite know, [42] Could my tears forever flow,
> All for sin could not atone; Thou must save, and Thou alone.
>
> Nothing in my hand I bring, Simply to Thy cross I cling;
> Naked, come to Thee for dress; Helpless, look to Thee for grace;
> Foul, I to the fountain fly – Wash me, Savior, or I die!

Bible reading schedule for next seven days

- ❑ 1st day – Romans 5
- ❑ 2nd day – Romans 6
- ❑ 3rd day – Romans 7
- ❑ 4th day – Romans 8
- ❑ 5th day – Romans 9
- ❑ 6th day – Romans 10
- ❑ 7th day – Romans 11

Worksheet no. 5

1. Prove with a Bible passage from this Lesson that we are to baptize and teach everyone:

   Matthew 28:18-20

2. Why is it so important that after Baptism we also teach them? *So that their faith in Jesus will grow.*

3. An act is a Sacrament when it:

   a. *Is instituted by God.*

   b. *Has certain externals such as water.*

   c. *Which are united with God's Word.*

   d. *Offers and conveys the forgiveness of sins earned by Christ on the cross.*

4. To perform a valid Baptism one must:

_____ Tell the person the Gospel story.

_____ Ask the person if he believes it.

_____ Have a prayer and the confession of sins.

_____ Call the person by name.

__✖__ Apply water to the person.

__✖__ Say, "I baptize you in the name of the Father and of the Son and of the Holy Spirit. Amen."

5. We may baptize by (✖) sprinkling, (✖) pouring, (✖) immersing.

6. Why do some churches reject infant Baptism? _Some churches believe children are born_ _without sin. Some churches say that infants cannot believe in Jesus. Some say that children_ _must reach the age of accountability._

7. True or _False_: The Bible does not command us to baptize infants.

8. True or _False_: Every baptized person receives forgiveness of sins. _[Consider the adult who is baptized, but does not believe in Jesus Christ. His unbelief rejects the forgiveness of sins.]_

9. _True_ or False: Baptism is more than a symbol, it also brings salvation. A Bible verse which proves it: _1 Peter 3:21 on page 40._

10. True or _False_: Baptism is no more than a symbol on the part of the baptized person that through faith in Christ he has forgiveness of sins.

11. True or _False_: When the Bible says that Baptism saves us, this is a contradiction of other passages which say that Christ alone saves us.

12. What gives power to the water in Baptism? _The Word of God or God's promise._

13. Briefly explain the statement: "Baptism is a means of grace." _It is a channel or means by_ _which God brings the blessings of Christ earned on the cross to sinful men._

14. According to Matthew 28:18-20 there are two ways we can make Christians out of people and that is by _baptizing them_ and by _teaching them._

15. What practical meaning should your Baptism have for you in your daily life? _It should remind_ _me that my sins are forgiven, that I am united with Jesus, and that all the blessings Jesus_ _earned for me by His suffering, death, and resurrection are mine._

[44]

We begin with prayer: Dear Lord Jesus, we thank You so much that you have brought us together tonight, and we pray that You will come to us again as You did last week, and give a word of instruction to us. We are here to learn about a Meal which can truly feed us. Feed us with Your Word that we may be fed by the Lord's Supper in the weeks, months, and years ahead. Forgive us for any ignorance on this subject on our part. We would learn from You the purposes for which You instituted this Holy Meal the night before Your death. We would learn from You how to prepare ourselves for the reception of this Meal. May this Supper be a means to build us up in our faith more and more until we feast with You and all the redeemed at Your heavenly table forever. Please let this be a blessed and exciting Lesson to us. May it be meaningful to us as we digest the spiritual food You share with us. We ask this for Your name's sake. Amen.

All other meals have definite limitations and rarely accomplish what they should. Not long ago a Christian family took my wife and me out to a beautiful place to eat. We had a tasty meal. One of the problems is that all those nice meals are very limited in what they can do. They take away hunger and provide an occasion for fellowship for a brief period of time. Tonight, however, we're going to look at a Meal served regularly in this church. It's very different from any meal you would buy at a nice restaurant. It's a Meal that has been prepared by God, by the entire Trinity. It is a Meal which we do not pay for. People who take us out to eat have to pay for the meal. Every meal has to be paid for. The heavenly Meal, the Lord's Supper, is no exception, but this time the price was too high for you or any of your friends. In fact, the price was so high that God, Himself, had to make special arrangements for the payment. What did He pay? He had to nail His only Son to the cross of Calvary. It's a very moving story. After hearing it so many, many times, it still makes me sing His praise for being so kind to one poor sinner like me.

Baptism, which we studied last week, is observed once and then we carry its truths and joys with us. The Lord's Supper is to be commemorated frequently, to be served again and again, until one day we get to heaven and sit down at the table that is set by the Lord Himself, and He will serve us. Until then He comes down to earth and presents this special Meal to us. We have an exciting subject to study this evening – one that has eternal implications. We're going to be supping with the Lord forever! We will start now.

Lesson 6

I HAVE GOOD NEWS FOR YOU

About A Meal Which Feeds You

1. What is the Lord's Supper?

In the following verses we have a summation of what transpired Maundy Thursday evening in an upper room in Jerusalem. Jesus and the apostles had just finished celebrating the Passover.

Matthew 26:26-28, Mark 14:22-24, Luke 22:19,20, 1 Corinthians 11:23-25 The Lord Jesus, on the night He was betrayed, took bread, and when He had given thanks, He broke it, and gave it to His disciples, saying, "Take and eat. *This is My body*, which is given for you. Do this in remembrance of Me." In the same way He also took the cup after supper, and when He had given thanks, He gave it to them, saying, "Drink from it, all of you. *This is My blood* of the new covenant which is poured out for many for the forgiveness of sins. *Do this*, whenever you drink it, *in remembrance of Me.*"

On Maundy Thursday, only hours before His betrayal by Judas and His death on the cross, Jesus was gathered with His disciples in an upper room in Jerusalem to celebrate the Passover (Exodus 12:1-14).

I would like you to read Exodus 12:1-14, if possible, tonight before retiring. Exodus 12 describes how God commanded the Jews to take the blood of a one year old lamb without blemish and paint it on the sides and tops of the door frames of their houses in Egypt. On this night God would send an angel of death throughout Egypt. He would kill every firstborn, both of man and beast, both Egyptian and Israelite. God decreed that there would be a safety net in the blood of a lamb. There still is safety in blood, the blood of Jesus, the Lamb of God. God promised that whoever was obedient to His offer of mercy, to this safety net, and painted the blood of a lamb upon the door frames, that as the angel of death went over Egypt he would spare the first born of man and beast.

God, in His mercy, was extending His grace. This was pointing forward to the day when Jesus would come to shed His blood, not on door frames, but on the wooden cross of Calvary, so that all who come to that blood soaked cross would be forgiven of their sins. God is coming in judgment to deal with sin, especially the sin of unbelief. Through the blood of Jesus you are passed from death to life. If Judgment Day comes tonight, you are safe from all condemnation and from eternal death. God said to the Jews who would be spared, "I want you to remember this night. I do not want you to ever forget how much I have loved you. I command that you celebrate the Passover Meal annually." Now we continue –

A new and better Meal was about to replace the old Passover meal. It would be only for disciples of Jesus who were to celebrate it often in **[45]** remembrance of Him. Beside bread and wine Christians also eat and drink Christ's body and blood. We cannot fathom this mystery, but we know that His words are true, and we believe them.

Other names for the Lord's Supper are *Holy Communion* – reminding us of the union of the elements and the union of believers with their Lord and with each other, *Lord's Table* – reminding us that it is set by the Lord with heavenly food, *Sacrament of the Altar* – reminding us that it is usually celebrated at an altar in God's House, *Breaking of Bread* – reminding us that the loaves were broken into smaller pieces by our Lord and were then handed to His followers, and *Eucharist* – giving of thanks.

2. **What is present at the Lord's Table?**

What is actually present? **We're going to concentrate on the elements that we can see and that we cannot see.** The time of the next verse is Maundy Thursday. The words "Maundy Thursday" come either from the Gospel lesson, namely, *"Mandatum novum do vobis,"* or from the custom of carrying gifts to the poor in maund (y) baskets on that day.

MATTHEW 26:26-28 While they were eating, Jesus took bread, gave thanks and broke it, and gave it to His disciples, saying, "Take and eat; *this is My body."* Then He took the *cup*, gave thanks and offered it to them, saying, "Drink from it, all of you. *This is My blood* of the covenant, which is poured out for many for the forgiveness of sins."

The Lord took bread and gave it to the disciples and said, "Take and eat; this is My Body." He then took a cup of wine and gave it to them saying, "Drink from it, all of you. This is My blood." Let me write the Greek word for "is" which Jesus used here on the marker board: εστιν which means "is." Notice the tense of this verb. Is it past, present, or future? Present. How would you define what this verb means in the present tense? The best word might be "reality." This verb simply gives a statement of fact. Do you think **"is"** means **"contains"** or **"symbolizes"** or **"stands for"?** No.

For example: May I say "This is a marker pen."? Is that true? Yes. May I say this marker pen is a piece of bread? Yes, I can say it, but it would not be true because it is not a statement of fact. Why would it not be true? Because it is not a piece of bread; it is a marker pen and because of who said it, namely, me. The reason for our concentrating on this verb "is" is because most reformed churches say that Christ did not mean that the bread "is" His body. Where do they get this? From the fathers of the reformed churches. Who are they? Calvin and Zwingli said, "Christ ascended visibly into heaven. He cannot be physically present in this world. He couldn't have meant that He was really present. He really meant that the bread and wine merely represent and symbolize His body and blood." But Christ used the word εστιν which means is. I do not have a right to change that word to suit my rationalizing mind. I would agree that Calvin and Zwingli do some good rationalizing. The only problem is that it does not agree with what Christ said.

You say, "But God gave us a mind to think." That's true. But aren't there many cases we've already come across in this Bible study that if we were to rationalize we would come up with false theology compared to what God clearly says in His Word? Many times my mind comes to conclusions quite different from what God says. I've learned not to trust my mind, but God. Furthermore, if we're all going to trust our minds, how many sets of theology are we going to have? As many as we have people here in the class. Ethel will have one idea, Francis is going to have another idea, Joe is going to have another idea, and can you imagine what our good friend Jean here will come up with? This is one of the reasons why we have so many different church bodies, because people say, "Well, I think this," and another person says, "No, I think that." My response to that approach is that I don't care what you think. I don't care what I think! I'm not interested. I'm interested in one thing: "God, what do You say?" I don't want anything to get in the way of that including you or me or any church. If we let God talk and we then believe what He said as true we'll be on safe ground.

1 CORINTHIANS 10:15-16 I speak to sensible people; judge for yourselves what I say. *Is not the cup of thanksgiving for which we give thanks a participation in the blood of Christ? And is not the bread that we break a participation in the body of Christ?*

Look at the first question: "Is not the cup of thanksgiving for which we give thanks a participation in the blood of Christ?" Is that past, present, or future tense? Yes, it is present tense. When Paul asks, "Is not the cup of thanksgiving for which we give thanks a **participation** in the blood of Christ?" does he want a yes or a no answer? A yes answer. Take the next question: "Is not the bread that we break a **participation** in the body of Christ?" Does he want a yes or no answer? A yes answer. What do Calvin and Zwingli say? They say no. Who are you going to believe? Calvin and Zwingli or St. Paul? I'll take Paul.

An interesting observation here. Notice how we let the Bible interpret the Bible. We do not say, "I have to interpret this passage." We don't have to interpret anything. About a week ago a lady said, "Pastor Ginkel, how do you get your theology? You do interpret, don't you?" I said no. She looked at me in disbelief. She said, "Well, what do you do?" I said, "I simply let the Bible tell me whatever it wishes to tell me." I don't tell Paul what the above verse means. I let it tell me. I let other verses on this subject shed light on this verse. **Remember this well, the Bible interprets the Bible!**

1 CORINTHIANS 11:26-28 For whenever you eat this *bread* and drink this *cup*, you proclaim the Lord's death until He comes. Therefore, whoever eats the *bread* or drinks the *cup* of the Lord in an unworthy manner will be guilty of sinning against the *body and blood of the Lord.* A man ought to examine himself before he eats of the *bread* and drinks of the *cup*.

THE LORD'S TABLE

Look at these words, class, and tell me how many elements do you see present in Holy Communion? The italicized words will help you. The **bread** and the **wine**. What else? The **body** and **blood**. All four elements are present. But what is present in the Sacrament according to Calvin and Zwingli? All four or something else? Just two. Which two? The bread and wine. But Paul says all four are present. The Lord is obviously telling us again and again that His body and blood are present in the bread and wine; they are connected, so that the communicant actually receives all four elements. Underline the next two sentences as we read them.

In the bread and wine Jesus is present both as the Giver and the Gift. His simple promise is that when we eat the bread we also truly receive His body, and when we drink from the cup we truly receive His blood. We may refer to this as the real presence of Christ's body and blood in the Lord's Supper.

Some churches do not believe that the bread and body and the wine and blood are together in this Meal. The Catholic Church believes that, after consecration, the bread has been totally changed into the body of Christ and the wine into His blood (transubstantiation) so that only two elements are received by the communicant. Most reformed churches, however, believe that Christ's body and blood are not present. "He is in heaven," they say. "The communicant receives only [46] the bread and wine (or grape juice) which are symbols or representations of His body and blood."

But this is not what Jesus says. Jesus says that the bread "is" His body. "Is" does not mean "symbolizes" or "represents." Furthermore, Paul says all four elements – bread, wine, body, and blood – are in the Lord's Supper. It is important to believe just what God's Word says. This is a powerful meal. It is a high calorie spiritual food earned by the Lord on the Cross and set with rich blessings, forgiveness of sins, joy and peace, for all His children to take and make their own.

Before we take the next section I want to share my concern with you regarding the gross ignorance on the purposes and benefits of the Lord's Supper. So many people in the church do not understand this heavenly Meal. Let me illustrate. Imagine a farmer this morning named Fritz opens his barn doors to milk his cows, and he says, "Here bossie!" They all come to the barn lining up in order. Cow # 1 is always cow first, cow # 2 is always second, etc. This never changes. Bessie goes to her stall. Ethel goes to her's. Every cow has her stall. Now as the cows are coming in the barn, let's assume that I would put my arm out and stop cow # 1, old Bessie. I would bend down a little and look into her big brown eyes and say, "Bessie, vas sagen sie? Vas is los? What are you doing? What meaneth this procession?" And Bessie would stand there on all fours and try to think, and then she would lift her soft, beautiful head up toward my face and with all the energy she possessed she would say, "Moooo!" And go on. That would be her answer. That is the best she can do.

Now let's go in spirit to some churches this morning at the early service, and we picture Fred and his wife Elsie who are going into church. It could be any denomination, Methodist, Presbyterian, Lutheran, whatever. It's the 8:00 service. Fred and Elsie come in to sit in their pew, and God help any other folks who happen to already be sitting in their pew. So they sit down. When the sermon starts old Fred goes to sleep as usual. When the "Amen" comes to the sermon he wakes up. He's programmed just like those cows. Then it's time for Communion. The usher comes down to usher up pew after pew. So Fred gets out of his pew and stands in line to go up to the front and Elsie follows right behind him. As he is moving forward in this line I put my hand out in front of him. He stops. We look at him, and we say, "Fred, vas is los? What meaneth this procession?" Fred puts his hands on his hips. He gets a quizzical expression on his face, and he thinks, thinks hard. And finally he looks at us and all he can say is, "Mooo!" And he walks on up to the communion rail. He doesn't know what he is doing. He is doing it by rote, by habit, not unlike Bessie the cow. You say,

"Rev. Ginkel, that's an exaggeration." And I say, "No, sad to say, no. Only too often that is the way it is." Anyone here agree with me? Yes, and that is sad. How it must grieve the Lord who established this holy Meal the night before His death. Ignorance! Gross ignorance! **This ignorance has a very high price tag as we shall see in Questions 3, 4, and 5.**

3. What are the purposes and benefits of the Lord's Supper?

LUKE 22:19-20 And He took bread, gave thanks and broke it, and gave it to them, saying, "This is My body given _for you_; do this in _remembrance of Me._" In the same way, after the supper He took the cup, saying, "This cup is the _new covenant_ in My blood, which is poured out _for you._"

Underline the italicized words. The first italicized words tell us who the Lord's Supper is for. It's for you. What comes next? "Do this **in remembrance** of Me." Last Sunday we had Holy Communion in our church. It was for whom? For you. When we have Communion you are to "do it." You should partake of this Meal. What do we see in some churches? We see people who say they are believers but do not come to Communion. If you did that last Sunday, you were disobedient. Your Lord told you to do this, but you didn't do it. You went and played golf or something else. Who were you disobedient to? Your Savior. Furthermore, you may have been in church and there was Communion but you didn't partake. You may have just sat there and looked at it.

I had one congregation that was like that. It had about 1,000 members. Only 200 were in church on the typical Sunday. Of those 200 about 40 would attend the Lord's Supper. After two months of this I finally asked from the pulpit, "Tell me. What did the Lord say? Did He say come to church and look at the Lord's Supper? Or did He say, 'Celebrate this Meal and do it as I have told you?'" After some time my patience runs thin with people who continually want to be disobedient to this simple command of the Lord. Now if they don't understand, I'll work with them, teach them, encourage them, and love them. But if you just want to be stubborn and just sit there, then let's just forget it. I'm not interested in that. When the Lord's Supper is being served it is for me, and the Lord expects me to partake of it. It is true that the Lord has not told us how often we should have this Meal. Here again I had some in this same congregation who said, "Well, I just go four times a year." Why do you do that? "That's what Martin Luther said." Not so! I told them, "Luther did not say that. You are misquoting him. What he did say is that it is to be feared that if a Christian does not go to Holy Communion at **least** four times a year, he's not even a Christian."

When we go to Communion we are to do it in remembrance of the Lord. Let's imagine that a year ago today someone saved your life in a burning building or from drowning in a lake; this happened one year ago today. Would you celebrate this anniversary in a befitting manner? Would you do that? Absolutely. This would not be a normal day for you. It would be a very thoughtful day. You would do a lot of thinking. Now Someone has saved you from something a lot worse than a burning building or drowning. This Person has saved you from everlasting death in hell. Who is this Rescuer? Jesus! He literally went through hell on the cross for you. He saved you and died in the process of doing it. Jesus is saying, "I want you to remember how I saved you from certain death, from the judgment of God, when I died for you on the cross of Calvary." Is it appropriate that you remember that? Sure. Should you? Sure. If you are at all grateful, you will do that.

Look at the last sentence of this verse. What is this cup? It's a **new covenant** in Jesus' blood poured out for you. This is the last will and testament of Jesus. He was gathered with His disciples and said, "This is my will for you. Do this. Remember what I have done for you." If your mom and dad had drawn up a will, would you have the right to change it? No. Do you even have a right just to think about changing their will? No. Then why is it that some churches and church people feel they have a right to change the last will and and testament of our Lord? I do not understand that. We have only one right and that is to be cheerfully obedient to that which the Lord has commanded.

MATTHEW 26:27-28 Then He took the cup, gave thanks and offered it to them, saying, "Drink from it, all of you. This is My blood of the *new covenant,* which is poured out for many for the *forgiveness of sins.*"

What is the purpose and benefit of this heavenly Meal according to the last words? "The forgiveness of sins." Would you like to be told in a very personal way by Jesus, not by the church, not by the pastor, but by Jesus that your sins are forgiven, that He loves you, and that everything is okay – would you like that? Yes. That's one of the purposes of Communion. Church people who are ignorant of this miss out, people like Fred and Elsie. They simply go through motions. They do not understand the purpose of this Meal, and they pay a high price for their ignorance. Look at the verse and tell me how many believers should drink from the cup? "All of you" or everyone, every believer. I have to ask you: Did you do that last Sunday morning or did you skip?

Why do some of our Catholic friends eat bread but not drink wine at Communion? Many Catholic Churches offer the communicant the consecrated wafer which they now refer to only as the very body of Christ. That is easy to do. Wine, however, is difficult to handle. They ask, "What would happen if some of the wine which is now only the blood of Christ would accidentally be spilled?" That would be a tragedy. To preclude any such accident the priest will drink the wine for the communicant. That's why in the past there have been jokes about why the local Catholic priest gets drunk. Jesus, however, says that every believer is to receive the bread, and everyone is to receive the cup. He uses the words, "All of you." Yet, according to this verse, people who do not recognize Christ's body and blood in the Sacrament should not participate.

1 CORINTHIANS 11:26 Whenever you eat this bread and drink this cup, <u>you proclaim the Lord's death</u> until he comes.

Underline the words, "You proclaim the Lord's death." **The Lord's Supper is based on the death of the Lord.** For example, last Sunday, when Louise here came up for Holy Communion she was preaching a sermon. What was the sermon that she was preaching to the congregation? She was saying, "Christ died for me." What were Fred and Elsie saying? Moooo! God wants going to Communion to be a thoughtful experience, and when it's not thoughtful, it's thoughtless.

Now a question. Let's say that last Sunday Louise, instead of partaking of Communion, would have just sat there and not come forward. She is a member of our congregation, but she just sat there. What kind of a sermon was Louise preaching by her sitting there? She was saying, "I don't believe He died for me." If she really believed that Jesus died for her, where would she be? She would be at the Communion rail receiving Jesus' body and blood. Notice that whether you sit there and just look at Communion or go up and receive it, you are proclaiming something. What do you proclaim when you go and play golf or go to a football game instead of coming to the Lord's Supper? Remember, there is nothing sinful with golf or football, but what are you proclaiming? You're saying I believe in my golf, or footfall, or fishing, or whatever it may be, and I want to put that ahead of my Lord." When it's time to go to the Lord's Supper, I ought to be doing that, unless things beyond my control prevent me, and sometimes that happens. By the way, if you are sick for a period of time you should let me know, and I will be happy to bring the Lord's Table to you at your sick bed.

1 CORINTHIANS 10:17 Because there is one loaf, *we,* who are many, *are one body,* for we all partake of the one loaf.

No matter how many people come forward for the Lord's Supper, we are all one body. Just as there is one loaf, so we are all one. This is why I do not like to have Communion at weddings or Bible study groups. I like the body to be present. Question, what is the member saying who just sits in the pew and does not come forward? "Well, I guess I don't really belong."

The purpose of this meal is to give us the most personal assurance that our sins are forgiven through faith in Jesus; it is a covenant or promise by the Lord. By it we receive strength and encouragement to live a holier, more dedicated life. We remember Jesus' death which gives us life and forgiveness of sins. When we go to the Lord's Table we publicly preach a powerful sermon: the theme – Jesus gave His body and shed His blood to make atonement for our sins! We also proclaim that we are one with Jesus and with each other. When this Table is set, Jesus is saying, "Come and help yourself. It's all for you!"

4. Does everyone who attends the Lord's Supper automatically receive these blessings?

1 CORINTHIANS 11:27,29-30 Whoever eats the bread or drinks the cup of the Lord in an *unworthy manner* will be *guilty of sinning* against the body and blood of the Lord... For anyone who eats and drinks *without recognizing* the body of the Lord *eats and drinks judgment on himself*. That is why many among you are weak and sick, and a number of you have fallen asleep.
[47]

"A communicant is either eating and drinking to his salvation or he is doing it to his eventual downfall"

Paul is saying that there is a right way and a wrong way of attending this heavenly Meal. You can come and be blessed or you can come and eat and drink God's judgment on yourself. Class, I want to tell you something right now: when you go to this God-given Meal, something terribly good is going to happen or something terribly bad is going to happen. Who will decide which of the two? You will. Look at the first italicized words. If you eat and drink in an unworthy manner, in an improper way, you are guilty of sinning against the body and blood of the Lord. Look at the second sentence. Let's say that you do not know or you do not believe that Christ's body and blood are present. You believe you are just receiving bread and wine. What are you doing then, according to Paul? You are eating and drinking the judgment of God upon yourself.

Look at the last sentence. Paul says that is why some of the Corinthians were sick. They didn't understand what they were doing and were bringing God's judgment on themselves. Others who didn't know what they were doing received the judgment of God in another way. What happened to them? They died. You say, "Pastor, do you think this still happens today?" Yes, I believe that. A communicant is either eating and drinking to his salvation or he is doing it to his eventual downfall. With other meals there are no such results. We can eat other meals with any attitude. Who cares, other than the company around us. But here is a Meal, if we do it correctly, we receive good things, and if we do it incorrectly we receive bad things which could end in disaster.

HEBREWS 11:6 Without *faith* it is impossible to please God.

Above the word "faith" write the word "saving." This teaches me that without saving faith in Jesus Christ as my personal Savior I cannot please God, in fact, I'm even unacceptable to Him. What makes me pleasing to God? Jesus! Jesus makes me acceptable to my heavenly Father. Without faith this is impossible, and without saving faith one should not partake of Holy Communion.

In and of themselves no person is worthy of the Lord's Supper, no one except he who believes on the Lord Jesus. *(Watch the next sentence. It's very important.)* Christ makes us worthy. Those who do not believe that Jesus died to save them or who do not believe that His body and blood are present in the Supper bring judgment on themselves.

5. Who should not eat and drink the Lord's Supper?

1 CORINTHIANS 11:28-29 A man ought to <u>examine</u> himself *before* he eats of the bread and drinks

of the cup. For anyone who eats and drinks *without recognizing* the body of the Lord eats and drinks judgment on himself.

Underline the word "examine." The Greek word for examine is δοκιμαζω. This word means to examine or test such as the testing of coins and metals as to content and weight. Paul uses that word here. He says, "I want you to δοκιμαζω or examine not a coin, but yourself. Put yourself under the microscope before you eat and drink of Christ's body and blood." Why? Because Paul says that anyone who eat and drinks in an unworthy manner not recognizing the Lord's body and blood brings judgment on himself. The Lord's Supper is not like going for breakfast at Perkins. It really makes little difference how one goes to eat at Perkins. But with this heavenly Meal it makes all the difference in the world. This must be done correctly. Who should not eat or drink? From this verse we learn that **a person who does not or cannot recognize the presence of Christ's body and blood should not attend**. Wait until you can understand a few important details.

1 CORINTHIANS 10:21 You *cannot* drink the *cup of the Lord and the cup of demons too*; you *cannot* have a part in *both the Lord's table and the table of demons.*

Let's get some background information. Heathen temples had large eating areas for their feasts. Here food and drink were consumed. This food had been offered to some idol. A misguided or weak Christian might think it was harmless to go the Table of the Lord Jesus to eat and drink His body and blood and then attend an idol feast. Paul does not state that such a Christian will immediately lose his Christian faith. However, one cannot willfully and continually eat at both tables. Paul calls the two: the Lord's table and the table of demons. **We cannot continually and willfully serve the Lord and Satan at the same time. A man cannot have two masters.**

Now this question comes to mind: What should I do if we have Communion next Sunday and I have sinned against my Lord? Should I partake of the Lord's Supper? Yes, because this Meal is for sinners. Now let's assume that I have been living in willful sin and just don't care. The "don't care" part is the key thought here. "I just don't give a care! It doesn't bother me in the least." Should I go to the Lord's Supper? No. I cannot say, "O Lord, I love You," and then turn right around and say to the Devil, "I love you, too!" That we sin is nothing new. We will do that. But to sin and be impenitent, not to care at all, will really kill you. **Can we attend the Lord's Supper if we have sinned? Yes, if we are sorry and trust in Christ alone to forgive us our sin.**

Underline the italicized words in the next verse as we come to them.

ACTS 2:42 They (the early Christians) *devoted* themselves to the apostles' *teaching* and to the *fellowship*, to the *breaking of bread* and to *prayer*.

These early Christians were the converts in Jerusalem on the day of Pentecost and the following days. Pay attention to the italicized words. These new Christians devoted themselves to these activities: **First, they devoted themselves to the teaching of the apostles.** This should be the fundamental activity of every Christian. They met daily for this purpose. **Second, they devoted themselves to the fellowship.** They were one spiritual body. They were one body in their faith and expressed that in their fellowship. **Third, they devoted themselves to the breaking of bread.** They came together to eat. What does eating together suggest? Friendship, fellowship, and oneness. At the end of the meal they would celebrate the Lord's Supper. At that time the Lord's Supper was commonly called the "breaking of bread." **Fourth, they devoted themselves to prayer.** The word "prayer" was used to designate the entire worship service and not just prayer. The dominating features were the teaching of God's Word and the Lord's Supper. All of this activity expressed their oneness with each other and with the Lord.

Who should not attend Communion according to this verse? Those who have a different belief from that of the Apostles, those who are not one with us in a common confession of faith.

MATTHEW 5:23-24   If you are offering your gift at the altar and there remember that your brother has something against you, *leave your gift* there in front of the altar. *First go and be reconciled* to your brother; *then come and offer* your gift.

The Lord is here talking about one aspect of proper worship. If you come to the Lord's House to worship and present a gift to Him, and there you remember that you have committed some wrong against someone or perhaps you have not granted forgiveness to someone, you should stop where you are, be reconciled to that person, and then come back and offer your gift.

A number of years ago I had a lady in this Bible study. She was in church every Sunday morning and class every Sunday evening. We studied this verse and the following Sunday she was not in worship, but the next Sunday she was at worship. At the evening class she asked, "Did you miss me?" I said "Yes." She said, "Know why I didn't come to church?" I said, "I think so." She started to grin and said, "Well, I had some hate in my heart toward someone. We read that verse, and I still knew I wasn't going to ask for his forgiveness. I also knew that I couldn't come to worship. Finally I got so miserable with myself that I couldn't stand it any longer. I went to him and told him that I was sorry and asked his forgiveness. He said he wouldn't forgive me. What do I do now?" I said, "Don't worry about it. That's his problem now, not your's. The Lord knows that you tried." I asked, "Do you feel any better?" She said, "I feel a lot better." I said "Good. Jesus feels better, too."

You know what? God wants you to have a foretaste of heaven now, this week. You say, "In Overland Park, KS?" Yes, right here, right now. How are you going to do that if you have bad feelings toward someone? How can you have any real joy in Christ with feelings of hatred in your heart? You can't. You must ask for forgiveness and/or grant forgiveness. That is the way to live. And in the Lord's Prayer you even pray this concept: "Forgive us our trespasses as we forgive those who trespass against us." Let's do that.

A person who has hatred or who will not forgive should not attend Holy Communion until that is taken care of.

ROMANS 16:17   I urge you, brothers, to watch out for those who *cause divisions and put obstacles* in your way that are contrary to the teaching you have learned. *Keep away from them.*

"Worship and attend Holy Communion with those with whom you are one in doctrine and practice"

Here Paul tells us to watch out for those who believe and teach false doctrine. "Watch out" might be rendered, "Keep your eyes open." **What does false doctrine do to Christian fellowship? It divides the fellowship.** What happened when the very first false doctrine appeared? In the Garden Satan said to Eve: "Did God really say, 'You must not eat from any tree in the garden'?" That false doctrine ended up dividing Adam and Eve from God. Who were the most famous teachers of false doctrine in Paul's day? They were the well-known Judaizers who taught Law and obedience to it as the only way to merit God's favor and heaven. What is Paul's advice? "Keep away from them." Why? What will happen if you permit a little false doctrine in your fellowship? It will grow.

People who have differences with us in doctrine should really fellowship and worship with who? Those whom they are in agreement with. I would normally expect that a Catholic friend of mine would worship with fellow Catholics. On the other hand I would not normally worship in a Catholic church because I do not believe what they believe. What should be our demeanor if, because of circumstances, we are guests at a Catholic worship service? We should be thoughtful and respectful. Good manners require respect for their church even though we may disagree in a number of important areas. I would not, however, normally worship with them. I do not agree with them on the doctrine of transubstantiation. I do not believe in asking Mary to intercede for me or in acknowledging her as the "co-redemptress of the world." I'm not saying all Catholics are lost. I am saying I don't believe those things. Those differences and others are very important. It would be hypocritical for me to commune with them because my very presence at their table says, "I'm one with this fellowship." Am I really one with them? No. I will, however, be a gentleman and will conduct myself as one when I am a guest. **The overall conclusion: Worship and attend Holy Communion with those with whom you are one in doctrine and practice.**

These people should not eat and drink the Lord's Supper: (1) Those who do not believe in Jesus and who really want to serve the devil, (2) Those who cannot examine themselves properly or who do not see the Lord's body and blood in the bread and wine, (3) Those who have offended someone and forgiveness is not given, (4) Those who do not believe the teachings of the apostles because Communion is an expression of our oneness.

6. How should I prepare for the Lord's Supper?

1 CORINTHIANS 11:28-29,31 A man ought to *examine himself* before he eats of the bread and drinks of the cup. For anyone who eats and drinks without *recognizing* the body of the Lord eats and drinks judgment on himself... But if we *judged ourselves*, we would not come under judgment.

We're told to do several things for preparation. First, we are to examine or test ourselves. When should we do that? Before partaking of the Lord's Supper. I like to do it two times. I examine myself privately, personally on Saturday evening before going to sleep. I examine myself again on Sunday morning at the Communion Service.

What are we to look for? Do we recognize the body and blood of the Lord in the bread and wine? It is critical that we know, believe, and confess that Christ's body and blood are present. In the last sentence Paul says the same thing with different words. **We are to judge or ask ourselves about the real presence of Christ's body and blood. Do we really believe it? Really?** Examine yourself. His presence is not just a dogma that I say yes to intellectually. It's Jesus whom I say "yes" to and whom I recognize as being present in Holy Communion. I subscribe to this teaching totally. This is a heavenly Meal. It's a sacred Meal. It's a precious Meal. There is my Savior, my Lord!

PSALM 51:17 The sacrifices of God are a *broken spirit*; a *broken and* [48] *contrite heart*, O God, You will not despise.

David was aware of his sin. David was wealthy enough to offer God thousands of animals for sacrifice. In the Old Testament these animal sacrifices pointed forward to the Lamb of God who would die on the cross. David, however, realized that to sacrifice thousands of animals would not relieve him of his sin. Here he states the sacrifice which is acceptable to God. What is it? A penitent heart. A broken heart. A heart filled with sorrow over sin. **Before going to Communion I need to ask, "Do I have a broken heart over my sin?" "Am I sorry over my sin?"**

> If your children tell you that they are sorry because they did something wrong, do you forgive them? Sure you do. But do you have a problem if they are not sorry? Yes. God looks at you in a similar way. Don't "die" over the fact that you have sinned. Do "die" over the fact that you are sorry. Have I told my Lord that I'm sorry? Do I mean it when I say that? Examine yourself to be sure you have sorrow over your sin, and God will accept you for Jesus' sake.

MARK 1:15 "The time has come," Jesus said. "The Kingdom of God is near. *Repent* and *believe* the Good News!"

> Jesus says there are two things that I need to do to be prepared for His second coming. First, I need to repent of my sins. **Above "repent" write two words: Contrition, sorrow.** Repentance is used here in the narrow sense, that is contrition and sorrow in my heart because of my sin. Repentance in the broad sense would include the element of saving faith. Second, I am to believe the Good News of Jesus. The Greek word for "believe" is πιστευετε. **Write these three words next to "believe": knowledge, assent, trust.** I am ready for the Lord's coming in the sky, and I am ready for Holy Communion by asking myself: Do I really have sorrow in my heart because of my sin? Do I really believe in Jesus as my Savior in my heart or just in my head? How many times should we ask ourselves these two questions? I ask those two questions each night before retiring: "Don Ginkel, where are you at? Are you truly sorry for your sins or are you just saying that? Do you really believe in your heart of hearts that Jesus died on the cross to save you?" Like a lot of other things that become habit, this important confession can evolve into nothing but habit. How about you? Do you really mean it when you tell God you are sorry? Do you really mean it when you tell Jesus you believe in Him? Only you can conduct this important self-examination. I cannot do that for you. I have to do that for myself. I also ask these two questions before going to the Lord's Table. **Next to this verse write these words: "For daily personal examination."**

PSALM 119:32 I *run in the path* of Your commands, for *You have set my heart free.*

> The last part of the verse comes first. Through His Word, God has set my heart free: more literally, God gives my heart wisdom so that I am free to do what? Look at the first words of the verse: "I will run, not walk, in the path God wants me to run." Let me paraphrase the verse: "God, as You give my heart wisdom through Your Word, I cheerfully walk on the path You want me to walk." Let me ask a question. Do you say, "God, I really want to run the path You want me to run." Or as God gives you wisdom from His Word do you say, "Well, no, I don't really want to run the way God wants, but the way I want."? The Bible says that, spiritually, we're either going to be soaring like an eagle or walking like a turkey. You cannot fly like an eagle until you can first say, **"God, You have set me free from my sins, from death, from hell. You have given me wisdom. Out of sheer love and gratitude to You, I lay my life down before You."** That's why you should examine yourself for on a daily basis and before partaking of the Lord's body and blood.

Before going to the Lord's Supper we should carefully examine our hearts. Do we recognize His body and blood in the bread and wine? Are we sorry for our sins? Do we have a desire to turn away from our pet sins? Do we really believe the Good News of Jesus' victory over sin and death on the Cross for us?

7. Should we attend the Table if we have sinned or if we have a weak faith?

MARK 9:23-24,26 Jesus said, "Everything is possible for him who believes." Immediately the boy's father

> **"Don't ever let the Devil tell you to stay away from Communion because of a weak faith"**

exclaimed, "I do believe; help me overcome my *unbelief!*"... The spirit shrieked, convulsed him violently and *came out.*

A father brought his demon possessed son to Jesus. Verse 20 says that the boy lay on the ground in front of Jesus twisting, turning, and foaming at the mouth. Verse 21 says that the evil spirit frequently threw the boy both into fire and into water to kill him. The father asks Jesus to take pity on his son's plight. Now look at the first sentence of our passage. What did Jesus say to him? "Everything is possible for him who believes." What is the father's response? He says he does believe, but asks Jesus for help with his unbelief which means his weak faith. Jesus then said to the demon in the boy: "I command you, come out of him and never enter him again." What was the demon's response? He shrieked and convulsed the boy violently and came out."

Class, when Jesus gives a command must even the devils of hell be obedient? Praise God, yes! Does Jesus honor the faith of this father even though it was weak? Praise God again, yes! Now I want to ask you a question. Looking at this verse, which faith saves? A strong faith in Christ or a weak faith in Christ? Both save. Are there times in our Christian life when we are like this boy's father and we have weak a faith, too? Yes. Question: On the basis of these verses would a weak faith be a justifiable reason for staying away from Holy Communion? No. **The Lord loves us, and don't ever let the Devil tell you to stay away from Communion because of a weak faith.** In fact, if we have weakness of faith, it would be all the more reason to come to the Lord's Table. That is one of the very purposes of the Lord's Supper.

ISAIAH 42:3 A *bruised reed* He will not break, and a *smoldering wick* He will *not snuff out.*

The **reed** was a plant which grew in marshy and wet places. It denotes that which is **fragile and weak.** The Hebrew word for "bruised" means that which is **broken or crushed**, but **not entirely broken off.** A bruised reed, then, describes believers who are weak and feeble because of sin and who are bent down by a sense of sin or calamity. What a description of all believers! At best we are feeble and fragile. We can easily be broken. What does God do with such believers? He loves them and cares for them. He does not cast out those who are weak in faith and good works, but continues to work with them.

The wick was made of flax. The Hebrew word for smoldering means that which is just ready to go out. The phrase is used to describe a wick in a lamp where the oil is almost gone. The flame is ready to go out. God will not put us out in a spiritual sense. Here God promises that He will continue to feed and cultivate us. Question: Should you go to Holy Communion if your faith is weak and you feel beaten? Yes. God wants you to come.

• JOHN 6:37 *Whoever comes* to Me *I will never drive away.*

Here is a verse for suggested memorization. The day will never come that Jesus will say to a person who comes to Him, "Get lost!" No matter how great your sin, no matter how numerous your sins, the Lord will never say that. The word "whoever" makes this very personal. You've sinned against God in a thousand different ways and you can sin against Him in another thousand ways, and He will never, ever say, "I'm through with you." He'll never say, "If you commit this sin one more time, you'll go to hell." Your friends may say something like that. Your Lord will never say it!

A father brought his possessed and epileptic son to Jesus for healing. His faith was weak, but the Lord healed his son. A broken plant is tied up to save it, and the smoking wick is given oil and trimmed so it may burn brightly. We should always come to Jesus even though we have sinned, have a weak faith, or are discouraged. We should come to the Lord's Supper even at

these times. The Lord will always warmly receive, forgive, and strengthen us. Friedrich C. Heyder wrote –

I come, O Savior, to Your table, For weak and weary is my soul;
You Bread of Life, alone are able To satisfy and make me whole.
Lord, may Your body and Your blood Be for my soul the highest good!

8. Why should we receive the Lord's Supper frequently?

1 CORINTHIANS 11:25-26 *"Do this*, whenever you drink it, *in remembrance of Me."* For whenever you eat this bread and drink this cup, you proclaim the Lord's death until He comes.

Have you ever received an invitation from an important person to attend a dinner as his guest? There is no one more important than Jesus, and it is He who sends you this note: **"Jesus of Nazareth cordially invites you to a Meal to be given in His honor!"** That meal, of course, is the Lord's Supper. Look at the first sentence and the italicized words: "Do this... in remembrance of Me." Two questions: Can you attend the Lord's Supper and remember Jesus' and what He did for you too much? No. Can you proclaim the Lord's death for you too much? No. So how often should you partake of the Lord' Supper? Just as often as you can.

LUKE 22:19-20 "This is My body given *for you; do this in remembrance of Me."*... "This cup is the new covenant in My blood, which is *poured* **[49]** *out for you."*

The Lord says His body is "for you." His blood is "for you." This is very subjective. It is for me. I should receive the Lord's Supper to remember Him.

MATTHEW 26:27-28 Jesus said, *"Drink from it, all of you.* This is My blood of the covenant, which is poured out for many *for the forgiveness of sins."*

This Meal is for who? For you, if you are a believer. Look at the last words. For what purpose? The forgiveness of sins. I need to be told over and over and over again, Don Ginkel, your sins are all forgiven. In Holy Communion God tells me that my sins are forgiven. He doesn't want me to feel stinky. He wants me to know and rejoice over my salvation. God is pulling for me. He wants me to be happy. I really don't see how a person can be a Christian and stay away from the Lord's Supper and stay away from church. There are times when I struggle spiritually even though I do go to church and to Communion regularly and study my Bible daily. How can people possibly survive spiritually when they don't? I really don't believe it is possible for very long.

The next verse is so beautiful. It's a verse for suggested memorization. Let's read it together:

• MATTHEW 11:28 *Come to Me,* all you who are *weary and burdened,* and *I will give you rest.*

Oh, how we sometimes feel the burden of our sins. Our sin makes us very weary, very tired. **It is the Lord's will to lift from you the burden of your sins.** You've made some dumb decisions in life, haven't you? So have I. With these bad decisions we have sin involved and with sin a heavy burden. Jesus doesn't want us groaning under the burden and guilt of our sin. He wants us to be new people in Him. How is this done? We bring our sin and misery to Jesus and say, "Lord, I don't want it; You take it." He will take away your sin and the burdens that come with it.

We're so foolish at times. We say, "I committed this sin so now I'll have to bear the burden of it." And so we carry it. And some days the burden of our sin gets pretty heavy. Jesus says, "Stop, put your sin and the burden on Me."

Don't do what so many people do today. So many people bring their burdens to a psychiatrist. I cannot recall, in the recent past, any person that I know of who has been appreciably helped by a psychiatrist or psychologist. I have met tons of people who are spending $80 to $100 a hour on psychiatrists or psychologists with little or no success. Folks, you can come to Jesus free, and He will lift the burden from your soul. Take your burden, take your guilt, take what frustrates you, take what scares you, and bring it to Jesus. He invites you to come. It is the height of abnormality to turn Him down, to say, "Oh, no, Lord, I can't believe in You" or "Maybe You can help others, but my case is different." What sad and irrational thinking that is! Jesus is calling, "Come to Me." Why don't you come? Do it tonight. Do it every day. He promises rest for your tired soul. The hymn writer wrote about what Jesus will do in these words –

"And whosoever cometh, I will not cast him out." O patient love of Jesus,
Which drives away our doubt, Which, though we be unworthy Of love so great and free,
Invites us very sinners To come, dear Lord, to Thee!

We should come to the Lord's Supper often because Jesus told us to do so in memory of Him, so that we may frequently proclaim His death, so that we may have added assurance that all our sins are forgiven, and so that we may have spiritual rest and strength.

Let's pray together

Dear Lord, thank You for instituting this sacred meal which we have just studied. In the bread and wine You are present with Your body and blood. Keep us from impenitence and unbelief, from not being reconciled to others, or from any other sin which would keep us from this blessed Supper. Instead, may we come to eat and drink even though our faith may be weak or though we may have sinned grievously against You. As we come may we be assured by You that our sins are completely forgiven. Give us joy, peace, and strength. Then we shall have power to live for You, to spend ourselves in building Your Kingdom, and to be Your instruments in bringing many others to believe in You. This shall be our life's work until You call us to be guests with You at Your heavenly table – there we will forever thank You for Your unspeakable mercy and grace to us. Amen.

Let's sing together

I come, O Savior to Your Table,
For weak and weary is my soul;
You, Bread of Life, alone are able
To satisfy and make me whole.
Lord, may Your body and Your blood
Be for my soul the highest good.

Your body crucified, O Savior,
Your blood which once for me was shed,
These are my life and strength forever,
By them my hungry soul is fed.
Lord, may Your body and Your blood
Be for my soul the highest good.

My heart has now become Your dwelling, **[50]**

O blessed, holy Trinity.
With angels I, Your praises telling,
Shall live in joy eternally.
Lord, may Your body and Your blood
Be for my soul the highest good.

Bible reading schedule for the next seven days

- ❑ 1st day – Romans 12
- ❑ 2nd day – Romans 13
- ❑ 3rd day – Romans 14
- ❑ 4th day – Romans 15
- ❑ 5th day – Romans 16
- ❑ 6th day – Acts 1
- ❑ 7th day – Acts 2

Worksheet no. 6

1. Jesus instituted the Lord's Supper on (   ) Epiphany, (   ) Ash Wednesday, (   ) Pentecost, (✖) Maundy Thursday.

2. When Jesus instituted the Lord's Supper, which Old Testament festival was He observing? (   ) Pentecost, (   ) The Day of Atonement, (✖) The Passover.

3. Check the correct statement(s):
   - __✖__ Christ's body and blood are present in the bread and wine.
   - _____ Only believers receive Jesus' body and blood in Holy Communion.
   - _____ Everyone who eat and drinks does so to his salvation.
   - __✖__ Like medicine is for the sick so Communion is for sinners.

4. What elements does the communicant receive when attending the Lord's Table:

   a. According to Catholic beliefs? *Body and blood.*

   b. According to many reformed churches? *Bread and wine.*

   c. According to the Bible? *Bread, wine, body, and blood.*

5. How is the Lord's Supper like Memorial Day? *American soldiers died to save us from our enemies. Memorial Day is set aside to remember what they did. Jesus died to save us from our enemies – sin, Satan, and hell and earned for us a place in heaven in the Father's House.*

6. *True* or False: Before going to Communion we must prove that we are worthy of it.

7. True or *False*: Only Lutherans and members of the congregation can be permitted to go to Communion.

8. Before eating and drinking Paul tells us to examine ourselves. What are three appropriate questions we should ask ourselves?

   a. *Do we recognize the Lord's body and blood in the bread and wine?*   [51]

b. *Do we have true sorrow over our sins?*

c. *Do we truly believe in Jesus as our personal Savior and the only way to heaven?*

9. True or *False*: The frequency of our Communion attendance should be determined by our feelings. Generally speaking we should attend Communion only when we feel a need for it.

10. True or *False*: The Lord's Supper might become meaningless to us if we attend too often. Almost anything can be overdone.

11. List at least three purposes of the Lord's Supper:

a. *We are to do it in memory of the Lord.*

b. *We are to do it to proclaim His death.*

c. *For forgiveness of sins (and for spiritual rest and strength).*

12. What is significant about the term, Holy COMMUNION?

The union of the bread and body, the wine and the blood. The union of Christ with us, we with

Him, and we, the believers, with one another.

13. When going to the Lord's Table we are to do it in remembrance of Jesus. What should we

remember? *How Jesus came to suffer and die on the cross and received the punishment of our*

sins in our stead.

[52]

Let's pray: Lord Jesus Christ, our precious Savior, we give You all thanks and praise for this day and for this Bible study tonight. Lord, many believers have trouble with their devotional life and pay a high price for that. Bless our study of Your Word as it instructs us on how to go to church and the role that Bible study should play in our daily lives. We want to see more of Your beauty and glory. When You were on earth Your disciples asked You: "Lord, teach us how to pray." Your disciples in this room ask the same question of You. May what happens here tonight have a huge impact on our discipleship in the days ahead. We want to love You more and serve You better. Thank You, Lord! Amen.

Once there was an airline pilot who was on a transcontinental flight. He spoke over the intercom saying, "Ladies and gentlemen, I have some mixed news for you tonight. Some of the news is good and some is bad. First, the bad news. We are low on fuel, our instruments are out, and we have lost our way. Now, for the good news. I'm happy to report that we are making excellent time."

That is the way it is with many people in the church. People believe in Jesus as their Savior. They have a good take-off. They are busy at church and all the activities there. There are all kinds of committee meetings, organizations, music groups, fellowship groups, and they are making good time, but in so many cases they don't even know where they are going. Have you ever had that feeling in the church? What are we doing here?

I believe that this Lesson is most critical. We said earlier that the big Lessons of the course were Lessons 2, 3, and 4. Lesson 2 dealt with the Law. Lesson 3 dealt with Jesus, our Savior. And Lesson 4 dealt with the Holy Spirit. After those three I would say this Lesson on a devotional life is the most critical of all. I have been in the ministry quite a few years, and I can say that I have seen the Devil win more victories in this area than in any other and with greater implications for his cause than anywhere else. He seems to have enormous success in the area of the devotional life.

Just think about this in your own experience. How many of us here tonight have to confess that maybe we were trying to read our Bibles or going to church or going to meetings and yet not a whole lot was happening? Not only was there little progress, some of us will have to say that many times we were even going backward in the church. And we wondered why. In fact, a few of us are here tonight because we've been in a church where nothing good has happened to us spiritually. This Lesson is tremendously huge in importance!

Lesson 7

I HAVE GOOD NEWS FOR YOU

About A Devotional Life Which Blesses You

Before we take the first question let me run a few thoughts past our minds. If students went to school the way some people go to church, only when they feel like it, they would fail. If an employee went to work like some people do the work of the church, he would be fired. If a person ate meals like some people partake of the Lord's Supper, they would starve. If one paid his bills like some support the church with small offerings, they would have no credit. If someone neglected his family the way some church people neglect the family of God, they would be charged with desertion. This doesn't work in the secular world nor does it work in the church. If you do that, you're dead! You have big problems.

Now a positive thought. I read of a pastor who went to a funeral home to pay his respects to a good Christian friend who had died. Some thoughtful person had placed her well-worn Bible in her hands. It looked fitting. As he left the funeral home he could recall the joy she had in Bible study. So many times he had visited her at home only to find her studying her Bible. As he drove home he thought to himself: If I was lying dead in a casket and someone put the most appropriate item from my life in my hands, what would it be? Would it be a cigarette? A golf club? A fishing rod? A TV remote control? A football? Or a worn Bible? Or a Bible not worn at all? What would be the most appropriate thing in **your** hands at **your** funeral? Now we're ready to learn.

1. What are some of the privileges and benefits of public worship?

ECCLESIASTES 5:1 _Guard your steps_ when you go to the house of God. _Go near to listen_ rather than to offer the _sacrifice of fools_, who _do not know that they do wrong_.

Underline the first three words. That means, "Watch your steps." **When you go to church you're to watch out HOW you go.** For example, go with the proper attitude. Don't go in to church chewing gum like old Bessie chews her cud out in the field. Go to church wide awake mentally, wide awake emotionally, and wide awake physically. Next underline, "Go near to listen." Above "listen" write "and obey." **The Hebrew word for listen means to listen AND obey.** We're to listen and obey rather than offer the sacrifice of fools who do not know that they do wrong. Just to go through motions is wrong, it's sin! There are a lot of people who do not watch their steps. They do not listen and obey, and God says they are fools and they sin by their actions.

I believe that some church goers who don't guard their steps are very naive. They're like the woman whose car had stalled, and she called a mechanic. He carefully examined the car and informed her that it was out of gas. "Will it hurt," she asked, "if I drive it home with the gas tank empty?" "Not if you can do it," was his reply. It would be cheaper to drive cars without gas, but anyone who has tried it has found out that it just does not work.

The same thing applies spiritually. So many people go to church and nothing ever happens, nothing changes, and they wonder why. Their spiritual gas tank is empty! What do you have to do to "drive on a full tank of gas"? This verse tells you. Watch your steps when you go to church. Prepare yourself beforehand. **On Saturday evening spend time thinking and praying about the Sunday morning worship service. Start anticipating good things from God. Ask God to help you prepare to receive His Word the next day and then to obey it. And come with an attitude of praise to God. THIS PREPARATION REALLY PAYS OFF!**

PSALM 26:8 I _love_ the house _where You live_, O LORD, the place where _Your glory dwells_.

These words come from David. How does he feel about God's house according to the second word? He **loves** it. David's **heart** is there. David reminds us of Jesus. Our Lord loved His Father's house, His church among men. Frequently He would be found there in His Father's house. Why? Look at the verse. Because God lives there in a special way, and His glory is shown there in a special way. **People who truly love God delight in going to the Lord's house, to see His glory and to sing His praise.**

I find myself saying this during the week: "Lord, I can't wait to meet with the saints Sunday morning, but even more important, to meet You, to give You my praise, to feed on Your Word, to attend the Lord's Table." Anticipation builds up within me as the week progresses. Perhaps it is true: What you expect is what you get! I hear some folks say, "Oh, I go to church, and I don't get anything out of it." Why? One reason may be that they are not expecting anything. It could also be that you have the wrong church. And maybe the reason is you. Learn from David. **Strive to be able to say in all honesty, "I love the house of the Lord!"**

PSALM 27:4 _One thing I ask_ of the LORD, _this is what I seek_: that I may _dwell in the house of_

114

the LORD <u>all the days of my life,</u> to *gaze upon the beauty* of the LORD and *to seek Him* in His temple.

King David has one over-riding desire. What is it? To dwell in the house of the Lord. Underline the first words: "One thing I ask of the Lord." If God would grant him only one thing it would be this. David asked for this in prayer. Underline "this is what I seek." What do those five words mean? They mean that he would really work at it. In David's day the priests had their lodging in the courts of God's house. David was a well known military hero and king, yet, he would rather be like the priests. David is making it very clear that he had this one desire: to daily be at the public worship of God with other faithful Israelites.

I want to tell you something about God's children who are growing. They desire to dwell in God's house. Should that be a surprise? No. God's children desire this and seek it. For what purpose? What did you come to see in church this morning? What did you come to gaze upon? Did you come to be an audience so that if the pastor did a good job you could cheer, "Yea," and if he did a poor job you could say, "Boo!"?

Learn from David. David is not over-awed by the sacrifices, nor the good music and singing. Look at the italicized words. **David wanted to be in God's house to "gaze upon the beauty of the Lord and seek Him."** Some people come to church to listen to the choir. Some people go to church to see how their friends are dressed. "Did she get that new outfit this week, and how does it look?" Some people go to church out of habit. **We should go to gaze upon the beauty of the Lord.** David loved the beauty of God, His love and grace, the promise of the Messiah. The last italicized words say he wanted to seek God in His temple or inquire of God. He wanted to ask God questions like Paul right after his conversion: "Lord, what will You have me do?" Finally, notice how long David wanted to do this? Was it for one hour on Sunday morning? Find and underline the words. "All the days of my life." Brothers and sisters, strive for that kind of thinking in your life. Then you'll find that you're a growing, happy Christian, too!

2 CHRONICLES 30:8 Do not be stiff-necked, as your fathers were; *submit* to the LORD. *Come* to the sanctuary, which He has consecrated forever. *Serve* the LORD your God, so that His fierce anger will turn away from you. **[53]**

Underline the three italicized words. Here we have three commands. Above **"submit"** write "No. 1" Above **"Come"** write "2." Above **"Serve"** write "3." Notice that these three verbs are action verbs. First you are to submit. Above that write "yield" or "surrender." Do you yield yourself to the Lord or do you say you're going to do what you want no matter what? Second, come to the sanctuary. Don't stay home. Don't play golf. Come! And third, "Serve" the Lord in your everyday life. God's children serve Him every day.

LUKE 10:39-42 Martha had a sister called Mary, who sat at the Lord's feet *listening to what He said.* But *Martha was distracted* by all the preparations that had to be made. She came to Him and asked, "Lord," don't you care that my sister has left me to do the work by myself? Tell her to help me!" "Martha, Martha," the Lord answered, "you are *worried and upset about many things,* but *only one thing is needed.* Mary has *chosen what is better,* and it *will not be taken away* from her."

Who was the honored dinner guest at Mary's and Martha's house? It was the Lord. What an honor. Now if the Lord were coming visibly, physically to dine at your house, do you suppose you would provide the very best meal that you possibly could? Yes. You would do that because you love Him. **Mary sat at the feet of Jesus as He taught her. Class, this complete attention to Jesus' Word** is the mark of true discipleship even today. The dinner was not yet ready, and so Martha attends to the elaborate preparations. Did Martha love Jesus? Yes. She is out in the kitchen hustling, bustling, and getting more frustrated with her sister who wasn't helping her. Finally, she had it. She doesn't come to Mary. She comes to Jesus and says, "Lord, don't you care that I have to do this work by myself? Tell Mary to help me." There's a little bit of gall here, isn't there? In a way she is faulting Jesus. Jesus is very kind and gentle. He says, "Martha, Martha." The double use of her name intensifies His love. Jesus does not chide her for her labor of love, but **He tells her that at this moment "only one thing is needed," not the dinner, but the Word.** Then, He adds, Mary has chosen that one thing, the Word, which will not be taken away from her.

What do we learn from this? It's one thing to have a meal; that's fine. It's quite another thing to have the opportunity to sit with the Lord and be taught. The Lord would rather have had Martha spend this time with Him. Then, afterward, attention could be given to the dinner. See how we can have good intentions and still be wrong?

Let's ask this question of Joyce. If you were having all-day company next Sunday would you skip worship and Bible class Sunday morning? You wouldn't skip? That's good, because you are choosing the one thing needful. Would you invite them to come with you? Yes. But what do you say to your friends or relatives who don't want to come to worship and Bible class and they have to sit at your home waiting for you? "Tough beans?" I was thinking of being a little more gentle, like, "I'll see you in a couple of hours." Will visitors in most cases go with you to church? Yes. And if they declined would most people be offended if you said, "I'll see you in a couple of hours?" No.

Last Christmas season I received a card from a Christian friend who wrote a message inside and closed with these words: "Don't be like Martha. Have a 'Mary' Christmas!" Those eight words made an indelible impression on me and encouraged me to put the Lord and His Word before so many holiday activities. **You might want to write those eight words down on the top of this page: "Don't be like Martha. Have a 'Mary' Christmas!"**

• ROMANS 10:17 Consequently, *faith comes from hearing the message*, and the *message is heard through the word of Christ.*

Let me put this acrostic on the board: **B**asic - **I**nstructions - **B**efore **L** eaving - **E**arth. I like this. What is the central message of the Bible? Salvation through Jesus. I'm not ready to leave earth until I have the Gospel message. Let's see how this verse drives that point home.

Above the word "faith" you can write the word "saving." True or False: Saving faith comes from listening to the evening news on CBS. False. True or False: Saving faith comes from going to church on Sunday morning. False. True or False: Saving faith comes when a message is heard that deals with the Gospel of Jesus Christ. True! We are not just to go to any old church, but to a church that clearly preaches salvation through Jesus. Is it okay if they preach the Gospel every other Sunday? No. The message of the church you attend should hold Jesus up at every worship service and in every Bible class. I have this little rule in my preaching. The sermon could be on prayer or Christian living or stewardship, but the message must always get to Jesus, our Savior. **Every sermon and every Bible class must say that Jesus died on the cross for sinners.** Why? Because this is the central message of the Bible and everything revolves around it.

One of the strangest compliments I ever received came from a member one time who said to me, "Pastor, I want to quit this church." When I asked why, he responded, "Because I get tired of you always talking about Jesus as Savior. Can't you ever talk about something else?" I was dumbfounded. My mouth must have dropped open. My first reaction was to put him down for that kind of thinking. Then I felt very bad for him. And then I thought, "Thank you for the compliment."

Another neat comment. One of my members was ringing doorbells trying to find people she might witness to and invite to church. She was talking to a man whose family attended a very liberal church in our community, well known for not preaching Jesus. She tried, in various ways, to get him to try a church just once that preached the Gospel. Her one last contemplative question to the man went like this: "Why," she asked, "would you want to eat food from 'Meals On Wheels' when you can dine at a four-star restaurant?" Are you feeding spiritually at a "four-star restaurant"? Will you encourage your friends to do the same?

PSALM 122:1 I (David) *rejoiced* with those who said to me, "Let us go to the house of the LORD."

These words come from King David. Some of David's friends stopped by and said, "Let us go to the house of the Lord." What was King David's reaction? He rejoiced. David was glad to join fellow believers in the public worship of God. We should do the same thing. **Get excited, and stir up those with you into excitement for what is about to happen.**

I have to chuckle sometimes as I look at a congregation from the chancel. I've preached in a lot of churches and, frankly, sometimes it's like looking out at 300 dill pickles. All the faces are sad as though grandma just died and maybe God was getting ready to die. I sometimes wonder, why are they so sad? "I was sad because of the organist and her playing." "I was sad because of the preaching of the pastor." "I was sad when they passed the offering plate, and I lost some of my money." Is there something that makes you sad when you go to worship? I think some of us have a real problem here. How was it this morning when you went to church? Did you rejoice? Did you wake up this morning and say with enthusiasm, "Boy, this is the day to go to the Lord's house. This is the day to go and rejoice in the Lord."? Or did you say, "Oh, man, church again!"? **What was your attitude this morning?**

One time a lady named Carolyn was attending this class. We studied this verse. I remember saying, "I would appreciate it once in a great while if you would just let me know how the worship service is going. Give me a signal or something that you're getting something out of this, that you like it, and it's great. And if not, give me thumbs down." A few weeks later Carolyn was at worship with her family. We were about half way through the sermon. Carolyn was to my left, a few pews from the front. I had forgotten all about what I had said to the class on this verse a few weeks earlier. I had just driven a point home from Scripture, and apparently it really got Carolyn's attention. At that moment my eyes were moving to the left down toward the front, and there was Carolyn, and she gave me this signal. She rounded her fingers in an okay sign. She held her hand up high and moved her hand back and forth with a big grin on her face. She was letting me know, "Man, I like this. This is good." I had to work hard to keep from laughing. She was trying so hard to let me know that she was rejoicing over what was being said. Is it okay to do something like that? Yes. You can nod your head yes, or, if it's real good, why not say out loud, "Yes!" or "Amen!"

It is a great privilege to come into God's presence in public worship. He tells us to watch our steps as we go to meet Him, to come close to Him to better see His beauty, to listen to His counsel, and to praise Him in word and song. In worship we are personally involved with God and He with us. We are also in fellowship with other members of God's family. Here we give and receive mutual encouragement and experience spiritual growth which brings glory to God.

Before going on let me give you some suggestions on how to retain the main points of the sermon. Write these points down on the bottom of this page. **1.** During the sermon jot down a few words on your bulletin which contain the main points of the sermon. **2.** During the reception of the offerings review these points in your mind. **3.** During the silent prayer at the end of worship let your prayer zero in on these points as you talk to the Lord. **4.** When you are in your car for the drive home review and discuss the main points again, but this time with those riding with you. Ask, "What can we do to put this into action today and through the week?" **5.** Sunday evening, in your private prayers, go over these points with the Lord and include implementation. **6.** On Monday be conscious of what you need to do. Act out the instruction of the sermon in your life. *(Pastor, you may want to reproduce this paragraph on 3 x 5 cards and give to your students at this time.)*

2. What role should Bible study groups, family and private devotions play in my life?

Now we're going to leave the formal study of the Word and go to the informal study of the Word. As a lead-in to that, does the name Bud Wilkenson strike a bell with anyone? Years ago Bud Wilkenson was a very successful college football coach in Oklahoma. One day some reporters asked him to define football. This is was his definition: "Football is a game where there are 22 players in desperate need of rest and 50,000 fans in desperate need of exercise." **Class, the formal study of the Word needs some augmentation.** Let's see what we need to do so that we Christians are not like those 50,000 football fans.

HEBREWS 10:25 Let us not give up *meeting together*, as some are in the habit of doing, but let us *encourage one another* – and all the more as you see the Day approaching.

One of the purposes of the Book of Hebrews was to counter the defection of Christian converts back to Judaism. Then and now we are not to give up meeting together. These gatherings were more informal for the purposes of study of the Word and prayer and fellowship. **I believe the Devil works very hard at getting us to give up doing this regularly with the saints.** When the saints are gathered together we should be there, even when we're discouraged and depressed. Especially when we're discouraged or we have a heavy trial, we belong with God's people.

What are we to do in this informal setting? We are to encourage one another. Have you noticed that in a Bible study like the one we're in now we have the opportunity to encourage one another whereas in the Sunday morning worship it's more formal and more difficult to do this? In Bible class after worship we have a much better opportunity to do the same thing. Are we in need of this encouragement? Oh, yes. Be sure you join us in Bible class on Sunday morning, and then don't give up the habit of being regular. The end of the verse gives an additional reason for doing this. What is it? The Last Day is coming soon. We need to be ready and prepared.

ACTS 2:42 They (the early Christians) *devoted themselves* to the *apostles' teaching* and to the *fellowship*, to the *breaking of bread* and to *prayer*.

Above "They" write "3,000 converts" from the day of Pentecost in Jerusalem. They devoted themselves on a daily basis to the apostles' teaching, then to fellowship, then to the breaking of bread which was the Lord's Supper and which followed a meal and then to prayer. We've been meeting every Sunday night. **These early Christians met every day for study and fellowship. Can you image the impact it had on their lives?**

You need to be present in adult Bible class and have daily Bible study at home. Be very careful! The Devil will come and say, "You're just too busy to do that." But isn't it true that many of the things we're so busy with really aren't all that important? **I'm told in the Bible that there are only two things that are going to count in eternity. One is people. The other is the Word of God. If people and the Word of God are the only things which will leave this world for eternity, then why are you and I not investing more heavily in people and in the Word?** We need to prioritize things here. **What priority rating is to be put on the Word of God from this Lesson?**

ACTS 20:7,9-12 *On the first day of the week we came together* to break bread. *Paul spoke* to the people and, because he intended to leave the next day, kept on talking until midnight... Seated in a window was a young man named Eutychus, who was *sinking into a deep sleep* as Paul talked on and on. When he was *sound asleep*, he fell to the ground from the third story and was picked up dead. Paul went down, threw himself on the young man and put his arms around him. "Don't be alarmed," he said. "He's alive!" Then he went upstairs again and broke bread and ate. After talking until daylight, he left. The people took the young man home alive and were *greatly comforted*.

Here is poor Eutychus. Eutychus was common as a name for slaves. He's a young man. He's tired. Paul talked on and on. Finally Eutychus falls asleep while sitting on a window sill. He falls three stories. They all rush down and think he's dead. Paul embraces him and says, "Don't be alarmed. He's alive." They take him back upstairs where Paul continues to teach until morning. What do we learn from this? First don't go to Bible study and sit in a window sill, and, if you do, don't fall asleep! I find it interesting that their activity wasn't timed. Today, in the church, everything is timed. "Reverend, you have sixty minutes for this worship service." "You've got two and a half hours for this Lesson tonight and then you better be through." Perhaps we should be careful and more open to what the Holy Spirit may want and open up the time at least a little bit.

COLOSSIANS 3:16 Let the *Word* of Christ <u>*dwell in you*</u> *richly* as you *teach and admonish* one another with all <u>*wisdom*</u>, and as you *sing psalms, hymns and spiritual songs* with *gratitude in your hearts to* [54] *God.*

Underline "dwell in you" and it above write, "I am the house." The Word of Christ should live in every part of me. Next we are commanded to teach and admonish one another with all wisdom. This tends to happen more easily in an informal Bible study group where the believers teach and interact with one another and they break the bread of life together. Underline "wisdom" and then write this definition: "Ability to use knowledge in a practical way." Finally Paul says that we should sing to God songs of praise with a thankful heart.

There are a number of settings in which we can be obedient to this verse. We can do these things in: **1. A Sunday morning Bible class. 2. A home Bible study group. 3. Our homes in what is called family devotions or the family altar.** How many here have daily family devotions now? Hands? Okay. I'll have a word of encouragement and help for you on this in a few moments. **4. Daily private Bible study.** I join Paul in urging you to use all four settings.

• LUKE 11:28 Jesus replied, "<u>*Blessed*</u> rather are those who *hear* the Word of God and *obey* it."

There was a father who picked a strange way of trying to teach this to his son. The family was wealthy. The son was about to graduate from high school. It was the custom in that affluent neighborhood for the parents to give the graduate an automobile. The boy and his father spent months looking at cars and the week before graduation they found the perfect car. On the eve of the son's graduation the father handed him a gift-wrapped Bible. The boy was so angry that he threw the Bible down and stormed out of the house. He and his father never saw each other again. It was the news of his father's death that brought the son home again. As he sat one night going through his father's possessions that he was to inherit, he came across the Bible his father had given him. He brushed away the dust and opened it to find a cashier's check, dated the day of his graduation – in the exact amount of the car they had chosen together. But actually there is more, a lot more than a new car in your Bible. Let's see what it is so you can have it.

As Jesus was teaching, a woman from the crowd called out: "Blessed is the mother who gave You birth and nursed You." Verse 28 is Jesus' response. Underline "Blessed." This comes from the Greek word μακαριοι which means happy. Let's write "happy" above "blessed." Do you want to be happy? Advertisers say, "Use our product and you'll be happy." **Jesus says, "There are two steps to deep and abiding happiness. What's the first step? "Hear the Word." What's the second step? "Obey the Word."** Let's compare hearing and obeying to the two wings of a bird. Can a bird fly with one wing? No. Can you be happy by just hearing the Word? No. Jesus promises that you will fly and be happy by hearing **and** obeying. That happiness now and in the world to come makes all the new cars in the world look like nothing. Don't let anything keep you from having it by really hearing and then obeying the Word of God.

ACTS 17:11 Now the Bereans... received the message with *great eagerness* and examined the Scriptures *every day* to see if what Paul said was true.

Underline the italicized words. Here we have one of the nicest compliments an apostle ever gave. It's to the Bereans. **Factor # 1: How did they receive the teaching of Paul and Silas? With great eagerness.** That's the first big plus factor. Something is wrong today when believers are not eager to sit at the feet of the apostles. **Factor # 2 is that they carefully examined the Old Testament to see whether what Paul and Silas said about Jesus was really true.** The Greek word for "examine" is ανακρινω. It has its setting in a forensic sense as in the preliminary examination of a prisoner before a judge. There are at least three elements that went into the Berean's examination. Write them above the word "examine": Study, exploration, and discussion. Do you suppose Paul was happy about his teaching being examined with a "fine tooth comb"? Yes. In fact, Paul not only asked for this, he demanded it. I would also be delighted if you would examine Scripture carefully to see that what I am teaching is, indeed, the very Word of God. **Factor # 3: They examined Scripture on a daily basis.** Folks, **God never intended for His children on earth to get by with a one hour spiritual transfusion per week on Sunday morning. You must eat spiritual food for your soul on a daily basis just as you eat physical food for your body on a daily basis. The difference can mean life or death.**

Most early Christians were excited about studying Holy Scripture. They were convinced it was the very Word of God. We should follow their example. The time spent in Bible study groups brings spiritual growth, encouragement, and good fellowship.

It is also important to have daily Bible study at home alone and with a family where possible. Some important suggestions to make your daily Bible study a success: (1) Beside your Bible have a good devotional book to assist you (ask your pastor for suggestions). (2) Have Bible study at the same time each day. Many believers do this after the evening meal, others before bedtime, and some at breakfast. Always have devotions, even when there is company or when out of town. *Never, never skip.* (3) Ask what the Lord is really trying to say to you in the study, and then, have a prayer to Him to drive it home. You will know the joy and power of the Lord's presence in your life on daily basis (Deuteronomy 6:6,7; Psalm 19:10, Jeremiah 15:16).

There are some suggestions I want to lay before you on the basis of what we have just studied. There are five key activities I like to see everyone in my flock employ. I'll name them. Please write them down on the bottom of this page. **1. Every Sunday worship**. If you're out of town you go to church, and you try to find a church that is going to preach Jesus. Bring back the bulletin from the church you visited, jot your name on top, and hand it to me the following Sunday. I'm very interested in where you worshipped. Every Sunday worship. We don't skip. In fact, we don't skip even if we don't feel too good. **2. Every Sunday Bible class attendance.** This is a must. Why? On my part I need at least an hour once a week where I can sit down with you in this informal setting and we can study the Word together and encourage one another. **3. Personal daily Bible study** where you have quiet time every day with God and He with you. **4. A small Bible study group that meets in homes** without the pastor. **5. Family devotions.** The first rule for successful family devotions is to have them every single day (In our house we skip Sunday if everyone was in church and Bible class Sunday morning.) I am a jogger. Every other day I jog, if it's snowing, if it's raining, if I don't feel too well and have a runny nose, if I'm far away from home, I go jogging. I discipline myself. The same with family devotions. If the Devil can get you to skip once, he'll do it a second time, and pretty soon you won't have devotions. As head of the house I will see to it that we always have devotions. You want to be informal. Ask questions of the text. Ask, "What does this mean? What should we do with this?" At the end of the devotion have informal prayer. It's a beautiful sight to see a family come together at the end of the day, tired, sometimes exasperated, and then spend ten or fifteen minutes in study, unburdening themselves, coming to the Lord, and then at the end to see a family reinvigorated. You should see to it that your dinner table is set with your Bible and a good devotional book like Portals of Prayer, Our Daily Bread, Little Visits With God **(Pastors please have copies of these and other devotional aids on the table and make them available to the class "while the iron is hot.")**

I see all five of these as part and parcel of a complete package. We should not just choose No. 1 and No. 3 and skip the rest. **I see all of these points as critical in the life of a growing and maturing Christian.** I'll go so far as to say on the basis of the promises of our Savior, that if you faithfully pursue these points you will live forever in heaven through Jesus Christ, your Savior. And if you want to go to hell, just forget these five points – just forget your Bible, forget the Gospel, and you'll be lost for eternity. **Please write down this Bible reference: John 8:31.**

3. **What is prayer?**

A father was passing his young son's bedroom one night and overheard a rather interesting prayer. The boy was kneeling by his bed with bowed head. He said, "Dear God, please make me a good boy, but it's all right with me if You'd like to take your time about it. Amen." One day the disciples said to Jesus, "Lord, teach us to pray." That's what we're going to do here.

PSALM 19:14 May the *words of my mouth* and the *meditation of my heart* be pleasing in Your sight, O LORD, my Rock and my Redeemer.

David is in prayer. What is he using for prayer? His mouth and his heart. Which of the two is most important? His heart. Do the words need to be audible? No. I have four sons. I remember one time when they were quite young, and we had family devotions after dinner. I always tried to change the structure of devotions from time to time. On this particular evening we had a prayer circle, and I said, "Let's all bow our heads and we'll pray silently." We bowed our heads. Little David was the youngest. Pretty soon I heard David say, "Dear God, I thank You for this day and..." I interrupted him and said, "Pray quietly. Okay?" He said okay, so we bowed our heads again. This time he said very softly, "Dear God, thank You..." I said, "David, no. Pray silently. Okay?" "Okay." We bowed our heads again, and this time we heard a whisper, "Dear God..." By this time the family was rolling on the carpet in laughter. I am convinced that God must have a excellent sense of humor. Audible words are not necessary to communicate. Even two human beings can communicate without the spoken word. **Be assured that God has no difficulty understanding what your heart is saying.**

PSALM 10:17 You hear, O LORD, the *desire* of the afflicted; You encourage them, and You listen to their cry.

> Oh, what a verse! God hears the desire of the afflicted. Parents, think back. When your children are small they can desire something, and no words are spoken. First, can you pick up on their desire? Yes. Second, when you pick up on it, what do you do? Do you try to address their need or do you ignore it? You pay as much attention when they do not verbalize as when they do. If you have that ability as a mere human being, how much more can your heavenly Father do this? Your heavenly Father picks up on **all** the yearnings and turmoil of your heart. What does God do according to this verse? He listens, and He responds. Words and folded hands are not needed. What does this tell you about your Father? How He loves you and cares about you. What a God you have!

Prayer is having a talk with God. We share with God our thoughts, joys, and sorrows aloud or just from the heart. Annie Hawks and Robert Lowry wrote:

> *Prayer is the Christian's vital breath, The Christian's native air,*
> *His watchword at the gates of death: He enters heaven with prayer.*
>
> *O Lord, by whom we come to God, The Life, the Truth, the Way,*
> *The path of prayer Thyself hast trod: Lord, teach us how to pray.*

4.   What are some important qualities of prayer?

MATTHEW 4:10 Jesus said... it is written: *"Worship the Lord your God,* **[55]** *and serve Him only.'"*

> The first basic truth for all who would worship is to be sure to worship the true and Triune God, Father, Son, and Holy Spirit and serve Him! What applies to worship also applies to prayer. **Worship and prayer to any other god are nothing more than idolatry.**

JOHN 16:23-24 Jesus said... I tell you the truth, My Father will give you whatever you *ask in My name.* Until now you have not asked for anything in My name. Ask and you *will receive*, and your *joy will be complete.*

"What is the right number to make a direct call to your Father?"

> **To get through to your heavenly Father, you need to "dial the right number."** Let's say that I went into the next room to the phone to place a long distance call to my mother in Minnesota. I don't have her phone number, so I'll just dial any number. As long as I'm sincere, I'm sure I'll get through. Would it work? No. What if I tried dialing ten thousand times? Would I get through? There's hardly a chance that I would reach her. You have no chance of getting through to your heavenly Father if you do not "dial the right number." **What is the right number to make a direct call to your Father? J-E-S-U-S in saving faith!** It gets you through morning, noon, or night, anytime, guaranteed. And when you do this, what does Jesus say will happen? Look at the last sentence. You will receive, and your joy will be complete.

ISAIAH 63:16 But You are our Father, though *Abraham does not know us* or *Israel (Jacob) acknowledge us; You,* O LORD, *are our Father*, our Redeemer from of old is Your name.

> Abraham, though he was the father of the Jewish nation, did not know the Jews of Isaiah's day.

Why? Because he was dead. Likewise Israel, which is another name for Jacob, could not acknowledge their requests because he was dead. Here we learn that **it is absolutely futile to pray to the dead. Why? Because they do not know us nor can they acknowledge us.** Millions of people today pray to the dead and for the dead. We disagree with our Catholic friends who say that we should pray to the saints who are now in heaven. The rosary and other prayers addressed to Mary and other saints in heaven are totally futile. In fact, not only is it futile to pray to anyone other than God, it is even sin. It's called idolatry. Scripture commands us to pray only to the one true God and Him alone. Neither should we pray FOR the dead. If they are in heaven, they do not need our prayers, and if they are in hell, it is too late. **The verse concludes that God is our unchanging Friend and Savior. To Him we come with our petitions and praise.**

JAMES 1:6-7 When he asks, he must *believe* and *not doubt*, because he who doubts is like a wave of the sea, blown and tossed by the wind. That man *should not think* he will receive anything from the Lord.

If you doubt that God can answer your prayer, you should know that your prayer will not be answered. There is no room for unbelief or doubt. **You may not know how God is going to answer your petition, but you must have implicit faith that He can.** Your doctor has told you that you have terminal cancer. You should have faith that God can heal you of that cancer. You don't know if He will, but you are positive that He can. This is one of the basic qualities of prayer. One reason why some of our prayers are not answered would be the result of doubt.

MATTHEW 6:7-8 When you pray, *do not keep on babbling* like pagans, for they think they will be heard because of their *many words*. Do not be like them, for your Father *knows what you need before you ask Him*.

In the first century the heathen frequently prayed long prayers to tire their gods out. Words and phrases were repeated over and over and over. The Jews tended to do this. Catholics have this constant repetition in the rosary. Why are many words and repetitious words not needed? The last sentence tells you. The one true God is omniscient. There is no need to fill Him in on countless details so that He understands. Furthermore, a prayer does not achieve a higher quality by its length or by a proper construction of sentences and good grammar. Let the pagans do that. Just say what you want like a child does. This is not to say that we cannot come back again and again with the same request. Our Lord makes it plain that consistency in prayer "pays off." Our Father delights in "being bothered" by His children. He even invites it.

1 JOHN 5:14 This is the *confidence* we have in approaching God: that if we ask anything *according to His will, He hears us*.

This simply means that for all temporal needs I will add, "If it be Your will and for my good." For example, would it be okay, Patti, for your son to pray for a brand new bicycle? Yes. Might God use you to answer that prayer? Maybe, maybe not. Can God circumvent you, Patti, and see that your son gets the bicycle without you? Sure. Joyce here has been praying for a new pink Cadillac convertible (teasing). She asked if this is okay, and I said yes. But what should she add to the request? If it be Your will. That condition should be added to all requests for things of this world. Obviously we do not want God to give us something which would harm us.

We must pray to the one true God, Father, Son, and Holy Spirit. All prayers to other gods are false and not heard. We can talk to God only through our Lord Jesus. We must believe that God hears our prayers and can answer them. Lengthy prayers are not necessary. It is God's will to give us all manner of spiritual gifts *(underline "spiritual gifts")*, and so we pray unconditionally. When praying for physical blessings *(underline "physical blessings")* we add, "If it be Your will!" We will let God decide to give us these things or not.

> There are two categories here. When I pray to God to forgive me my sins for Jesus' sake I will not add, "If it be Your will." Why? That is His will. With requests for temporal things I do not know if it is His will for me to have them, hence, the condition.

5.   What else does the Bible tell us about prayer?

1 TIMOTHY 2:1-2 I urge, then, first of all, that *requests, prayers, intercession and thanksgiving* be made for everyone – for kings and all those in authority, that we may live peaceful and quiet lives in all godliness and holiness.

> How many people are we told to pray for (second line)? Everyone. How can you pray for everyone? I approach that challenge this way. I divide my prayer time into sections. The first person I pray for is myself. I seek forgiveness, help with spiritual gifts, the fruits of faith, etc. Next I pray for all members of my family starting with my mother, my wife, my children. I pray for them every evening no matter how tired I may be. The next section might be called the revolving section. Each evening I take a different area of concern. One night I pray just for my congregation and for each of you people, name by name. The next night I will pray for as many relatives as I can bring to mind and their needs. The next night I pray for those in government both here and overseas including the police and the military. The next night I may pray for people who are hurting physically or spiritually, for those who have just lost their sight, for new mothers, for those who are facing death.

MATTHEW 5:43-44 You have heard that it was said, "Love your neighbor and hate your enemy." But I tell you: Love your enemies and *pray for those who persecute you.*

> Look at the words in quotes. The scribes and Pharisees were guilty of teaching people many wrong concepts, among which was this, they taught people that they should love their neighbors and hate their enemies. This was a gross perversion of God's will. Jesus corrects these people by saying: "Love your enemies and pray for those who persecute you." And Jesus practiced it when, on the cross, He prayed for His enemies and said, "Father, forgive them." We, too, should pray for our enemies that God will show them their sins so that they may repent and come to faith in the Savior.

PSALM 50:15 *Call* upon Me in the day of trouble; I will *deliver* you, and you will *honor* Me.

> **Put a number 1 above "call," a 2 above "deliver," and a 3 above "honor."** What's the first thing you should do when you have trouble? God says, "Call on Me." What promise does God make? "I will deliver you." And our response to that help is to honor the Lord, to thank and praise Him. An example of this. When my first son, Paul, was about five years old he smashed the last half inch of his thumb in the front door of our house. That part of his thumb was pulp. He was in great pain, blood was all over his hand, and as he cried he said, "Dear God, please make it better. Dear God, please make it better." How great! Since you are going to cry, why not cry to the Lord? He promises deliverance. You, then, should praise Him.

1 THESSALONIANS 5:16-18 Be joyful always; *pray continually*; *give thanks in all circumstances*, for this is *God's will for you* in Christ Jesus.

124

No matter what our circumstances we are told to be joyful. Why? Because everything works together for good for the child of God. Underline "pray continually." This means that we are always to be ready to approach God in prayer, not only when rising in the morning, before meals, and at bedtime, but any time throughout the day. Be ready to bring Him your requests on behalf of others or yourself. Next underline "give thanks in all circumstances." Why? Because you are a winner in Jesus no matter what is happening around you or to you.

I want you to know that you folks have given me great joy. I give thanks to God for each of you. Can you imagine the impact that has on my heart when I say out loud, "God, I thank you for Tom. I thank You for Rita. I thank You for Donna and Mona." I'll name you one by one. Wouldn't it be wonderful if every night you would say, "God, I want to count the reasons why I'm grateful to You tonight. I want to mention them to You." That will honor Him. That will make you feel good. It's a nice way to go to sleep. **Be sure you take time to frequently praise God for whatever reason.**

PHILIPPIANS 4:6 *Do not be anxious about anything*, but *in everything*, **[56]** by *prayer* and *petition*, with *thanksgiving, present your requests* to God.

Do not be anxious about anything. **The verb "anxious" means to have a divided mind and you are torn back and forth.** What should you do? In everything come to God in prayer. Everything. Nothing is too big or too small. And bring your request to God with a thankful heart.

HEBREWS 9:27 Man is destined to die once, and *after that to face judgment.*

How many times must we face death? Only once. We are not reincarnated. Immediately after death we face God's judgment. Because of Jesus and our faith in Him we are received by God into heaven or because of unbelief we are cast into hell. In essence, then, there are two judgments. The first judgment occurs at the moment of death, and the second judgment is on the Last Day before all men in the presence of the Lord. The second judgment will be a detailed affirmation of the first judgment. We'll study that in Lesson 10. I also see from this verse that after death no man is in need of my prayers any longer. Everything has already been decided and executed.

MATTHEW 6:5-6 When you pray, do not be like the hypocrites, for they love to pray standing in the synagogues and on the street corners to be *seen by men*. I tell you the truth, *they have received their reward in full*. But when you pray, *go into your room, close the door* and pray to your Father, who is unseen. Then *your Father, who sees what is done in secret, will reward you.*

The scribes and Pharisees had a bad reputation: They loved to stand in the synagogues and pray to be seen by all the worshipers. They loved to stand on street corners where there were many people who would see them turn toward Jerusalem or toward the Temple and pray. But it was nothing but sheer hypocrisy. Jesus says that they will get their reward in full. Private prayer should be just that – private. To close the door emphasizes this privacy. Look at the last three words. Jesus promises that your Father will reward you.

ISAIAH 65:24 *Before they call I will answer*; while they are *still speaking I will hear.*

What is God promising here? **He says that He sees our needs and anticipates our prayer. Oh, how eager God is to supply our needs.** Oh, how He carefully watches us. I know that this has happened to me many times. I can recall instances when I knew I was going to pray for something and before I had the chance to say the words the need was taken care of. Is God encouraging us to be people of prayer? Oh, yes, is He ever! **Be sure that you develop good prayer habits. Work hard at it. Your heavenly Father will be honored, and you will be blessed.**

 We pray because (1) God invites us to, (2) God promises to hear us, (3) of our own needs and that of others, and (4) of gratitude for all blessings received. We should pray for everyone, even our enemies. We should pray when we have trouble. God promises to help us. We should then thank Him. We should not pray for or to the dead, nor should we make a show of our prayer life. God answers prayer in one of three ways: (1) No! (2) Yes! (3) Wait!

6. How does Jesus teach us to pray?

MATTHEW 6:9-13, LUKE 11:2-4 This is how you should pray: Our Father in heaven, hallowed be Your name, Your Kingdom come, Your will be done on earth as it is in heaven. Give us today our daily bread. Forgive us our sins, as we also forgive those who sin against us. Lead us not into temptation, but deliver us from evil. For the Kingdom, the power, and the glory are Yours now and forever. Amen.

"Our Father in heaven": Jesus teaches us to call God our "Father." The word "Father" should inspire full trust in Him. We are His children. As little children trust and speak to their earthly father, so we trust and speak to our Father in heaven.

"Hallowed be Your name": Hallow means holy. God's name is holy by itself. Here we pray that God's name will be holy to us, that we will love, honor, glorify, and trust Him in our thoughts, words, and actions. In these ways we show that God's name is holy to us.

"Your Kingdom come": This means: Father, may Your Kingdom grow in my heart, my home, my church, my country, and in all the world. Here we promise God that we will help build His Kingdom. We will be fishers of men. No matter who we are or where we are, at home, at **[57]** work, in school, on vacation – The Kingdom of God is first, and we will personally do all we can to help it grow.

"Your will be done on earth as it is in heaven": We are asking that God's will be done as perfectly on earth as it is done in heaven. We ask God to have His will done among us and by us.

"Give us today our daily bread": Daily bread means everything we need for life – food, clothing, home, good government, good weather, employment, health – everything that makes our lives happy and successful. All these are gifts from God.

"Forgive us our sins, as we also forgive those who sin against us": We are asking God to forgive us as we forgive others. We receive God's full, free forgiveness because of Jesus Christ. We will now forgive others who sin against us.

"Lead us not into temptation": God does not tempt people to sin. Here we pray that God will protect us so that the devil, the world, and our own flesh will not fool us or lead us to sin or to stop believing in Jesus. In this way we overcome and win spiritual victories.

"But deliver us from evil": There is evil all around us. Here we pray that God will shield us from evil. If God permits a burden to come, we ask Him to give us strength to bear it. When life is over, we ask God to take us to our new home in heaven where there will be no evil.

"For the Kingdom, the power, and the glory are Yours now and forever": This is a wonderful way to end a wonderful prayer. Our Father in heaven has all power. He can do whatever He promises. He will do everything He promises. And He has promised us much. We are completely safe in His hands. We also promise God that we will continue to give Him all glory now and forever in heaven.

"Amen": This word means "it shall be so" or "so let it be."

"Amen" is confirmation of what has been said. Believers may be listening to a sermon or a statement by another Christian and will say out loud or quietly, "Amen." In other words, "so let it be."

Can you see from this Lesson that if we do what we've just studied, we have our devotional life together. If we don't implement what we have learned, you can see how we'll be in trouble. Lessons 2, 3, and 4 were very important, but they'll do us little good unless we have this Lesson in place in our daily living. Little wonder that Satan tries so hard to disrupt the devotional life of a Christian.

Let's pray together

Heavenly Father, we give You all praise for the Scriptures we have just studied. May we use every opportunity we have to worship You in public worship services with other believers. May we study Your Word and fellowship with You and fellow believers in Bible study groups, in daily family devotions, and daily private study. Forgive us for the times when we worshiped or prayed thoughtlessly or mechanically. Please richly bless our prayer life. Move us to come to You with our troubles and our sins. Then You will receive honor, and we will be happy. We ask this in the name of Jesus Christ who Himself spent many a night in prayer. Amen. **[58]**

Let's sing together

> What a Friend we have in Jesus, All our sins and griefs to bear!
> What a privilege to carry Ev'rything to God in prayer!
> Oh, what peace we often forfeit, Oh, what needless pain we bear,
> All because we do not carry Ev'rything to God in prayer!
>
> Have we trials and temptations? Is there trouble anywhere?
> We should never be discouraged, Take it to the Lord in prayer.
> Can we find a Friend so faithful Who will all our sorrows share?
> Jesus knows our ev'ry weakness – Take it to the Lord in prayer.
>
> Are we weak and heavy laden, Cumbered with a load of care?
> Precious Savior, still our Refuge – Take it to the Lord in prayer.
> Do your friends despise, forsake You? Take it to the Lord in prayer;
> In His arms He'll take and shield you, You will find a solace there.

Bible reading schedule for the next seven days

❑ 1st day – Acts 3 ❑ 3rd day – Acts 5 ❑ 5th day – Acts 7 ❑ 7th day – Acts 9
❑ 2nd day – Acts 4 ❑ 4th day – Acts 6 ❑ 6th day – Acts 8

Worksheet no. 7

1. True or *False*: People who say they worship God out in the woods on Sunday morning or the golf course instead of church usually do.

2. What does public worship offer that private worship does not? _Fellowship with a large number of believers, a message from God's Word, the Sacraments, meeting God in His House._

3. What does group Bible study offer that public worship does not? _Can ask questions, share your faith, be more informal, better fellowship, and many times more meaningful._

4. Why is it important for you to have family or personal devotions in your home each day? _Need for daily quiet time, to feed daily on the Word, to slow down to think and meditate._

5. On a scale of 1 – 10 where were you spiritually five years ago? _____. A year ago? _____. Today? _____. What does this tell you about your devotional life? _(Ask for volunteers to share)_

6. When praying for physical blessings we should always add _if it be Your will._

7. _True_ or False: When we pray we have as many reasons to thank **[59]** God for the things He does not give us as for the things He does give us.

8. How do we hallow God's name? _By the way we use His name in thought, word, and action that brings honor to Him._

9. What do we mean when we pray, "Your Kingdom come"? _May Your Kingdom grow in my heart, home, church, country, and the world, and may I be a Kingdom builder._

10. True or _False_: Forgiven of all our sins we promise God that we will, if possible, forgive those who sin against us.

11. Four basic reasons why we pray are:

    a. _God invites us to._

    b. _God promises to hear our prayers._

    c. _Because of our needs and the needs of others._

    d. _Because of gratitude for blessings received._

12. If God already knows all about our needs even before we ask Him, why ask? _First because He has told us to. Second because we need to hear ourselves ask Him and then trust Him._

13. _True_ or False: God always answers prayer. _(But in His own way, in His time.)_

14. Write out a mealtime prayer: _Come, Lord Jesus, be our Guest, And let these gifts to us be blessed. Amen. Father, bless us and these gifts which receive from Your good hand. Amen._

15. What does "Amen" mean? _It shall be so or so let it be, Lord._ **[60]**

Before we take Lesson 8 let's bow our heads for a moment of prayer: Heavenly Father, I thank You for this day of rest and for the privilege I had to worship You in Your house this morning. Tonight I will learn about keys which lock and unlock, about the Church, about my place in the Church. Forgive me, dear Father, for those days that I have wasted, that were spent on trivia. So frequently I see only the things of this world. More and more let me see people and Your Holy Word both of which are present now and will be forever. O God, I want to honor You with my life. I want to invest in those things which will produce eternal dividends. Help me look at my life from the perspective of eternity. May the people in this class and in this church look at all other people as sincere objects of our love. May every sermon, every Bible study, and every person in this Christian fellowship grow in these eternal concerns to the glory of Your name and for the everlasting salvation of people. For Jesus' sake. Amen.

In downtown Chicago near the lake front there is a bronze statue of a group of soldiers holding their guns with fixed bayonets ready to charge. Many years ago I admired that statue. A few years ago when I visited Chicago I found that same group of soldiers still standing there. They hadn't advanced a single inch. And so we have people in the church who lustily sing, "Onward Christians soldiers, marching as to war," but, like this sculptured group of soldiers, they never advance. A cure for such lack of action could be found in our Lesson this evening.

Last week we said that the Lesson on A DEVOTIONAL LIFE WHICH BLESSES YOU was most critical because if we failed in that area we would really fail spiritually and if we succeeded it would be a great victory. Tonight's Lesson is going to go a step further. I HAVE GOOD NEWS FOR YOU ABOUT KEYS WHICH LOCK AND UNLOCK. This is a particular teaching of the Lord Jesus with huge implications for many people, and yet, in the church, there is an abysmal ignorance on the Office of the Keys. For example, if you were to tell us everything you know about the Office of the Keys, how many hours would you need? How many minutes would you need? For some of us this evening we wouldn't even need minutes – seconds would do real fine. And yet the doctrine of the Office of the Keys is, next to the plan of salvation, one of the most important doctrines in the New Testament. Let's begin.

Lesson 8

I HAVE GOOD NEWS FOR YOU

About Keys Which Lock and Unlock

1. What is the Church of Jesus Christ?

We begin the topic of keys which lock and unlock by starting with the subject of the Church. I'm going to put the Greek word for "church" on the marker board: εκκλησια. Εκκλησια means: "That which is called out." Let's write those five words above "Church" in question 1. Behind "Jesus Christ" write: "The one, true **invisible Church** on earth." This is in contrast to **visible churches** such as our church, "Family of Christ Lutheran Church." In Question 1 we will not be discussing the visible church on earth which you can see, but rather, the invisible Church of Jesus Christ which you cannot see. Before we can understand the Office of the Keys we must understand the doctrine of the Church of Jesus Christ. Let's see what the Bible says.

EPHESIANS 2:19-21 You are *no longer foreigners* and *aliens*, but *fellow citizens with God's people* and *members of God's household*, built on the *foundation of the apostles and prophets*, with *Christ Jesus* Himself as the *chief cornerstone*. In Him the *whole building is joined together* and *rises to become a holy temple* in the Lord.

Paul is writing to Gentile Christians at Ephesus. Jews often looked upon Gentiles as foreigners and aliens, substandard individuals without any rights or privileges. These Gentiles had now accepted the Lord. While they were members of the congregation in Ephesus, they frequently felt inferior to Jewish Christians. Paul tells them, however, that they are not foreigners or aliens any longer no matter what other people may think. What are they now? "Fellow citizens with God's household." The Jew thought that he and he alone was God's person. Just like today there are a few Lutherans who think they are God's exclusive people. Some Baptists feel they are God's exclusive people. This amounts to spiritual bigotry and spiritual stupidity. And that's what the Jews had. Paul says no. You Gentiles have all the privileges and benefits that any other member of the Family of God possesses. There are no second rate citizens in the Church of Jesus Christ! There is complete equality in Jesus' Church! There are a lot of families on earth tonight. All of these families live in different homes. But there is really only one family that counts and that is the Family of God. All other families will cease. **You want to think more and more in terms of your eternal Family, God's Family, where we are all brothers and sisters.**

Paul says that as a member of the invisible Church you are built upon the foundation of the apostles and prophets. Some church people take great pride in being built upon the human father of their denomination. There are Lutherans who are extremely "proud" of being built upon the teachings of Martin Luther. I know of people who belong to reformed churches who are so terribly "proud" of being built upon the teachings of Calvin and Zwingli. Paul does not tell us to be filled with pride over these men, but we are to be filled with joy and ecstasy over the fact that we are built on the teachings of the apostles and prophets. Their foundation, however, rested on Jesus. Jesus is the cornerstone because the entire edifice of the invisible church rests on Him. Just as a cornerstone was indispensable to any building in that day, so Jesus is indispensable to the one true Church.

Look at the last sentence. "In Jesus the whole building is joined together." No matter where Christians may be on this earth, we are joined together, we are one. Look at the last words: "**Rises** to become a holy temple in the Lord." This great Church actually **grows** to become a holy Temple. You may not feel holy tonight. You may not have been holy this afternoon. But St. Paul says you are a part of the holy Temple. Your sin is gone. You belong to Jesus.

ROMANS 12:5 In Christ *we who are many form one body*, and *each member belongs to all the others*.

We have a lot of different last names, but really, we have only one name, believer, and we believers form one body, the Una Sancta. There are over 300 religious denominations in America, but there is only one Church of Jesus Christ. **As a member of that Church I not only belong to Jesus but to all the others, and all the others belong to me. I have a relationship with all other believers that is deeper than blood.** I am here as a Christian not only to serve Jesus, but to serve all other believers, and they are to serve me.

ROMANS 8:9 If anyone does *not have the Spirit of Christ*, he *does not belong to Christ*.

Underline, "Not have the Spirit of Christ." **Verse 7 mentions the Holy Spirit as the "Spirit of God." Verse 9 mentions the Holy Spirit as the "Spirit of Christ." The Holy Spirit brings to us the Lord Jesus so that we "have" Jesus by faith.** If this has not happened, if you do not have the Lord whom the Holy Spirit brings to sinners, then you do not belong to Christ. Your saying you are a Christian does not make you one. Having your name on the church membership list does not make you a Christian. "How many," we wonder, "of those who belong to some local congregation really belong to Jesus?" You may be able to sing hymns most beautifully. You may have great zeal as a church worker, but if you don't have Jesus residing in your heart you will perish.

What shall we say of some congregations that are almost totally devoid of Jesus? What solution is there for churches and church people who **persistently refuse** the Holy Spirit and the Savior He brings? There is one alternative. If a congregation devoid of Jesus has 300 members, I suggest that they go out and purchase 300 talking parrots. Put them in the pews on Sunday morning and teach them a few hymns and a few other words so that they could respond to the pastor. They would know when to stand up and when to sit down just like the member, and that would "solve" their problem. Since they do not have Jesus in their hearts they would then be free to do what unbelievers normally do on Sunday morning.

I say to you this evening, if you are not really a Christian, either you are going to change by the power of the Spirit or you need to go out and buy a parrot who will represent you in church. I know what some of you are thinking: "But the parrot would just be reciting, just 'parroting' my words and actions." How different is that from what you are doing right now if you don't have Jesus in your heart? That is all you are doing – parroting things. You've been programmed. You know when to stand up and when to sit down, when to chant at the right time, and you can do it without thinking. That's not satisfying to you, and it's not satisfying Jesus.

Luke 17:20-21 The Kingdom of God does not come with your *careful observation,* nor will people say, "Here it is," or "There it is," because the *Kingdom of God is within you.* **[61]**

This is the invisible Church of God. The Mormon Church says that it, and it alone, is the one true church. Even today that are a few Lutherans, Baptists, and Catholics who believe that their church is the one true church. This cannot be. **The true Church is invisible. It is totally a spiritual Church. Human eyes cannot see it.** Yet too many church people sit in their observation towers proclaiming theirs is the true church, when, fact, these hypocrites couldn't recognize the one true Church of Jesus if it were right in front of them. Christian friend, you are the Kingdom of God. That eternal Kingdom is in your heart.

2 TIMOTHY 2:19 The *Lord knows* those who are His.

If you are a hypocrite the Lord knows it. On the other hand, if you are a believer, even if your faith is weak, the Lord knows you as His child. Maybe the world doesn't know and the world doesn't care, but the most important Person on earth and in heaven knows that you believe in Him. The Greek word for "knows" should not be understood as mere knowledge, but **that knowledge includes affection and effect**. Above "knows" write the three words: "Knowledge and effect." Who is the subject? The Lord. Who is the object? You are. **How does He "know" you? With affection for you and effect for your life!**

Underline the italicized words as we come to them in the next verse.

EPHESIANS 5:25-27 Christ loved the church and gave Himself up for her to make her *holy, cleansing her* by the washing with water (that's Baptism) through the Word, and to *present her to Himself* as a *radiant* church, *without stain or wrinkle* or any other *blemish*, but *holy and blameless.*

Paul says that Christ has made the one true Church "holy." He has "cleansed her." As a bride is presented to her groom, so the Church is presented to the Lord. **What one word describes the Church? Radiant.** That's you, my friend. Not only are you radiant, but you are without any spiritual stain or wrinkle or blemish. The last three words simply say you are "holy and blameless."

131

David, do you believe tonight that you are a sinner? Yes. Do you believe that Jesus died for all your sins on the cross of Calvary? Yes. Now I want all of you, especially his wife Heidi, to look at the italicized words. Is Jesus saying that John has been cleansed, that he is without any spiritual stain, wrinkle or blemish, but he is holy and blameless? Yes. Heidi, does that sound like the man you know? Does David get up in a bad mood some mornings? Yes. Can David be a real rascal once in awhile? Yes. Can he pout once in awhile? Yes. Does he ever say something nasty? Yes. Despite the fact of all of these sins, the Lord looks at David tonight and says what? He is without stain, wrinkle, or blemish. He is holy and blameless. David, how does this sound to you? It's great. David needs help, and he has it in Jesus. Not only David, but everyone of my spiritual brothers and sisters are without blemish. Do you suppose we should start seeing one another more the way Jesus sees us? Yes. Do you suppose we should see ourselves more the way Jesus sees us? Yes.

1 PETER 2:5 You also, like *living stones*, are *being built* into a *spiritual house* to be a *holy priesthood, offering spiritual sacrifices* acceptable to God through Jesus Christ.

The bricks and stones in our church buildings are very dead. We Christians are not dead stones, but living stones. **All believers are living stones being built into a spiritual house, namely, the Church of God. You are also being made into a holy priesthood**. What a lofty title you have. In the Old Testament the priests offered sacrifices of animals which pointed forward to the sacrifice of Christ. **The sacrifices which you offer are yourselves, your good works, and your praises** which are acceptable through Jesus Christ. Your pastor is not the priest. Your pastor is the servant of the priests. Your pastor is to teach and equip the priests for their ministry to the Lord and to man. Most churches have this wrong. They say, "We'll hire someone to do the work of the church for us." No. The pastor's job is to equip God's people for the work of the holy priesthood. In view of that I do not want to hear any of you say something like this: "I am just a layman." That is anti-Scriptural, and it's a plain lie. You are a priest of the living God. That is the very terminology which God uses. He elevates you into a high and lofty position, a holy priesthood in His most holy Church.

• 1 CORINTHIANS 3:11 For no one can lay *any foundation other than* the one already laid, which is *Jesus Christ*.

Every building has a foundation. Now this important question. What are you building your life on? Everyone is building on something – the politician, the student, the housewife, even the unbeliever. Everyone believes that he must build on something. Here Paul tells us what we as Christians build on. What is it? The Lord Jesus Christ. How wise you are tonight that you have decided to build on Jesus, the one true foundation of the Church.

There is only one true Church of Jesus Christ that will last forever, and it is to be distinguished from denominations and congregations.

An important clarification. Not everyone in a visible church or congregation is in the invisible Church of God; however, almost every member of the Church of God is a member of a local visible congregation that preaches Jesus.

It is made up of all true believers who are members of God's family. These believers are built together on Christ, the Cornerstone of the Church. Hypocrites and godless people do not belong. We cannot see the true Church because the Church resides in each believer's heart. This Church is clean, pure and has no fault; it has been cleansed by the blood of Jesus. The believers in this Church are living stones. They serve God as holy priests and offer many good works acceptable to God through Jesus.

Many Christians today seem frustrated and discouraged. It seems that even many believers do not really know who they are or why they are here. The next question and the next Lesson can do much to help you understand why God has not taken you to heaven yet, but leaves you in this world.

2. What are the keys to the Kingdom?

What is the function of a key? It is to lock or unlock a door. Now let's take the next verse.

MATTHEW 16:19 I will give you the *Keys of the Kingdom of Heaven*; whatever you *bind* on earth will be *bound* in heaven, and whatever you *loose* on earth will be *loosed* in heaven.

Jesus says, "I give you the keys to your place of employment." No. "I give you keys to your home." No. "I give you keys to the doors to your church building." No. I give you keys to what? The Kingdom of Heaven. There is no more important place in this world or out of it than heaven, and Jesus says, "I give you keys to heaven, to My Father's House." What does He say next in this verse? "Whatever you bind on earth will be bound in heaven, and whatever you loose on earth will be loosed in heaven." Who is it who tells us about keys to the Kingdom of Heaven? Jesus. This is not simply a church teaching.

We need to get familiar with the words, "Keys of the Kingdom." Christ is saying, "I am giving you keys to My Father's House that will either unlock the door to it or lock it." This is, indeed, a very important thing Jesus is telling us. If you are a believer in the Lord tonight, Christ is saying to you, "I am giving you the keys to either unlock the door to heaven or to lock it."

Jesus says, "whatever you bind on earth will be bound in heaven." In other words,**"If you lock the door to heaven for someone, it is truly locked. And if you unlock the door to heaven for someone, as far as I am concerned, it is unlocked." What a huge responsibility.**

Mark 16:15 Jesus said to them, *"Go* into all the world and *preach the Good News* to all creation."

I want to ask you a question: What alone opens the door to heaven? Faith in Jesus as Savior. To exercise the Office of the Keys according to this verse we are going to have to do two things. What are they? First we **have to go and then we have to preach the Good News so that people may believe and the door to heaven will be opened to them and they will go in. If they do not believe, we must lock the door to heaven, and they will be kept out.** Again, most church people have little or no understanding of these Keys. The ushers ush, the deacons deac, and the world goes to hell. And they think this is the way it is supposed to be. Jesus, however, does not want anyone to perish, so He gives us this command.

MATTHEW 28:18-20 Jesus came to them and said, *"All authority* in heaven and on earth has been given to Me. Therefore *go and make disciples* of all nations, *baptizing them* in the name of the Father and of the Son and of the Holy Spirit, and *teaching them* to obey everything I have commanded you."

"If you want the ultimate authority in heaven and on earth you must look to Jesus."

This is the Great Commission which Jesus gave to His disciples, about 120 in number, on the hill of ascension. Look at the italicized words, "All authority." There is no one in heaven or on earth who has the authority that Jesus has. God the Father and God the Holy Spirit have put all things into the hands of Jesus. **If you want the ultimate authority in heaven and on earth you must look to Jesus.** Jesus is saying He has the right to say what He is about to say.

What is it? "Go and make Lutherans out of all people." No. Make what? Disciples. I want you to drop down to the last paragraph on this page. There we have a three point definition of the word "disciple." Please underline it. **"A disciple is: (1) A student of the Master, (2) A follower of the Master, and (3) One who makes disciples of others for the Master."** Jesus does not say that we are to make church members out of people. He says, "First, I want you to go out and make people students of Me. Second, I want you to make them followers of Me. And thirdly, I want you to teach them how to make disciples of others for Me." **All of a sudden the word "disciple" has an awesome meaning to us. A disciple is not just a believer.** It is not the Lord's will that you just be a believer. The Lord in the Great Commission did not tell us to go out and make believers out of people. What DID He say? We're to disciple them. **My calling as pastor is to equip you for the task of discipling people.** Many people in the church do not understand that. They say it's the pastor's job to make disciples of all people because he went to the cemetary, I mean the seminary and he's trained. **Insist that your pastor teach you how to be a discipler, that he disciple you for the Master so that you, in turn, can disciple others.** Be sure to learn this three-fold definition of a disciple. You'll be asked about it in the worksheet and in Lesson 9.

How will we disciple them? Put a No. 1 above "baptize them." Above "teaching them" put a No. 2. "By teaching them to obey everything I have commanded you." There are two ways in which we disciple people for the Master: We baptize them in the name of the one true God, and we teach them everything Jesus has taught us. Question: Am I trying to disciple you for Jesus this evening? Yes. This morning in worship and in Bible class did I try to teach you things the Lord has taught me? Yes. Now when I teach you these things and disciple you for Jesus you are supposed to "sit on that." No. You are to teach what you have learned to others. Whose command is that? The Lord's. Does the Lord say you can do this if you feel like it? No. Does He say go when the weather is right and it's not too hot or cold? No. He says, "If you are My disciple you are to be about this work of discipling others for me." It's a command. And all who love Jesus say, "Yes, Sir! Thank You, Lord, for the honor." Those who don't love Jesus or their faith is so weak they scarcely believe simply scratch their heads and say, "I don't understand this." Or, "I choose not to understand this."

Now look at the last words again: "Teaching them to obey everything I have commanded you." Would you say tonight that after two hours of teaching this morning in worship and Bible class that you know more of Jesus' will for you than you did twenty-four hours ago? Yes. How did that come about? Through the teaching of the Word. **You should be in the process of being discipled all the time. How long do you suppose you will be in the discipling mode? As long as you are on earth, 'till the day you die.** In the meantime the Lord wants you to improve.

JOHN 20:22-23 Jesus breathed on them and said, "Receive the Holy Spirit. *If you forgive* anyone his sins, *they are forgiven*; if you *do not forgive* them, *they are not forgiven.*"

Let's use an example. Virginia, when I was at your house, I tried to find out what you and John knew about Jesus. You said you believed in Him as your Savior. What did I then asssure you of? I told you that your sins were forgiven, that if you died that night you would go to heaven. Who told me to tell you that? Jesus did. Now if that night you would have said, "No, Pastor Ginkel, we do not believe in Jesus," what should I have told you? What should I have done with the Key? I should have said, "You are not going to heaven. The door to heaven is locked for you. I have bad news for you. You are going to perish eternally." Who's fault is that? Yours. It's not my fault, not the fault of the church, and surely not the fault of the Lord. How sad. In other words, I had the responsibility to announce to John and Virginia forgiveness of their sins and if they are impenitent that their sins are bound to them and the door to heaven is locked. Everyone of us has the responsibility to be about this business – tomorrow with someone at work, with a neighbor, a relative, or a friend.

Jesus wants us to make disciples of all people. A disciple is: (1) A student of the Master, (2) A follower of the Master, and (3) One who makes disciples of others for the Master. The Lord gives to all believers on earth the Keys of the Kingdom, namely, the authority and power to tell the Good News, to baptize and serve the Lord's Supper, **[62]** and to forgive or not forgive sins. Daniel March put it well –

> Let none hear you idly saying, "There is nothing I can do,"
> While the multitudes are dying And the Master calls for you.
> Take the task He gives you gladly; Let His work your pleasure be.
> Answer quickly when He calls you, "Here am I. Send me, send me!"

3. To whom has the Lord given these keys?

MATTHEW 16:19 *I will give you the Keys* of the Kingdom of Heaven; *whatever you bind* on earth will be bound in heaven, and *whatever you loose* on earth will be loosed in heaven" (To Peter as the spokesman of the disciples).

Who do the Keys belong to in the first place? To Jesus. What does Jesus say He is doing with these Keys that He holds? "I give them to you." This is the verse that our friends in the Catholic Church use to prove that Jesus was giving the Keys to Peter since the Lord is talking to him. They say, "Peter was chosen by the Lord to be the head (pope) of the Church, and he alone possesses these Keys." We believe that Jesus first spoke to Peter as the spokesman of the disciples and that he was to pass it on to them. In the next verse Jesus says the same thing to all the disciples.

The heart of the Office of the Keys is your proclaiming the Good News of Jesus so that people may believe. You may then announce forgiveness and the opening of the door to heaven. A few of you may say, "I can't do this." You are correct when you say, "*I* can't do it." In your own strength you cannot, but with Jesus with you in spirit (Remember His words at the end of the Great Commission: "And surely I will be with you always") and by the power of the Holy Spirit you can do this. The most effective location for this work is not the worship service, but a one-to-one situation wherever that may be. You are to witness. You are to share the Gospel with the hope of discipling the person for Christ. The masses of people will never be won to Jesus by the clergy. There are too many people and too few clergy. Besides, too many clergy don't know the Lord as Savior themselves. It's going to be up to Christians like you to win people to the Lord.

JOHN 20:22-23 Jesus breathed on *them* (all the disciples) and said, "Receive the Holy Spirit. If *you* forgive anyone his sins, they are forgiven; if *you* do not forgive them, they are not forgiven."

This is the first Easter Sunday evening. Jesus is sending them out to proclaim the Gospel so that they may announce forgiveness. But He who **sends them** also **enables them** with the gift of the Holy Spirit. To my knowledge the disciples did no proclaiming Easter Sunday evening. To my knowledge no unbelievers came to saving faith either. No souls were won Easter evening, but on Pentecost these men proclaimed the Gospel, 3,000 souls came into the Kingdom of God, and to them the disciples proclaimed forgiveness. Does the Lord want unbelievers around us today to hear this same Gospel? Yes. Does He want us to announce forgiveness or no forgiveness on the basis of what they do with the Gospel? Yes. When a sinner comes to saving faith he needs to hear that his sins are forgiven, that they are dismissed.

It is true that only God can forgive sin. It is also true that Jesus has made us His agents. The Lord acts through His followers. So **when we proclaim the Gospel, when we proclaim forgiveness or the lack of it, the Lord is really doing so through us, His servants.** Oh, how important that we do our work well and do it this week. Jesus who commands you to do this also **gives you the**

1 PETER 2:9 *You* are a chosen people, a *royal priesthood*, a holy nation, a people belonging to God, (underline these italicized words) *that you may declare* (publicly and one on one) *the praises of Him* who called you out of darkness into His wonderful light.

True or False: You are a royal priesthood, and the way in which you exercise your duties as a royal priest is that you come to church and sit in a pew for an hour. False: Your duty is to declare to believers and one-on-one to unbelievers the wonderful Gospel of Christ Jesus. "That you may declare" is not a **static** phrase, but rather a **dynamic** statement. You are to announce the name and fame of Him who called you out of darkness into His wonderful light. **As a true believer you cannot be quiet. You must declare the Gospel by your lips and your life.** This is the missionary spirit in every believer. Someone said, "Either you are a missionary or else you need one!" It is for this purpose of declaring the Lord's name and fame to the unconverted that God lets us remain in this world! The Lord wants the non-Christian to hear about Him and what He did for them on the cross so that they be discipled and join in this discipling process.

MATTHEW 18:17-18,20 If he refuses to listen to them, tell it to the *church*; and if he refuses to listen even to the church, treat him as you would a pagan or a tax collector. I tell you the truth, *whatever you bind* on earth will be bound in heaven, and *whatever you loose* on earth will be loosed in heaven. For where *two or three come together in My name, there am I with them.*

What is the "church"? It is the local gathering of believers. How many believers are needed to qualify? It could be only two or three Christians. There, in that local gathering of Christians, Jesus is present to do His work for them and through them.

The Lord has given these Keys to all Christians on earth individually and as they are gathered together in local congregations in His name.

4.   Whose sins are forgiven and whose sins are not forgiven?

ACTS 3:19 *Repent,* then, and *turn* to God, so that your sins may be wiped out, that *times of refreshing* may come from the Lord.

Whose sins are forgiven? If a person has sorrow over his sin and turns to God, his sins are forgiven. **Above "repent" write "true sorrow." Above "turn" write "be converted,"** which means we were going one way and now we are converted 180 degrees going the opposite way. John and Virginia, let's assume that when I visited you that you were in unbelief, but after some visits you came to repentance and conversion. It would then have been my duty to announce forgiveness of sins to you and unlock the doors to heaven for you. First you repented and turned and you are converted; then I am proclaiming to you what has transpired in your hearts. Do you need to hear the Good News of forgiveness through Jesus? Yes. I am the mouthpiece of the Lord to speak to you that forgiveness. Look at the verse. **"Your sins are wiped out." That means that God has forgotten them so that all trace of them is removed.** What effect should this have on you? Look at the last italicized words. "Times of refreshing." Oh, how refreshing it is to be forgiven.

Let's look at it another way. When you repent and turn to God you are saying to Him, "I give you my heart." In conversion, then, God owns our hearts. We cannot let God own our hearts and at the same time let the Devil own us. John and Virginia, when I was at your house, I not only wanted to know that you were sorry for your sin and that you believed in Jesus as your Savior, but I wanted to know if you **really** wanted Jesus to have you. Or are you playing a game? You give yourself to the Lord on Sunday morning and the rest of the week you give yourself to the Devil. This is not repentance and conversion. After it became apparent that you were serious in your commitment to the Lord, I assured you that your sins were wiped out and God would remember them no more.

PSALM 51:17 My sacrifice, O God, is a *broken spirit*; a *broken* and *contrite heart*, O God, You will not despise.

God will not forgive the person who says, "O God, I don't sin, at least very much. I'm not as bad as other people are." God can't help that person. But **God can help the person who says, "I'm a sinner, and I know it, and I confess it. Have mercy on me, O God." God will delight in having mercy. God will delight in forgiving and healing that person.** When I hear people saying this I assure them of the forgiveness that Christ has earned for them, and I remind them that the door to heaven is open. Where that is not the case the door to heaven is closed. How did the person close it? By a lack of repentance and faith. This should lovingly be proclaimed to them. Who told us to do that? Jesus has told us. It's all part of the Office of the Keys.

2 SAMUEL 12:13 David said to Nathan, *"I have sinned against the LORD."* Nathan replied, *"The LORD has taken away your sin. You are not going to die."*

David was guilty of two terrible sins, that of adultery and murder. David would not confess his sin to God, and he couldn't stand to live with himself, he couldn't sleep at night, he had one mammoth guilty conscience. Any sin should make you feel that way. God finally sent Nathan to David to confront him with his sins. How did David respond? He made an open and full confession. Look at the italicized words: "I have sinned against the Lord." Every sin is against God. In Psalms 32 and 51 David talks further of his repentance. Who exercises the Office of the Keys by proclaiming forgiveness? Nathan does. What does Nathan assure David of? That God has taken away his sin and David would not die. Two crimes for which the Law imposed the death penalty were adultery and murder. God's grace to the repentant sinner is truly wonderful. Let's review one more time. Who made confession? David did. Who pronounced forgiveness and unlocked the door to heaven? Nathan did. **Two things were needed: Repentance over sin and the pronouncement of forgiveness.** Is the saying, "Confession is good for the soul" correct? Definitely.

When should we confess our sins? Privately each day we should confess all known sins. Why daily? Because we sin daily. We make public confession of sins at worship services. Who speaks the word of forgiveness? The pastor. When a Christian does not find the peace of Jesus after confession it would be wise for that person to talk about it with another believer or perhaps the pastor. God desires to bring the peace of forgiveness to everyone of His children.

• MARK 16:16 Whoever *believes and is baptized* will be *saved*, but whoever *does not believe will be condemned*.

These words let us know how high the stakes really are as we share the Gospel. Those who believe and are baptized will be saved. What will happen to those who do not believe? They will be condemned to hell. What is at stake here couldn't be any higher. We're not simply talking about bringing people into a congregation or keeping them out. We're talking about going to heaven or hell! **Our work in the Church of Jesus and with the Office of the Keys involves eternity in heaven or hell. It doesn't get any bigger!**

Do you suppose that your gracious God might have you cross paths with certain people this week so that you might share with them a message of hope and forgiveness in the Savior? We can assume that. You want to be ready, to do the best job you can and be a bold witness so that they can clearly hear the story of Calvary. Be loving and tender and kind. Have the compassion the Savior has had with you. If you do not tell them about Jesus, I would like to know who is going to. Chances are no one. **If you tell someone about Jesus this week, maybe someone at work, a neighbor, a relative, and they believe – what does this verse say will happen? They will be saved.** And **if you don't tell them what will happen? They may well perish.** The stakes are as high as they can go. We're not talking about church membership, but where they will spend eternity!

I think we need to be frank sometimes and just say to a person: "John, I'm really, really concerned about where you're going to spend forever. I thank God that I've come to a place in my spiritual life that I know for certain that if I were to die tonight I would go to heaven. John, do you have that certainty? If he says yes, ask: "What would you tell God if you stood before Him and He should ask, 'Why should I let you into My heaven?'" If he can't give the right answer (and the typical person can't) then share the Gospel with him that he may be converted.

What about Christians who say they simply can't talk about Jesus? Well, what would we say of a person who will never talk about their spouse or will never talk about a son or daughter. They have a problem. They need some help.

What shall we say about people who say they love Jesus, but never use His name except in a worship service? What shall we say about people who say they love Jesus who will not even raise their little finger to tell someone who is going straight to hell, "My friend, you have a problem. God loves you and has the perfect solution for it."? At best that person has a weak faith, and at worst they are not even Christian. Jesus says to all His followers: "You shall be witnesses unto Me." That's by word and deed. Psalm 107:2 says, "Let the redeemed of the Lord say (so)."

We should announce forgiveness and God's eternal love to all who repent and are sorry for their sins, who desire to turn away from **[63]** them, and who believe in Jesus Christ as their personal Savior from their sins. We should tell people who refuse God's love in Christ that their sins are not forgiven. We continue to love them and urge them to see their sin and their Savior so that they may be saved.

5.   **What about church discipline and excommunication?**

This is a part of the exercise of the Office of the Keys in a congregation.

1 CORINTHIANS 5:12-13 What business is it of mine to judge those outside the church? *Are you not to judge those inside?* God will judge those outside. *"Expel the wicked man from among you."*

Paul asks, "What business is it of mine to judge those outside the church?" Does Paul want a yes or a no answer? A no answer. Do we have any business to apply church discipline to those outside the church? No. We do, however, have an obligation to judge those within our fellowship.

On what basis do we make a judgment? **The evidence on which we judge fellow believers and members concerns the confession with their mouth and their life.** Let's say a member has sinned. Let's say that the person is not penitent. He or she is very impenitent. If we see that, then we are to judge. **That a member sins is not that shocking. That he is impenitent is shocking. This person needs to have the Law and Gospel applied by fellow believers.**

Let's say that the person remains impenitent, what does Paul tell us to do? "Expel that wicked man from among you." That's what we call excommunication or exclusion. Question: In this case who really initiated the exclusion? The impenitent person did. How did he initiate it, class? By his impenitence. When that person is then excluded he has no right to say, "That no good church. They kicked me out." Wrong. Who kicked whom out? The impenitent person himself. In a way what the church is doing is proclaiming the exclusion which was really initiated by the impenitent person in the first place. How long a period should a Christian congregation work with someone before he is excluded? Scripture gives no time limit. It depends on the situation. It might be a matter of weeks, months, or even a year or more. I like to give every benefit of the doubt to the impenitent individual. I'm a bit fearful when some churches want to come on too strong and too fast. If anything, let's go the extra mile with the person.

I want to add that church discipline must be exercised in a very loving way. We ought to be careful about looking down our "pious noses" in making judgments. **Our demeanor should reflect the love and care of Jesus for the lost sheep.**

MATTHEW 18:15-18 If your *brother* (that is your spiritual brother) *sins* against you, go (and tell the pastor and the other members. Is that what it says? No.) go and *show him his fault, just between the two of you.* If he listens to you, you have won your brother over. But *if he will not listen, take one or two others* (believers) *along,* so that every matter may be established by the testimony of two or three *witnesses. If he refuses to listen to them, tell it to the church* (That is the local congregation); and *if he refuses to listen even to the church, treat him as you would a pagan or a tax collector* (In Jesus' day they were regarded as being outside the family of God). I tell you the truth, *whatever you bind on earth will be bound in heaven,* and *whatever you loose on earth will be loosed in heaven.*

In reality the excommunication is coming after the fact. The individual has already excluded himself from heaven and from the local family of God by his impenitence even though he has been visited and ministered to by a number of believers. It is no one less than Jesus who commands such action. The Lord is really doing this to the individual through the congregation. Among other things **this action is intended to make the impenitent person see the gravity of his folly. If he laughs at what is being done to him, he laughs at his own doom.** Beside the door to heaven being closed and his sin not removed, he will also have his membership from the local Christian congregation removed including all the rights it conveyed.

2 CORINTHIANS 2:6-8,10 The punishment inflicted on him by the majority is sufficient for him. Now instead, you ought to *forgive and comfort him*, so that he will not be overwhelmed by excessive sorrow. I urge you, therefore, to *reaffirm your love for him.* If you forgive anyone, I also forgive him.

Had the Corinthian congregation excommunicated someone? Yes. Was it a unanimous vote? No, a majority. This person became repentant, very sorrowful over what he had done. The desired goal, repentance, had been achieved. Paul is now asking that he be reinstated. In fact the congregation is told to forgive and comfort him quickly so that he is not overwhelmed with grief. In the last sentence Paul joins the congregation in forgiving the individual.

We think of one example from the Bible. Was Judas sorry over the sin he had committed? Yes, very sorry. Was his heart crushed over what he had done? Yes. As far as he was concerned his sin was so great that it could not be forgiven. There is one thing he could not believe – that the Lord loved him, died for him, and forgave him. The last look of Jesus to Judas in the Garden was a look of love. The last words of Jesus to Judas began with "Friend." The look and the word were an invitation to repentance. What did he do in his grief? He killed himself.

I wonder how many people there are in our community who are like Judas, who say, "I believe God loves people and wants to take them to heaven for Christ's sake except for me. My sin is just too big for God to forgive." I have heard words like that on numerous occasions while canvassing door-to-door. That's the amazing thing about the one true God. No matter how big your sins may be, His mercy is bigger. Paul says in Romans 5:20, "Where sin abounded, grace did much more abound." Even for Judas forgiveness was there. He needed to be told about it. He needed to believe it. We must tell the sorrowing sinner that.

God loves people and in that love commands church discipline and excommunication where needed. One who has committed a grievous sin or one who is not sorry for his sin should first be approached privately. If there is no success, two or three Christians should visit him. If he is still impenitent the church should speak to him. If the person still refuses to listen, the church is to remove (excommunicate) him from its fellowship. This action is as valid as if Christ Himself dealt with the person. If the excluded individual later confesses his sins and wants forgiveness, the congregation should assure him of God's love and their's, and he should graciously be received back into the congregation.

6. How does the local congregation publicly use these Keys?

1 CORINTHIANS 4:1 So then, men ought to *regard us as servants of Christ* and as those *entrusted with the secret things of God.*

Above the word "us" write "pastors." In the first place a pastor is not the servant of the congregation. He is first of all a servant of Christ. That suggests lowliness. I've always like to assure my people that I'm here first to serve the Lord and next to serve them in the Lord's name. Above "those entrusted" write "steward." That suggests dignity and responsibility. In Paul's day a steward was often a slave to whom his master or owner entrusted his property. In this instance God is the Master or Owner. The pastor is a steward who is a slave. And the property which God has given to pastors to be stewards over can be found in the last five words: "The secret things of God." This is the Gospel of Jesus Christ which is a secret to unbelievers. The pastor is to teach the secret things of God to people so they are no longer secret, but believed.

I've spent quite a bit of time with you today. Over two hours in worship and Bible class this morning and tonight over two and a half hours so far. Have I tried to reveal to anyone this morning or this evening any "secrets of God," that is, they were secret to you until today? Has this happened to anyone here tonight? Let's see hands. Praise God!

ACTS 20:28 *Keep watch over yourselves* and *all the flock* of which the *Holy Spirit has made you* [64] *overseers*. Be *shepherds* of the church of God.

St. Paul is writing to pastors. Who should the pastor look out for first? Himself. Why? It would be difficult to feed others if the pastor does not feed himself. Sometimes the schedule in the ministry is hectic, and it becomes difficult to take care of your own spiritual needs first. You can't give away what you don't have. So watch out first for yourself.

Secondly, watch out for whom? "All the flock." What is the flock? The believers in the local congregation. These believers are often called sheep. Sheep follow the shepherd. They depend on him. Paul says, **"All** the flock." Not merely those who are close friends of the pastor. **A good shepherd, a good pastor is to love, lead, and feed ALL the sheep, even the weak ones, even the stubborn ones.** When David was a shepherd he fought a bear and a lion just to save the sheep. Jesus, the Good Shepherd, gave His life for all lost sheep. The pastor is a shepherd of his flock and should be ready to sacrifice everything for their well being. Have you ever heard of a flock of sheep that can manage and provide for itself? No, so Paul says in the last words, "Be shepherds of the church of God." You need a shepherd!

Now look at these words: The "Holy Spirit has made you overseers." For those of you who are members, who has made me your overseer or shepherd? The Holy Spirit. The Holy Spirit saw to it that I came here. What a neat assurance for the sheep. No one less than the third person of the Trinity provides me with a pastor. What must it be like for so many people who do not have such knowledge and assurance? **If you are looking for a church home you could pray no better prayer than this: "Holy Spirit, please give me the pastor/teacher that I need."** What is an overseer? One who leads, feeds, guards, and provides for. I believe that my job is to do everything that I can to disciple you for Jesus and help you get to heaven through Him.

EPHESIANS 4:11-12 It was *the Lord* who gave some to be *apostles,* some to be *prophets*, some to be *evangelists,* and some to be *pastors* and *teachers,* to *prepare God's people for works of service*, so that the *Body of Christ may be built up.*

The Lord gave to the Church **apostles**. This would be the Twelve Apostles plus Paul. What did Jesus give next? **Prophets**. Prophets are men who communicate to men God's will. What is mentioned next? **Evangelists**. An evangelist is one who announces the Good News of Jesus to the lost. Next He gives **pastors** which means shepherds. And then **teachers**. Often these different types of work overlap. Now the question: Why does He give these people to the Church? What does Paul say? To "prepare God's people for works of service, so that the Body of Christ may be built up." **All believers are to be in service to the Lord, but it is the task of these men to enable the saints in their service**.

What if you belong to a congregation and you are not growing in works of service and you are not being built up in the Lord? Something is wrong, either with you or the spiritual person ministering to you. If the problem is you, than have a change of attitude and heart. If the problem is the one ministering to you, then you may need a different pastor/teacher. This is so important. **God wants the Body of Christ to abound in works and grow**. He wants you to abound in works of service and wants you to be built up in the Lord. Ask yourself daily: Is this happening to me?

Jesus authorized and commanded all believers individually and collectively to tell the Good News, to use the Sacraments, and to forgive or not forgive sin. The public use of these Keys is normally given to pastors. The Holy Spirit calls these men (divine call) to be pastors. They serve the Good Shepherd and are like shepherds for members of His flock. The holy ministry is the only office instituted by Christ. A congregation may, however, ask others to assist their pastor as Sunday School teachers, church officers, youth leaders, etc.

There is someone this week who is just waiting for you to bring them Good News (Capital G, captial N). If you are a Christian you have a story to tell. There is someone right now who is waiting for you to tell them **your** story of Jesus. Please don't disappoint that waiting soul. Please tell them in your own words, from your heart to their heart. You're not going to be preachy. You're not going to shove it down their throats. You are going to love them as Jesus has loved you and as He used some Christian to be influential in your walk with the Lord. Souls are at stake. **The Keys are to be used now.** Jesus says that He has the authority to give you the Keys to use. Make the Lord happy that He did that. Make some lost person happy. Fulfill your purpose here on earth until the Lord calls you Home. And all of God's people said, "Amen!"

Let's pray together

Dear Jesus, how great and wonderful and clean is Your Church. And to think that You have made us holy priests in it to serve You daily is a honor we do not deserve. You have also given us Keys which can lock and unlock the door to heaven by sharing the Good News, by baptizing and celebrating the Lord's Supper, and by forgiving and not forgiving sin. Help us use these Keys faithfully and wisely. Give us true compassion for the unconverted. When they come to faith may we joyfully assure them of their redemption and adoption. When it is necessary to exclude the impenitent from our fellowship, may we do so in love. Bless our pastor as the shepherd of this flock. Lord, join our hands with his hands that we may do all in our power to bring You to the lost and the lost to You. May we remain steadfast in the one true, saving faith to the end and finally wear the crown. For Your sake we ask it, Lord. Amen.

Let's sing together

> The Church's one foundation Is Jesus Christ her Lord;
> She is His new creation By water and the Word.
> From heav'n He came and sought her To be His holy bride;
> With His own blood He bought her, And for her life He died.
>
> Elect from ev'ry nation, Yet one o'er all the earth;
> Her charter of salvation: One Lord, one faith, one birth.
> One holy name she blesses, Partakes one holy food,
> And to one hope she presses With ev'ry grace endued.
>
> Yet she on earth has union With God, the Three in One,
> And mystic sweet communion With those whose rest is won.
> O blessed heavn'ly chorus! Lord, save us by Your grace **[65]**
> That we, like saints before us, May see You face to face.

Bible reading schedule for the next seven days

❑ 1st day – Acts 10   ❑ 5th day – Acts 14
❑ 2nd day – Acts 11   ❑ 6th day – Acts 15
❑ 3rd day – Acts 12   ❑ 7th Day – Acts 16
❑ 4th day – Acts 13

Worksheet no. 8

1. Every believer is a member of (   ) a Christian congregation, (   ) a Lutheran congregation, (✖) the invisible Church of Christ.

2. We become members of the one true invisible Church by (   ) Baptism, (   ) joining a Lutheran Church, (   ) going to church, (✖) faith in the Lord Jesus.

3. The Keys Jesus has given us give us the authority and power to do three things. They are:

    a. _To preach the Gospel of Jesus Christ._

    b. _To provide the Sacraments of Baptism and Holy Communion._

    c. _To forgive or not forgive sins and lock and unlock the door to heaven._

4. _True_ or False: Christians can forgive sins in the name of Jesus.

5. What happens to the doors of heaven when sinners do not repent and believe? _They are_

142

closed.

6. *True* or False: The Keys which lock and unlock the doors to heaven have been placed in my hands.

7. List the three steps to be followed in carrying out church discipline:

   a. *Speak to the individual privately.*

   b. *Speak again, but this time with two or three fellow believers.*

   c. *Then tell it to the local congregation.*

8. In one of the Bible verses we learned that ___*David*___ confessed his sin in the presence of presence of ___*Nathan*___ , and ___*Nathan*___ assured ___*David*___ that God had forgiven him his sins.

9. The purposes of excommunication are to (✖) have the impenitent **[66]** sinner see how great his sins are, ( ) keep him from going to church, ( ) keep him out of heaven, (✖) bring the person to repentance.

10. The sins of some church members today have been described as sins of commission, sins of omission, and sins of no mission. What is meant by the last sin? *They do not understand that their mission is to preach Christ to their community and world; they have no mission.*

11. Recently someone characterized many a modern congregation's view of their mission as that of assisting in "hatching, matching, and dispatching." What did he mean? *That the church is here for baptizing, marrying, and burying.*

12. *True* or False: A congregation which does not go all out to evangelize its community with a dynamic witnessing program is forfeiting one of the basic reasons for its existence.

13. What is the main mission of the Church? *To make disciples of all people by sharing the Gospel and by baptizing them in the name of the Father, Son, and Holy Spirit.*

14. What is a disciple? *A student of the Master, a follower of the Master, and one who makes others disciples for the Master.*

15. *True* or False: The office of the holy ministry is a divine office.

16. A person says to you, "I think the important thing is that a minister be sincere. If he is sincere, any preacher can be my minister!" How would you respond? *He can be sincere but sincerely wrong. The first criteria for a pastor to be my minister would be that he must preach and teach all of God's Word, both Law and Gospel, in all its truthfulness.* **[67]**

L et's bow our heads for prayer: Heavenly Father, I thank You for this day, for worship and Bible class this morning, and for this Bible study this evening. Forgive me, Father, for those days that are spent on trivia. Frequently I only see the things of this world. More and more let me see people and the Word which are present now and will be forever. I want to invest in those things which pay interest in eternity. Forgive me where I have failed in the past because of Jesus who died for all my sin. Help me look at life with the eternal implications in clear view. May this congregation also look at people and the Word as sincere objects of all the activities and functions which take place here. May every sermon, every Bible study, and every member grow in these eternal concerns. Father, it will not be long before I will be called to give an account of my stewardship before Jesus on the Last Day. I want that to be a joyous event. To that end bless Your Word in my heart this evening. I ask this in the name of Jesus. Amen.

When a minister gets into the pulpit on Sunday morning and says to the congregation that the sermon is going to be on stewardship, what sign or symbol immediately pops into the mind of the typical church member as he or she hears that? Yes, Dottie has it – it's the dollar sign, and the person says, "We're going to get a sermon on money." Then the person says, "Rats, I could have gone golfing this morning or stayed at home and read the paper, and now we're going to get a sermon on money." In the minds of most church people the word "stewardship" equates "money." We do want to see a symbol, but not a dollar sign. When the sermon will be on stewardship what symbol should come to mind? The cross of Jesus Christ. That is the heart and core of Christian stewardship. That's what we're going to learn this evening. When I stand at the foot of the cross, and His blood has made me whole, I need to look at Jesus, and ask, "Lord, what do you want me to do?"

We're ready to go. I HAVE GOOD NEWS FOR YOU ABOUT A STEWARDSHIP WHICH IS FULLY COMMITTED.

Lesson 9

I HAVE GOOD NEWS FOR YOU

About A Stewardship Which Is Fully Committed

If you were put on trial this week for being a **Christian** steward, would there be enough evidence to convict you? An ancient proverb says, "He who aims at nothing hits it." Many people are right on target. They're aiming at nothing and hitting nothing. Let's see what we can do to change that.

Underline the word "Committed" *three times*! At the bottom of this page I want you to write down three questions. **1. What am I committed to? 2. Will I be happy in the hour of my death that I was committed to this? 3. When I finally get to heaven and see Jesus, will I be glad that I was committed to the things I was committed to in this world?** I think you can sense that this Lesson is going to have a profound effect on your life. Many times we are frustrated about what we're doing with our lives, the wasted effort, the wasted time. There are not too many people who are satisfied with the goals and productivity of their lives. These three questions need to be asked regularly, even daily. Please refer back to them often in your life.

1. What is a Christian steward?

We're not asking, "What is a steward?" because a steward is a caretaker, but we're asking, "What is a **Christian** steward?" The following passages are going to give us a Biblical definition of a

Christian steward. As these verses give us this definition we should say, "I want to be this kind of person so that I can put my life together and properly answer the three questions I wrote on the bottom of this page."

PSALM 24:1 The *earth is the LORD's, and everything in it*, the world, and *all who live in it*.

Who is the absolute Owner of the earth? The Lord. "And everything in it." All animals and birds and fish, all the forests and oceans, the earthworms, the cattle on a thousand hills, our lands, our houses all belong to the Lord. Look at the last five words. What else? All who live on earth. Even the unbelievers and pagans? Yes. We do not own our bodies and souls. These words tell you plainly that what you call "yours" is not correct. I'm sure that last week you spoke of "MY house." This is "MY car." These are "MY children." And yet this passage says that your house, your car, and your children are not yours, but God's. Further, your body belongs to the Lord, your brain belongs to the Lord, your time belongs to the Lord, your skills belong to the Lord; everything belongs to the Lord. They're only on loan to you. **God owns, you owe!**

Let's assume that you go to a neighbor to borrow his car or his boat or whatever it may be for a day or two or a week or two. You have this item in your possession. You use it. Question: How do you treat the item that has been loaned to you? Do you treat it as though it were your own? No. In fact, most of us take extra good care of something loaned to us. Years ago someone loaned me their car, a little Volkswagen Beetle. I took such good care of it. One day I was going downtown on the freeway. Some kids were on an overpass and dropped a good sized rock down which went right through the windshield. I felt terrible. I could afford to fix it. That wasn't the problem. What was the problem? **I damaged something that didn't belong to me.**

The same thing applies to God owning everything, even that which He has loaned you. He has never deeded it over to you. And **since He is the Owner He expects you to use it according to His wishes. You're the steward.** You ought to be treating everything in this world, your home, your money, your time, your abilities with the care that God expects you to have. In a few minutes you will learn that on the Last Day Jesus will ask for a full report.

<u>This means that you must change your attitude and thinking to a brand new way of looking at everything in this world.</u> This is your duty as a steward. And <u>**as a CHRISTIAN steward you are moved to do it out of love and devotion to Jesus who died on the cross for you**</u>.

HAGGAI 2:8 "The *silver is Mine* and the *gold is Mine*" declares the LORD Almighty.

All the silver and gold in the world are God's. All the money and the things that money will buy are God's. Even the little penny (hold one up) bears a stewardship concept: "In God We Trust." Do you look at your money this way? **It's not MY money, MY pension fund, My savings account. It's God's, and if you are a Christian steward you know this and use it accordingly.**

I want you to write down a Scripture reference under this passage: 1 Chronicles 29:1-20. To the left of it write: "Read tonight." Read it before you retire this evening. David is standing before the assembly of worshipers at the dedication of the Temple. (Have someone ready to read aloud verses 3-4 to the class.) "In my devotion to the temple of my God I now give my personal treasures of gold and silver for the temple of my God, over and above everything I have provided for this holy temple: three thousand talents of gold and seven thousand talents of refined silver, for the overlaying of the walls of the buildings" (3-4). **Do you know how much gold and silver that is? David "gave" God about 110 tons of gold and 260 tons of silver.** Who would like to figure out the value of this? Do you suppose David knew that it was all God's anyway? Yes, indeed. In this same Chapter we come to David's prayer. The next verse is part of it. Let's read it together.

1 CHRONICLES 29:14 *Everything* comes *from You*, and *we have given You only what comes from Your hand.*

I'm a tither, and when I present my tithe to the Lord, I am presenting not only something sizeable, but according to this verse I'm presenting something that already belongs to whom? To the Lord. Think about that. **This morning in worship you presented your offering and you were giving God only what was already His, but if that was done in the right spirit, it should have been a great experience for both you and God.**

When my four sons were small, we agreed that we would give $5 to each boy, mom and dad, to buy a Christmas gift for one family member whose name they would draw from a hat (we didn't have much money then.) On Christmas Eve, about midnight, we opened our presents (each person had only one). The youngest son brought over a gift to me. As he brought it over my second son, John, about seven years old, just "trailed" the present over from the Christmas tree to me. He was like a fish following a lure. While the names were secret, I immediately knew who had my name. It was John. He moved up close to the chair I was sitting in. I also knew what was in the box. I knew it was a tie because the box was the size of a tie box. I pulled the paper away, opened the box, and there was a tie made up of all the colors of the rainbow, plus all the colors that are not in the rainbow. It was the ugliest tie I had ever seen. I knew exactly what happened. He went to a men's store. Pulled his $5 out and said to the man, "I want to buy a tie for my dad for Christmas." Now what kind of a tie can you buy for $5? I know what happened next. I used to sell ties. The salesman went into the back room to a box where they threw junk ties. He pulled one out, went out to John, and said, "Here is a beautiful tie, and it's only $5." They dumped that tie on him. I opened it up, held it up, and my eyes began to water. John looked at me and said, "Do you like it?" I said, "John, this is something else." He said, "Do you really like it?" I said, "John, it's just great." He said, "Oh, that's good." He was wriggling around so much he could not contain himself for joy. Then he said, "When are you going to wear it?" I said, "Oh, John, soon, soon." Fortunately, a few days later, we had a bad snowstorm. I knew I wouldn't see anyone that day so I put it on, and it glowed. I want to ask you a question. On that Christmas Eve who was the happiest of the two of us? Yes, most people say John was. He was, indeed, very happy – because we all know that it is more blessed to give than to receive. But you're wrong! He was very happy, but there was someone right next to him who was even happier. Who do you think it was? I was the happiest. His happiness brought me even greater happiness – this despite the fact that I gave him $5 of my hard-earned money and this is what he bought. When I saw what it did for him, it did something even bigger for me.

I believe that you should have come to God this morning at offering time and said, "God, here is my present to You. I know that what I'm giving You is only what is Yours in the first place, but I'm just so happy to be able to do this for You." If you would have done it with that happiness, I know who was even happier than you – your God in heaven. This is how a Christian steward operates.

LUKE 12:48 From everyone who has been *given much, much will be demanded;* and from the one who has been entrusted with *much, much more* will be asked.

Concept No. 1: Much has been given to you. You have been given much with regard to your brain, with regard to your eyes, your ears, your abilities, and many, many other gifts. I am going to suggest that all of you are filthy – rich! **Concept No. 2**: The more you have the more will be expected of you by God.

Now listen to this truth: You cannot take these gifts and abilities and then squander and waste them. Even unbelievers can understand this. As for a Christian, he cannot do what he wants and believe he is accountable to no one. He knows that the Day is coming when Jesus will say to all His children: "My son, My daughter, what have you done with everything that I have given or loaned you? What have you done with your time? What have you done with your abilities? What have you done with this body of yours?" This verse says that the Lord will ask. A Christian steward knows this and acts accordingly. You can see how this verse should have a profound effect upon the way you think and live. By the way, **before you can live this way you have to think this way!**

1 CORINTHIANS 10:31 Whether you eat or drink or *whatever you do, do it all for the glory of God.*

Here is the final principle of all Christian activity: Do everything to the glory of God. That means all activities: eating, sleeping, working, jogging, relaxation, sex, whatever it may be. Either we do what we do to God's glory or else man's glory and the Devil's. What if you can't do it to the glory of God? Don't do it.

But how do you do it to the glory of God? Do you suppose there may be a person who can drink a glass of wine to the glory of God? Yes. Do you suppose there is a person who can drink a glass of wine to the glory of the Devil? Sure. What decides? In the first case you do it to the glory of God by becoming a Christian so that you are in God's family by faith in Jesus. Next it means that as a Christian you receive this object or activity as a gift from God. Then you use it as He intended. And perhaps the most important, you use it or do it with thanksgiving in your heart to God.

Before we read the next verse, let me read the verse just prior to it: "Men ought to regard us (pastors) as servants of Christ and as those entrusted with the secret things of God." Now the next verse follows.

1 CORINTHIANS 4:2 It is required that those who have been *given a trust must prove faithful.*

Above "given a trust" write the word "steward." There is a fundamental truth that applies not only to pastors who are stewards of the secret things of God; this truth applies to all believers. What is that fundamental truth? You must be faithful. God has entrusted certain gifts and abilities to all His children. The key, as far as He is concerned, is that you and I be faithful. **Other things may be important for a good steward. What might some of them be? Ability, experience, learning, and so on, but THE INDISPENSABLE QUALIFICATION IS FAITHFULNESS.**

For example, an employer may not care that much about your ability, your training, etc. The one key issue that he will not hedge on is your fidelity. If you have that you are on your way. That same principle holds true in Christian stewardship. God says, "As a Christian steward I expect you to be faithful." Faithful with what? Your use of time. The activity or inactivity of your gifts and abilities. **God even expects you to be faithful with regard to your potential, something that many people completely overlook.** As a Christian I love my God. I give Him my life. A Christian steward is one who understands that and works at it constantly.

• 2 CORINTHIANS 5:15 Christ died for all, that *those who live* (that is, those who are alive spiritually) *should no longer live for themselves* (that's what you use to do before your conversion) but *for Him* who died for them and was raised again.

I'm going to submit that before you became a Christian you believed it was fun to live for yourself. However, after you became a Christian you discovered that was not true. There is real, deep joy in living for Jesus. Before I came back to Christ at seventeen years of age I didn't want to get very serious about Christianity because I wanted to enjoy life, to have fun. Little did I know that only in

Jesus could I really have joy and fun. Before I was a believer I thought "I had the world by the tail." It really had me by the tail. **When Jesus came to me, He touched and affected every area of my life. I'm here to live for Him.**

An analogy. When you buy a washing machine you buy it, not for the sake of the washing machine, but for your sake, that of washing your clothes. What do you do with it if it refuses to wash clothes? Guess you know. Jesus didn't save you for yourself or for the Devil but for Himself. **You were rescued FOR God.** He created you for that. You blew it. Then He bought you back with the blood of Jesus. **YOU WERE CREATED AND REDEEMED TO LIVE FOR HIM. A Christian steward is very aware of this.**

JOHN 15:5,8 I am the vine; you are the branches. *If a man remains in Me and I in him, he will bear* (underline the next word) *much fruit*; apart from Me you can do nothing. *This is to My Father's glory*, that you *bear* (underline the next word) *much fruit, showing* (or proving) *yourselves to be My disciples.*

"The Lord has never planted a Christian on this earth to be a shade tree"

What is the fruit? The good works a believer does. True or False: Jesus is here saying that believers connected to Him will bear fruit. False. He is saying that believers connected to Him by faith will bear **much** fruit! Apart from Jesus a man may produce good works which the world applauds, but what does Jesus say they are? Nothing! Listen to this: The world is full of people doing good works who, in the sight of God, are doing nothing. What are you doing?

Are you like a pear tree in my back yard? It's five years old and has produced no edible fruit. I've pruned it. I've fertilized it. And yet nothing. I will cut it down shortly and replace it with a tree that does produce fruit. Not far away from that tree I have a five year old golden delicious dwarf apple tree. This year it produced hundreds of apples. Five limbs broke off from the sheer weight of the apples, yet, even with that loss, I was still able to harvest about three hundred delicious apples and that from a dwarf fruit tree! **The Lord has never planted a Christian on this earth to be a shade tree. When you are connected to Jesus you can produce good works in abundance, the way that apple tree did for me. A Christian steward is one who is into producing much fruit, many good works.** This is to whose glory? The Father's. And what does Jesus say this proves? "You are My disciples."

ROMANS 14:12 So then, each of us will *give an account of himself* to God.

If you were put on trial for being a good Christian steward, would there be enough evidence to convict you? Know what? You're going to find out! The Day is coming when you will give account of yourself to the Lord. You will give an account of how you spent your time, of how you used the gifts entrusted to you, and so on. A Christian steward is very aware of this up-coming trial on the Day of Judgment.

A steward is someone who takes care of another person's property and manages it the way the owner wants it managed. We are stewards for God here on earth. Everything belongs to God, and we do everything we can in our stewardship to honor Him. The secret to doing that is to live in and for Jesus. Then we will be ready for the Last Day when we give an account to the Lord.

2.   **What does God say about our use of time and abilities?**

MATTHEW 25:14-15 Again, it will be like a man going on a journey, who called his servants and *entrusted his property* to them. To one he gave five talents of money ($10,000), to another two talents ($4,000), and to another one talent ($2,000), *each according to his ability*. Then he went on his journey.

Jesus is telling this parable. The "man going on a journey" is a picture of Jesus getting ready to leave His followers on earth to go back to heaven. His children on earth are not called church members, but what? Servants. The word "servant" comes from the Greek word δουλοσ which we translate "slave." Jesus is your Master. He owns you. He purchased you to be His with His blood. Jesus is saying that He is turning over talents of money to His beloved slaves, to you. By doing this He is honoring you greatly. **What do the talents represent? Every spiritual and physical gift that you have. They are given to you as a sacred trust from the Lord to be used in His service.** Why the difference in gifts? Each slave is given talents according to what? His ability.

1 CORINTHIANS 12:27,29-31 *You are the body of Christ* (that means that you are not your own), and each one of you is a part of it. Are all apostles? Are all prophets? Are all teachers? Do all work miracles? Do all have gifts of healing? Do all speak in tongues? Do all interpret? (Does Paul want a yes or no answer to these questions? No.) But *eagerly desire the greater gifts.*

The word "gifts" is plural. You should know that God has given you many gifts. Some of you may say, "I don't have a clue as to what my gifts are." You will have to discover them, and as you discover them you are to concentrate on which gifts (look at the last two words)? The greater or more important gifts. You may start out discovering a lesser gift, but don't stay there.

An example: When we started this church and moved into this facility we took turns cleaning. On a number of occasions I've come over here on Saturday evening to set things up for Sunday morning. Occasionally I have found dirty restrooms, so I cleaned them up. This is not beneath my dignity. Do you suppose that when I clean a restroom on Saturday evening I do a very good job? Yes sir! As this congregation grows, do you think it would be wise for me to continue to clean up the church on Saturday evenings in view of the greater gifts God has given to me? Don't any of you say yes. I believe God has given me the little gift of cleaning up a mess. Do you believe God has also given me a few more important gifts than this? Yes.

Paul is saying that all of you have various gifts; however, you are to be eager to discover and develop those greater gifts. I see so many church people majoring in minors. Have you ever felt that you were doing that? Have you ever thought: "I'm not doing what I should be doing with my life."? Let's go after the more important gifts that we have.

1 PETER 4:10-11 Each one should *use whatever gift he has received* (Underline the next seven words) *to serve others, faithfully administering God's grace* in its various forms. If anyone speaks, he should do it as one speaking the very words of God. If anyone serves, he should do it with the strength God provides, (Watch this now) *so that in all things God may be praised* through Jesus Christ.

God wants to be praised by the things that you say and do as you serve others. Do you want joy in service? Sure you do, and you can have it if you follow the right order. Let's put this acrostic on the marker board:

J-esus

O-thers

Y-ou

Jesus first. Others second. Who comes last? I do. In what order do I sometimes put these three? Just the reverse. I'm first, others are second, and if there's anything left over the Lord can have that.

Do you want fulfillment? Do you want joy? Sure you do. The acrostic describes how to go at it. You could have all the right faith in the world, but James says that if you do not have works your faith is dead.

I'd like you to think of a little boy who, one day, came into a store and stood before the candy counter to buy some candy. The man behind the counter waited and waited while the boy looked. The man said, "Please tell me what you want, I'll take your money, and you can have your candy." The boy said, "Okay." He looked and looked and looked some more. Finally the man said, "Hurry up and tell me what you want to buy!" The boy said, "Okay." But he kept right on looking, looking, looking. The man said, "Will you please tell me what you want? This is not a big deal" The little boy looked up at him and said, "Mister, when you've only got one penny to spend it IS a big deal." To the man it was no big deal. To the boy it was a very big deal. **What's your "penny"? How many do you have? Right now you're spending those "pennies." Are you satisfied with the way you're spending them? And is God satisfied? What changes need to be made as you spend the rest of your "pennies"?**

EPHESIANS 5:15-17 (<u>Underline the next seven words, but triple underline "how"</u>) *Be very careful, then, how you live* (<u>It's not the quantity, but the quality. Be careful HOW you live</u>) – not as unwise but as wise, *making the most of every opportunity*, because the days are evil. Therefore *do not be foolish* (<u>Don't kid yourself</u>) , but (<u>Underline the following</u>) *understand what the Lord's will is.*

"After you are dead will anybody be able to say that it was good that you lived? If so, who and why?"

You must ask, "What is the Lord's will for my life? What is His will for the stewardship of everything in my possession?" To do this you will have to ask a lot of questions of yourself. Do this daily. Where have you been? Where are you now? Where you are going? Do you remember the very first words of Paul after his conversion on the road to Damascus? "Lord, what will You have me do?" You should ask the same question. I try to make it a practice each evening, before I go to sleep, to say, "Lord, help me to know and do those things You want tomorrow. Help me meet the people You want me to meet, to say the things You want me to say to them. Help me put aside the things that I should not be occupied with." Does that sound like wise praying? Be sure that in the days ahead you try to do what the Lord wants.

In view of Question 2, let me ask you a question. **After you are dead will anybody be able to say that it was good that you lived? If so, who and why? Will God be able to say it was good that you lived and, if so, why?** Along with those questions one more. How old are you? I want to suggest that some of us may have wasted a third or a half or more of our lives. **We've got to be careful how we spend the rest of our lives**. I see some people in the church like old Fred who changed the hymn: "Take my life and let it be, Consecrated, Lord to Thee." He substitutes another word for life. Like some other church men he sings, "Take my *wife* and let her be, Consecrated, Lord to Thee." He thinks it's funny, and he doesn't know how far off base he really is.

I remember years ago when I finished conducting evangelism services at a church in Minneapolis, I was driving home about midnight in a snowstorm. I had the radio on, and I heard Peggy Lee sing a song I never heard before. Through that song she spoke a powerful message. She sang about when she was a little girl and her dad took her to the circus. She saw the animals and the acts and when it was all over she sang the refrain:

> *Is that all there is, my friends? Then let's keep dancing and romancing.*
> *Let's break out the booze and have a ball If that's all there is"*

151

In the next verse she fell in love with a guy and ran off and married him. She was so happy, but after three weeks he left her and ran away, whereupon, she sings the refrain again. After going through a few more sad verses she finally says, "I suppose you're asking: Why doesn't she end it all?" She laughs and says, "I wouldn't give you the satisfaction!" How sad. But I like her asking, "Is that all there is?" You know, for many people there's not that much to life. What is there for you? There ought to be everything. You think of your job, and if that's all there is to life, I'm going to suggest you're missing quite a bit. Perhaps you should be singing the refrain of Peggy Lee's song. **One of the things I like to ask frequently is this: "What am I doing that's going to count in eternity?" Paul says, "Don't be foolish."** <u>Try to find out what the Lord's will is day by day and then do it.</u>

God gives all believers various gifts and abilities. He wants His lost sheep to be found and His Church to grow as His children use their gifts. His directive to you is to *discover and develop your more important gifts.* Don't waste time! Don't waste your gifts! God has a plan for you to serve. Spend more time discussing this with a mature Christian friend or your pastor.

> If a Man's faith does not affect his pocketbook, then his faith is phony. ELTON TRUEBLOOD

3. What does God say about our serving Him with money?

MARK 12:41 Jesus sat down opposite the place where the offerings were put and *(underline the next word)* <u>*watched*</u> *the crowd putting their money into the temple treasury.*

There were thirteen metal receptacles at the Temple to receive the gifts of the worshipers for the benefit of the Temple. Jesus, with the disciples, sat down near one of these receptacles to watch the worshipers put their money in. **The Greek word for "watch" really means "observing closely."** The next words read: "Many rich people threw in large amounts. But a poor widow came and put in two very small copper coins, worth only a fraction of a penny." Then He makes this amazing statement: "I tell you the truth, this poor widow has put more into the treasury than all the others." **Her fraction of a penny was more in God's sight than all the huge gifts of the rich. Why was that? Two reasons. First, she was a true believer. Second, she gave sacrificially; this was all she had left.** When you presented your gift to the Lord this morning He looked for these two things. Did He see you give out of a living faith? Did He see your gift involve any kind of sacrifice? This is how a good Christian steward gives!

PROVERBS 3:9 *Honor* (underline that) the LORD with *your wealth*, with the *firstfruits* of all your crops.

Did you hear about the little boy who started walking to Sunday School with two nickels, one for the Lord and one for himself? On the way to church he lost one of them. "There goes the Lord's nickel," he said. That boy didn't understand this verse. We are here to honor the Lord with what? Our wealth, with our firstfruits. Above "firstfruits" write "the best." **God's people were commanded to give the best of their crops and animals to the Lord to honor Him. Today this would be the top part of your income, a generous amount, not leftovers.**

Luther says that a man needs "two conversions," one of the soul and one of the pocketbook. Malachi 3 is the Scripture the Lord used to "convert" my pocketbook. It happened on my vicarage, the year of internship at the seminary. I was serving a congregation in Indiana. The cupboard was bare. The checkbook was empty. I have heard a few people say that they cannot afford to tithe. I don't believe it. I have learned that even in poverty one can and should tithe. I also learned that I cannot afford not to tithe. Let's see what I discovered, and bear in mind, these words are for your edification as well as mine.

MALACHI 3:8-10 Will a man rob God? (The prophet begins with this basic question. Is it possible to actually rob God? Can a man actually be so rude as to do that? God says through the prophet:) Yet you rob Me. (They stand indicted for robbery. Who makes that statement? God.) But you ask, "How do we rob You?" (They plead not guilty. How could they ever do that? Notice that those who are guilty of doing this do not want to admit to it. Here comes the proof for the charge.) In *tithes and offerings*. (These were used by the priests and Levites for the maintenance of their work and their families.) You are under a curse – the whole nation of you – because you are robbing Me. (The whole nation is robbing God. For their robbery God is cursing them. He punished them with famine, bad weather, and loss of crops.) Bring the *whole tithe* into the storehouse, that there may be food in My house. (They were keeping some of the tithe for themselves. That was robbing God.) *Test Me in this,*" ("I want you to put Me to the test.") says the LORD Almighty (Have you, my friend, done this?), "and see if I will not *throw open the floodgates of heaven* and pour out *so much blessing that you will not have room enough* for it."

What might those blessings be? They could be financial, spiritual, family, or personal blessings. I imagine that there may be some here who have been robbing God by withholding the offering they should be bringing to Him. **Bear in mind that in the Old Testament Jacob and Abraham did not HAVE to tithe, but they did because they loved the Lord.** And if they did it because they loved the Lord in the Old Testament, you who live in the New Testament have many more reasons than they to do the same, to tithe, not because you HAVE to, but because you WANT to.

A few years ago a man named Ron Hoover went through a class like this where his soul was converted. When we came to this point in this Lesson His pocketbook was "converted." He became a tither. Then something interesting happened. Ron's business took off and money poured into his pockets, so much so, that one day he asked if he could stop by for a visit. When he arrived he told his story of soul and pocketbook conversion. However, because of the huge increase in income, Ron said that his tithe offerings were really getting big. "Is there some way," he asked, "that I can cut these large offerings down a bit?" I said, "Ron, I can think of only one way." "Good," he said, "what is it?" I said, "Ron, in a few minutes you and I will kneel down in front of these two chairs, and I will ask the Lord to reduce your income so that your offerings are not so high." He was in shock. In a few seconds he said, "No, I think I like it the way it is." You should know that Ron continued to tithe. A few years later, at age 43, he became exceedingly wealthy – he moved into His Father's House in heaven. How is it with you? Would your offering be too high if you tithed? If so, there is one way we can reduce it so that you can tithe and your offering is smaller. Or would you rather say with Ron, "No, I think I like the tithe and everything it brings."

I do not believe you should wait until you have abundance to tithe. I believe that when you have little or nothing it is a perfect time to start. In fact, **according to Malachi the perfect time to start tithing is right now. Old Testament believers, like Jacob and Abraham, did it voluntarily out of love, and only love should prompt us today.**

LUKE 6:38 *Give,* and *it will be given to you.* A *good measure, pressed down, shaken together* and *running over*, will be *poured* into your lap. For with *the measure you use*, it will *be measured to you.*

True or False: The more you give, the more God will give you. True. Which words show that? "A good measure, pressed down, shaken together and running over will be poured into your lap." Who promised this? Jesus did. **As you "up" your giving, God will "up" His giving. He will always give more than you give.** Look at the last sentence. What is this saying? How does God determine what to give to you? He gives on the basis of your giving.

1 CORINTHIANS 16:2 On the *first day* of *every week* (<u>That's Sunday.</u>) , *each one* of you (<u>There should be no exceptions.</u>) should *set aside* a sum of money (<u>What size?</u>) *in keeping with his income.*

Why should you set this money aide? Because it is the Lord's. Another benefit is that there is then no temptation for you to spend it on yourself. **Behind "income" write "percentage or proportionate." Paul is not teaching giving a certain amount, but he is commanding percentage or proportionate giving.** The key issue with your gift to the Lord this morning was not the amount, $20, $50, $100. The percent is the issue. What percent did you give God today? Figure that out this week. **Let the percent represent your love and thanksgiving to God.** There is no legalism in the New Testament as to what percent of your income you should give.

2 CORINTHIANS 9:7 *Each man should give* what he has *decided in his heart* to give, *not reluctantly* or *under compulsion*, for God *loves a cheerful giver.*

Who should decide what a believer gives to the Lord? The believer. The words "he has decided in his heart" suggest willingness and joy. Christians should never feel compelled to give. Look at the last words. What kind of a giver does God love? A cheerful giver. A more literal translation of the Greek word for "cheerful" is **"hilarious."** One time missionaries in New Guinea were translating the Bible into the native tongue. Their tongue had no word for "cheerful." But the missionaries did a good job anyway. Their translation read: "God loves a **giggling** giver." That's very close to **"hilarious."** God is very happy over the person who is hilarious, who has joy inside in bringing this present to Him. Was God happy with your present this morning? Will He be happy with your present next Sunday morning?

We honor God by giving our best gifts to Him. In the Old Testament this was the tithe (10%). Today we are free from the law to tithe, yet, many Christians still tithe and give more than the tithe because of their love for the Lord. A definite percent of one's income should be set aside for church work and charity. God says that Sunday is the day to bring these gifts to Him. He challenges us to give cheerfully, liberally, and to tithe, promising to give us more than we give Him.

4. What is our job as Christian witnesses?

MATTHEW 28:19-20 Jesus said, "Therefore go and *make disciples* of *all nations, baptizing* them in the name of the Father and of the Son and of the Holy Spirit, and *teaching* them to obey everything I have commanded you."

One time I was doing door-to-door canvassing for our church. A woman came to the door, and when she discovered I was from the church she became furious. "Who told you to do this anyway?" she demanded. I replied, "Jesus, my Savior, commanded me in Matthew 28:19-20 when He said to all His followers: 'Go and make disciples of all people.' I'm here because of Him." She did not know what to say and quickly closed the door. If you are a believer in the Lord, then, you, too, are under command by Him to go disciple people for Him. Only unbelievers are not under this command.

Jesus does not command us to make church members of people, but what? Disciples. Now let's check your memory from the last Lesson. What is our threefold definition of a disciple? Anyone? **A disciple is: 1. A student of the Master. 2. A follower of the Master. And 3. One who makes disciples of others for the Master**. We're not even commanded to make believers out of people, but disciples. **How are we going to disciple them? By baptizing them and teaching them what? "Everything I have commanded you." This is a big command and a big process. It starts with conversion and ends when the disciple leaves this earth for heaven.**

Jesus bought all men from hell with the payment of His holy blood on the cross. A poet wrote:

> *If for a world a soul were lost, Who could the loss supply?*
> *More than a thousand worlds it cost A single soul to buy.*

Jesus does not want such world-wide redemption wasted. He does not want one person to miss the opportunity of hearing the story of Calvary. Our Lord loves the alcoholic, the woman who has had an abortion, the unwed mother, the person who's been divorced, and everyone else. What about us? Do we love them? Will we gladly obey the command to win the lost for Him?

ACTS 1:8 You will receive (underline the next word) _power_ when the *Holy Spirit* comes on you; and *you will be My witnesses* in Jerusalem, and in all Judea and Samaria, and to the ends of the earth.

Do you suppose you will need power from the Holy Spirit to be a witness for Christ? Yes. A lady named Marilyn Monroe (not the Hollywood one) went through this class. She received Jesus as her Savior and showed great spiritual growth. Some of our ladies were doing door-to-door canvassing, and I felt Marilyn was ready to move out in this area. I happened to meet her in the sanctuary of the church one day and told her that I felt she was ready for door-to-door work. She had a lively Christian faith and a warm personality. She looked right at me and said, "I can't do that." I said, "Oh, yes you can!" She said, "No, I'd be scared." Then I reminded her that the Holy Spirit would give her power to do the work. Finally she held her arms up in the air in exasperation and let them fall down at her sides and said, "Rev. Ginkel, if you make me do this I'll just die." I said, "Okay, Marilyn, if you do, I promise to give you a Christian funeral right here in this church." She was dumbfounded. "Okay, she said, but remember your promise." She went out door-to-door and did great work for her Savior. You know what? She never died. In fact, she enjoyed it immensely. I have never seen or heard of a Christian dying while witnessing for Jesus in America. When you say, "I can't do it," you are right. You can't, but the same Holy Spirit available to the early Christians and to Marilyn is available to you right now.

Jesus says "You WILL BE My witnesses." It's not optional. You can't say, "Well, maybe I will and maybe I won't." You are under orders, not necessarily to do door-to-door canvassing, but to be a witness. The Greek word for "witnesses" is μαρτυρεζ. On the top of this page write this definition: "Witness - to testify, to speak the truth about someone or something." Jesus says you are to testify and speak the truth about Him to others.

LUKE 5:10-11 Jesus said to Simon, "Don't be afraid; from now on you will catch men." So they pulled their boats up on shore, *left everything* and *followed Him.*

Peter had just observed the miraculous catch of fish at high noon, a time when one would normally not catch anything. When Peter sees the enormity of the miracle, he falls down in fear at the feet of Jesus. Jesus says to him, "Don't be afraid; from now on you will catch men." What happens next? Peter leaves his fishing business, relatives, friends, and follows Jesus. The Lord wants you to be a fisher of men also. **Your greatest spiritual joy is your own conversion. Your second greatest**

spiritual joy on earth will be when you know that the Lord has used you to catch someone for Him. Jesus told Peter not to be afraid. He says that to you also.

Unfortunately we have too many church people who want to be "keepers of the aquarium." They need to learn from Peter. **Question: Is there something that would keep you from being a fisher of men? If there is, you better leave it just as Peter left his boats. I don't believe that anything should stand in the way of your telling someone about Jesus.** You have a story to tell, and there are people out there waiting to hear it. Let's run this passage through once more forward and then backward. If you follow Jesus you will be a fisher of men. Now backwards. If you are not fishing for men, what is the conclusion? You may not be following Jesus. Christ says, "If you follow Me, I WILL make you a fisher of men."

MATTHEW 9:36-38   When *Jesus saw the crowds, He had compassion* on them, because they were harassed and helpless, like sheep without a shepherd. Then He said to His disciples, "The *harvest is plentiful* but the *workers are few. Ask* the Lord of the harvest, therefore, to *send out workers* into His harvest field."

"There is no excuse for people perishing today"

Jesus saw the crowds and had compassion on them, which means that His heart was deeply moved. What did He see? People like sheep without a spiritual shepherd. One of the problems we have with many folks in the church is that they do not take time to see people. The result is that many lost sheep stay lost and die lost. The children have a nursery rhyme that is <u>absolutely false</u>. Listen to it:

> *Little Bo Peep has lost her sheep, And doesn't know where to find them.*
> *Leave them alone, And they'll come home, Wagging their tails behind them.*

Lost sheep do not find their way home nor do they wag their tails. Without help, what happens to lost sheep? They die. That's why **Jesus wants each of His followers to constantly seek out the lost sheep around them.**

Next the Lord compares lost people to a huge field of grain, but again there are not enough workers, not enough people who care. Think of the hundreds and even thousands of people in our very own community who comprise this ripe harvest field today.

Listen to this little article from the newspaper: **"Man drowns at party for lifeguards.** New Orleans - A man drowned while attending a party for New Orleans lifeguards who were celebrating their first drowning-free swimming season in memory, officials say. Jerome Moody, 31, was found on the bottom at the deep end of a New Orleans Recreation Department pool at the end of the party Tuesday. He was dead." That's almost unbelievable. There is no excuse for something like that. **There is no excuse for people perishing today, not in a swimming pool, but in what Jesus calls "the lake of fire," hell. Please be like Jesus. Please let your heart be stirred. Please try to do something this week about this eternal tragedy**. A. Thomas wrote:

> *Who'll go and help this Shepherd kind, Help Him the wand'ring ones to find?*
> *Who'll bring the lost ones to the fold, Where they'll be sheltered from the cold?*
> *Bring them in, bring them in, Bring them in from the fields of sin;*
> *Bring them in, bring them in, Bring the wand'ring ones to Jesus.*

I'm praying that the Lord will move each of you to seek the lost sheep and bring them to the Good Shepherd, that you will work in the harvest field of souls and bring them into the Lord's granary. I'm praying that you will tell someone this week about Jesus in your own words and then bring them with you to worship next Sunday morning.

JOHN 4:35 Do you not say, "Four months more and then the harvest"? I tell you, *open your eyes* and *look at the fields*! They are *ripe for harvest.*

Jesus had just led the Samaritan woman to faith at Jacob's well. She went into town and began telling (she was really witnessing) about what had just happened. **The impact of her simple witnessing was powerful. Remember, she was a brand new Christian. Most of the people in that town went with her out to Jacob's well to meet Jesus. It must have been quite a sight – a brand new believer leading a huge crowd of unbelievers to the Lord!** If this new believer, who knew the Lord only for a hour or so, could give such a witness, how much more should not you who have known the Lord much longer than one hour? Some of you have known Jesus for weeks, some for months, and some of you have known Jesus by faith for years. **The Holy Spirit sets the example of this one-hour-old believer into Scripture as a mighty encouragement to spur you on to do what is only your duty.**

Now look at John 4:35. Remember that the grain had been sown on the fields in that area in our month of November. This scene is taking place in December, so the fields are now turning green. **Jesus says to the disciples, "'You say in four more months and this grain will be harvested?' I want to tell you something. Open your eyes and look at the fields. No, not the grain. The fields of people coming out here who are ripe for a spiritual harvest."** The disciples were concentrating too much on the wheat fields. Jesus says, "Gentlemen, **OPEN YOUR EYES** and **LOOK AT THE FIELDS** of people right here in front of us." Must not Jesus say the same thing to you and me tonight? "Stop looking at the physical things around you, your home, your food, your buildings. Listen to Me, My children, **OPEN YOUR EYES** and **LOOK AT THE FIELDS** of people right around you ripe for harvest. If you wait much longer they will be wasted. Go out and gather in the sheaves and put them in the granary of My Kingdom."

ROMANS 1:14-15 I am *obligated* ("I don't have a choice about it," says Paul. Who is he obligated to?) both to *Greeks* and *non-Greeks* (that means to those who are educated and those who have no education), both to the *wise* and the *foolish*. That is why I am so *eager to preach the Gospel* also to you who are at Rome.

A Christian steward is obligated to his Master to share the Gospel with everyone, with those who are educated and wealthy and with those who are unlearned and poor. What same message do those on the high end of the social ladder and those on the low end of the social ladder need to hear? Jesus! **Whether you are talking to your doctor or to some poor person from "the other side of the tracks," the need and the message are exactly the same.** Just give your Jesus away to both groups. Ordinarily when you give something away you are poorer. In this case, however, when you give your Jesus away, the more you will have Him! Christian stewardship always makes the steward much richer here on earth and forever in heaven.

ROMANS 10:1 Brothers, my *heart's desire* and *prayer* to God for the Israelites is that *they may be saved.*

Let's set up a hypothetical situation using "old Fred" who is a dead member of the church. Old Fred is so religious. Each night he kneels down by his bed, folds his hands and bows his head and prays: "O God, save me and my wife. Our John and his wife. Us four and no more. Amen." Now I know that Fred doesn't actually come out and say that in words, but he does say it in actions or lack of them. His actions talk a lot louder than his words. When Harry Truman was President reporters used to say, "Give 'em hell, Harry." And that's just what Fred says, too. Old Fred needs to be enlightened. Old Fred needs to be be converted. Old Fred needs his best Friend, Jesus. He needs a change of heart and so do you, if you feel that way.

Look at the first two italicized words: "heart's desire." We do not have one English word for "heart's desire." The Greek would literally translate like this. Paul would say, "Let me tell you what would give me the greatest pleasure and satisfaction." What was it? "That the Jews might be saved." This is a true expression of agape for the lost. **What would give you the greatest pleasure and satisfaction tonight, tomorrow, and every day?** I hope it is that your relatives might be saved, that your neighbors might be saved, that your community might be saved for Jesus. That is a true expression of agape for them. If you are a Christian steward like Paul, then you will have this compulsion and desire, and it will be with you twenty-four hours a day, seven days a week, night and day: I want them saved!

You are in this community to harvest the ripe grain right here for Jesus – not the grain in Tampa Bay or Chicago or Denver, but right here. **The Lord has placed you here on your street, in your house, with your friends, your neighbors, and your relatives that you may say, "I'll tell you what would give me the greatest pleasure and satisfaction – their being converted to the Lord."** If not, if you don't feel that way, then you have wrong priorities. You need a change of heart, and only Jesus can give you that!

What was the definition of a disciple from the previous Lesson? (<u>Ask the class to mention all three points here</u>.) With that definition in mind, know that it is God's divine will to win the world to Himself. It is God's desire to have the Gospel of Christ come to you and then go through you and on to many others. The Lord wants you to be a fisher of men, not just a "keeper of an aquarium." All who follow Jesus take these words seriously. This is not a game. Evangelism is to be the prime work of every Christian and every Christian congregation.

By the way, have you ever taken time to thank the person(s) who was instrumental in introducing you to Jesus Christ, your Savior? If not, would you, this week, take a moment to write a letter or make a phone call to that person and thank him? That person needs to hear that. It will be a mighty encouragement. Make a note right now to do that.

5. What should we do as Christian witnesses?

ACTS 10:39 We are *witnesses* of everything He did in the country of the Jews and in Jerusalem.

Peter is speaking to a group of people in the house of Cornelius who needed to hear the Gospel. Peter says that he and the other disciples were witnesses of everything Jesus did. He is sharing their experience with Jesus. **What is your experience with Jesus? A witness is someone who has seen or experienced something in some way. You have seen and experienced something regarding Jesus, and you are the only one who can tell your experience.**

ACTS 4:20 For we *cannot help speaking* about what *we have seen* and *heard*.

The Sanhedrin, the Jewish supreme court, commanded Peter and John not to speak about Jesus anymore and were threatened with death if they did. There was no hesitation. They could not remain silent about what they had seen and heard of Jesus. Can you remain silent? If you were put on trial for talking about Jesus, would there be enough evidence to convict you? Would there be enough evidence on the basis of your witnessing to convict you? If you were brought before a court and told to never talk about Jesus again to anyone, what would you do?

I would like you to imagine that you were caught in a fire here in Overland Park. You were trapped in the burning building, both your legs were broken, all your ribs are cracked (we're going to make this real bad), you can hardly breathe, you are pinned to the floor, fire is everywhere, you are ready to give up and die, and someone rescues you. Could you imagine later on one of your friends would say to you, "Hey, how did you get rescued?" And you reply, "I'm not going to tell you. It's a secret. Don't embarrass me by having to tell." Would any of you do that? Then why are you embarrassed to tell about your biggest Rescuer who saved you from the biggest fire, the fire of hell, who is your very, very best Friend and Savior, to whom you owe your life now and forever in heaven, Jesus Christ? My friend, **it's time for you to stop being embarrassed about Jesus! Be embarrassed if you don't talk about Him.** A beautiful hymn in our hymnbook (Grigg & Oliver) says:

Jesus! Oh, how could it be true, A mortal man ashamed of You?
Ashamed of You, whom angels praise, Whose glories shine through endless days?

Ashamed of Jesus, that dear Friend On whom my hopes of heav'n depend?
No; when I blush, be this my shame, That I no more revere His name.

Till then - nor is my boasting vain - Till then I boast a Savior slain;
And oh, may this my glory be, That Christ is not ashamed of me!

Brothers and sisters, let's not be ashamed of Jesus anymore. Let's be like Peter and John!

"You're an ambassador for the King!... believe it!"

JOHN 4:28-29,39 The woman went back to the town and said to the people, *"Come, see a Man (That was Jesus) who told me everything I ever did."... Many* of the Samaritans from that town *believed* in Jesus *because of the woman's testimony,* "He told me everything I ever did."

The Samaritan woman was a woman with a sordid past. She came to the well. She met Jesus. And in just a short time she came to saving faith. Her life is changed. She forgets her waterpot. She even forgets to give Jesus a drink. Jesus had gripped her heart. She goes back to town and tells people about her experience. That is what you are to do. You are to tell others about your experience with the Lord. Look at the verse and tell me what happened next? Many of the people from that town believed in Jesus because of her testimony. Can the Holy Spirit bring people who hear your experience with Jesus to saving faith, too? Absolutely. Beside sharing your experience with Jesus, you can invite and bring people you know to a study class like this *(Share when the next class will start).*

2 CORINTHIANS 5:19-20 God has *committed to us* the message of reconciliation. We are therefore *Christ's ambassadors*, as though God were *making His appeal through us.*

God has given us the Gospel which tells how He and man are reconciled through the cross. **What is an ambassador? A representative of and a mouthpiece for his government.** Look at the last words. God is making His appeal to people through you. Since you are ambassadors for Christ, you should never apologize for Jesus or for being His mouthpiece.

"Well, now, George, I go to Family of Christ Lutheran Church. I'm a little embarrassed to bring this up, but, ah, I am a, you know, one of those, ah, Christians. I know that I'm supposed to talk to you about, well, you know, ah, spiritual things, but would it be okay, ah, if... ah... if I invited my pastor to come over and talk to you?" What do you mean – invite your pastor to come over and talk to him? I'm not going to talk for you. I can't be your mouth! I can't be you. You be you! I do my witnessing. You do yours. You are an ambassador for Jesus Christ. Who says so? He does. And He wants to make His appeal to the people of this community through who? You! You're a child of the King. **You're an ambassador for the King! Look like it! Talk like it! Act like it! And above all – believe it!** God will bless that.

1 CORINTHIANS 9:19-20,22 (Underline the italicized words as we come to them.) Though I am free and belong to no man, I *make myself a slave to everyone*, to *win as many as possible*. To the Jews I became like a Jew, to win the Jews... To the weak I became weak, to win the weak. I have become *all things* to *all men* so that by *all possible means* I might *save some*.

What did Paul mean when he said he made himself a slave to everyone? He tried to meet them on their level and tried to be considerate of their circumstances. Paul, like Jesus, ate with and witnessed to the Pharisees and publicans and had contact with drunkards and prostitutes. Why did Paul and Jesus do that? "To win as many as possible." Would you say that Paul and Jesus had a strong love for people. Yes! Did they have any success? Yes, indeed! **Would you emulate your Savior? Would you be like Paul? Why? Because you love the lost, because you love Jesus.** Would you do that tomorrow? Will you meet people on their level and be considerate? Consider yourself a slave that you may save some of them. Make this a way of life. Be like Jesus. Be like Paul.

COLOSSIANS 4:5 *Be wise* in the way you *act* toward outsiders (<u>non-Christians</u>); *make the most of every opportunity*.

"Be wise in the way you act toward non-Christians." We ought to be careful how we act around unbelievers so that our conduct does not build up a wall. Our actions can be very important in our relationships with people. Look at the last six words and write: "Seize opportunities. Watch for open doors." Watch for open doors tomorrow at work, at play, in the neighborhood. Try to make opportunities for witnessing. Invite someone over for a cup of coffee. Watch for doors. Whenever a door opens, go on in, and by word and deed let that person know about your God and theirs.

The Harvest Is Ripe

A Christian witness knows Jesus and shares that knowledge with other people. An ambassador for Christ is His envoy, represents Him, and speaks for Him. I am His witness and ambassador by virtue of my faith in the Lord. I have a story to tell, and there are people waiting for me to tell it. My goal should be to speak to people about Jesus at every opportunity. I will also invite people to my church. Over 70% of the people who join a church came the first time as a result of an simple invitation by one of its members.

6. **Why do we want to be good Christian stewards?**

MATTHEW 25:19-21 After a long time the master (<u>Jesus</u>) of those servants (<u>believers</u>) *returned* (<u>on Judgment Day</u>) *and settled accounts* with them. The man who had received the five talents brought the other five. "Master," he said, "you entrusted me with five talents. *See, I have gained five more.*" His master replied, *"Well done, good and faithful servant!* You have been faithful with a few things; I will *put you in charge of many things. Come and share your master's happiness!"*

On Judgment Day Jesus will praise those of us who have been faithful. In fact, He holds it up now to you so that you may be encouraged to always be faithful. After the praise comes reward: "I will put you in charge of many things" in heaven. We presently do not know what this consists of, but the promise is there. Look at the last six words. "Come and share your Master's happiness."

When you meet the Lord on the Last Day, don't you want it to be a joyous event? One important key to that is that you have been faithful in your stewardship here on earth. The Lord may have given you five talents. On that Day you will want to be able to say, "Lord, here are five more." The

Lord looks at the next Christian and asks, "How many talents did I give you, My child?" "You gave me three talents. Lord, here are the three with three more beside."

And then to hear those words, "Well done, good and faithful servant." Then the Lord will reward you in heaven with glory and further responsibility. At that moment you will be glad if you have been a faithful steward. Now, my friend, is the time to tend to your stewardship. **To be a good Christian steward as defined in this Lesson means that what you have learned tonight will have to become your lifestyle.** To that end write down this little sentence: "I need to view my present lifestyle from the perspective of eternity."

LUKE 18:28-30 Peter said to Him, "We have left all we had to follow You!" (Peter's comment is strange. It suggests that he and the apostles deserve recognition and reward for their sacrifices. Peter has not yet learned that sacrifices for the Lord are to be done out of love.) "I tell you the truth," Jesus said to them, "No one who has left home or wife or brothers or parents or children for the sake of the Kingdom of God will fail *to receive many times as much in this age* (that is, right now, in this world you will be rewarded) and, in the age to come, *eternal life."*

I can tell you now that as you walk closer and closer to Jesus, some of your unbelieving friends will leave you. You could also lose a job for being a Christian and for insisting on honesty at your work place. But whatever your losses are, whatever sacrifices you make for the Lord, He promises that you will be rewarded many times over in this life and in the life to come. Be sure that you make those sacrifices because you love the Lord. You do them because of Him, not because of the rewards. It is true, however, that Jesus does want you to know that He will repay you many times over for everything you have done for Him.

DANIEL 12:3 Those (write "soul-winners" above "those") who *lead many to righteousness* (Notice that it is God's will that we not lead just one or two people to Jesus, but what? **Many** to righteousness. I don't mean to be negative, but do any of us here tonight have to confess that we have not been instrumental in bringing a single soul to know Jesus? My friend, that is not God's will for you. It is God's will that you have fruit and that you have a lot of it. Notice what will happen to you in heaven if you are a soul-winner.) (You) will *shine like the stars for ever and ever.*

Jesus shines right now in heaven like a brilliant sun. He lights up all of heaven. Soul-winners in heaven will be like stars having different degrees of luster and brilliancy. The stars we see in the sky now will be destroyed on the Last Day. These heavenly stars, however, will shine forever. Their reward will never end. Those who brought people to Jesus here will have an eternal reward there. Be sure that you are one of them. That's why the Lord put these words in the Bible. He is telling you that your labor for Him will be more than worth the effort.

GALATIANS 6:9 Let us not become weary in doing good, for at the proper time we *will reap a harvest* if we *do not give up.*

I can say this to you as one who has been a Christian a long time – I have seen so many people start out so nicely for the Lord and then they fall flat on their faces. They give up. What does Paul say? Don't give up. You will reap a harvest if you will remain faithful. Don't become weary. The time is coming when God will reward you for that which you have done.

• 1 CORINTHIANS 15:58 (Underline all italicized words.) Therefore, my dear brothers, *stand firm.* Let *nothing move you.* (So many believers are moved around like they were water or sand. Picture yourself as a football lineman. What is going to happen if you stand there on tippy toes? That's what some would-be Christians do. Then the Devil bowls them over and they say, "How'd that happen?" What must you do? Plant your feet on the Lord's team and don't move them! Don't let anything move you. Don't budge. Don't give an inch. How does Paul's advice continue?) Always *give yourselves fully* to the work of the Lord (not to a thousand other things, but to the work of the Lord. Why?) because you know that *your labor in the Lord is not in vain.*

You know, when you work for the Lord, there's going to be fruit. You cannot labor for the Lord with zero results. That's the Lord's promise. Your job is to be faithful.

Some day the Lord will return for an accounting. Faithful stewards will hear Jesus commend and praise them. He promises to give countless rewards to faithful stewards already in this life. Faithful stewards should feel encouraged and never give up their work for Jesus. Faithful stewards also lay up rewards in heaven. What a kind and gracious God we have. No work for Him is ever wasted.

Let's pray together

Heavenly Father, thank You for teaching me what it means to be a good Christian steward. I believe You own everything. I want to honor You by the way I live and the way I give. Every ability I have is a gift from You. I commit myself and my skills to You in daily service. I want to dedicate a large percent of my income to You as an expression of my love. Help me be a good witness for Jesus. Bless my efforts to bring people to trust in Him. When I feel discouraged, please encourage me and graciously bless my work. Thank You, God, for everything! I pray in Jesus' name. Amen.

I want to remind you to read 1 Chronicles 29:1-20 before you retire tonight. Make a note now to do that. Let's start tomorrow with a brand new outlook on ourselves as Christian stewards. We need to make some good changes. Seek out someone this week to speak to about Jesus. Go for a cup of coffee. Go someplace where you will be undisturbed and tell that person what Jesus has done for you and encourage that person to take a spiritual step forward with the Lord. Think through your stewardship of time. Use the many talents God has given you. Friends, it's commitment time to the one true God. Let us right now commit ourselves to our great God and the things He would have us do in this life. Let's stand and sing, "Lord of the Living Harvest."

Let's sing together

> Lord of the living harvest That whitens on the plain,
> Where angels soon shall gather Their sheaves of golden grain,
> Accept our hands to labor, Our hearts to trust and love,
> And with us ever hasten Your Kingdom from above.
>
> As lab'rers in Your vineyard, Help us be ever true,
> Content to bear the burden Of weary days for You.
> To ask no other wages When You will call us home
> Than to have shared the labor That makes Your Kingdom come.
>
> Be with us, God the Father, Be with us, God the Son,
> And God the Holy Spirit, Most blessed Three in One.
> Teach us, as faithful servants You rightly to adore,
> And fill us with Your fullness Both now and evermore.

Bible reading schedule for the next seven days

- ❏ 1st day – Acts 17
- ❏ 2nd day – Acts 18
- ❏ 3rd day – Acts 19
- ❏ 4th day – Acts 20
- ❏ 5th day – Acts 21
- ❏ 6th day – Acts 22
- ❏ 7th day – Acts 23

Worksheet no. 9

1. Since God is the Owner of everything, what rule should we follow in using anything in this world? _We should use things the way God would want them used._

2. Name some special gifts and abilities that you may have to serve the Lord as a good steward: _The gift of teaching, comforting, leading, singing, etc._

3. _True_ or False: Christian stewardship is dedicating everything we have to God's glory, the building of His Kingdom, our neighbor's welfare and our own good welfare out of love for Jesus Christ.

4. As Jesus watches you give your offerings in His Father's House, how do think He feels? What changes, if any, do you feel are necessary on your part? _I trust that He is usually pleased. I could have more joy as I bring my gifts to Him._

5. What are some of the chief thieves which sometimes needlessly rob us of time? _Television, recreation, sleep, work, almost anything could._

6. _True_ or False: I really believe the Lord wants me to speak to others about Him as best I can and that He will give me the strength to do so.

7. _True_ or False: We should share Christ with all people, even those who have membership in another church.

8. What is the greatest gift we can give a person? _Our Savior and faith in Him._

9. What can we do to become more efficient in our witnessing for Christ? _Do it and learn by doing, ask for God's help, receive special training from someone more accomplished than I._

10. Should it bother us to know when certain people are living without the Lord Jesus? _Yes._ Why? _If they die without a Savior they will perish eternally._

11. As you speak to a friend about believing in Jesus he says, "I have plenty of time. I'll take my chances." What would you say to him? _How do you know that for sure? How could it possibly be worth taking the chance? Hell is full of people who thought that._

12. What is meant by spontaneous witnessing? _Sharing our faith and Savior naturally and daily_

as we have the opportunity.

13. What truths should we stress when speaking to folks about Jesus? *He is God's Son. He died for their sins. He is the only way to heaven and wants to be received as their Savior.*

14. How do you suppose you will feel in heaven if someone is there because God used your voice to speak to him about Christ? *Very happy, more than words can tell.*

15. Mention three things that you will surely want to do before leaving this life for heaven:

    a. *Read the entire Bible through.*

    b. *Win as many for Christ as possible.*

    c. *I want to establish my reputation as one who honors God.*

DISCIPLES OF OUR MASTER

Almighty God, we thank You for this Bible study course. We have been privileged to study Your holy Word on so many critical subjects. Father, bless our last lesson, ABOUT A LIFE THAT NEVER ENDS. We confess that we still tend to view death as the final end. Help us move toward Your view of our impending departure from this world. Give us grace to see death, not as the end, but the beginning of a new life with You in heaven. As we look forward to joining You in heaven, we wonder "What will we do there?" Make this Lesson a response to that question. We have so many fears and so many questions. We trust that You will help us. As we learn more, may we yearn more for the day when we say farewell to everything here and join You there. In the name of Jesus, our only Savior and Redeemer. Amen.

During the Vietnam War there was a young man who received a draft notice. His parents became alarmed that their son would meet certain death. The young man, trying to quiet their fears, said to them, 'Now Mom and Dad, there is no problem. I've been drafted, and there are two choices that will be made – either I will be rejected or accepted into the army. That's no problem." He went on to say, "Now if I'm accepted into the army, there are two choices. I could get an office job and that will certainly be safe or I could go to the front lines. But that's no problem. If I go to the front lines there will be two choices – either I will live or I will die. If I live, we will all rejoice and that's no problem. If I die, I will go to be with the Lord in heaven and certainly that's no problem. So Mom and Dad, please don't worry – there's no problem."

What a beautiful way to introduce this last Lesson in the course, I HAVE GOOD NEWS FOR YOU. The crowning climax of God's love is that He has prepared for You a building, a mansion, a city that is yours. Everything is yours to use and enjoy forever.

Lesson 10

I HAVE GOOD NEWS FOR YOU

About A Life Which Never Ends

Comedian Woody Allen was asked by an interviewer, "Aren't you glad that you will achieve immortality through your achievements?" Allen gloomily responded, "Who cares about achieving immortality through achievements? I am interested in achieving immortality through not dying." Woody Allen will never do it.

George Bernard Shaw once wrote, "The statistics on death are quite impressive. One out of one people die." We human beings have a strikingly high mortality rate. Death comes on its own terms, not ours. When death comes we want it to be quick, quiet, and painless.

What is death? Romanticists call it "man's last great venture." Poets speak of it as "crossing the river" or "putting out to sea." Atheists say it is the end of existence. The Bible, however, teaches something quite different. Let's see what it says.

1. What happens at the moment of death?

ECCLESIASTES 12:7 The *dust* returns to the *ground* it came from, and the *spirit returns to God* who gave it.

We have two actions occurring in the moment of death. The soul of man is taken from his body, and his body immediately begins to return to dust. And the spirit returns to God. Who created the body originally? God did. Who created the soul and placed it in that body? God did.

I believe that every Christian has guardian angels. Now I'll make a bold statement. I believe that angels, perhaps the person's guardian angels, will take the soul of each believer safely to heaven. There are a few Scripture verses which seem to suggest this. In Luke 16, for example, angels carry the beggar to Abraham's bosom, which is another name for heaven. Scripture stronly implies this activity by angels for all believers.

This journey from earth to heaven will be completely safe. I remember, as a little child in the small town of Nicollet, Minnesota, visiting relatives on cold, snowy nights. My mother would bundle me up. Dad would place me in a little home-made sled and then pull the sled to wherever we were going. We children would play until we got tired; then, we would find someplace to fall asleep. The next thing I knew it was morning, and I was awake in my own warm bed. I like to compare this little wonder to my final trip – to my real home in heaven. I will fall asleep here and wake up there. Everything was done for me at Nicollet. Everything will be done for me on my final trip.

Near-death experiences are interesting, but they are inconsequential. Why? First, because they are not really death, the complete and final separation of the soul from the body, and, second, because unbelievers report the same experiences as believers.

2 CORINTHIANS 5:8 We are *confident,* I say, and would *prefer to be away from the body* and at *home with the Lord.*

Paul says, "If I had my choice, instead of being an apostle, instead of being an evangelist, instead of being a preacher I would prefer to leave my body here on earth and be at home with the Lord in heaven." Paul had an idea of what heaven was like. Where would you rather be tonight? Bumper stickers say, "I'd rather be golfing." "I'd rather be dancing." Make your bumper sticker message right now: "I'd rather be... " Finish it. I hope that you can say it would be heaven.

When we die God will welcome us, the angels will welcome us, and the redeemed will welcome us. Let me illustrate. Years ago an elderly couple, missionaries, returned from a lifetime of service on foreign soil. On the same boat, the President of the United States and his party were also arriving from a foreign tour. Great crowds of people greeted the President, but there was no one to greet the missionary and his wife. Afterward, in the hotel room, the old missionary cried and said, "We spent our lives on a foreign mission field, and no one was there to greet us when we came home." The thoughtful wife said, "But darling, we aren't home yet." Remember that you are not home yet. But when you get home, there will be a warm welcome waiting for you.

There is something wonderful about going home. My father was a faithful follower of Jesus all his life. He had cancer for his last four years. Not long ago I visited him for the last time. He held my hands tight and pulled them to his chest. "Thanks," he whispered, "for coming." Then he said softly, "I want to go Home." A few days later he did. What a beautiful name for heaven! Home is where the heavenly Father is and where many members of Dad's family are. I echo Dad's prayer which was also St. Paul's prayer: "I want to go Home." I hope you feel the same way.

PSALM 23:4-6 Even though I walk through the valley of the shadow of death, *I will fear no evil, for You are with me; Your rod and Your staff, they comfort me...* and *I will dwell in the house of the LORD forever.*

David is not afraid as he walks through the valley of death. Why does he say, "I will fear no evil."? The Lord is with him. The rod signifies the omnipotent power of the Lord to crush and break all enemies. The staff signifies the Lord's wise and sure guidance. What does David have to fear with such a Shepherd? Nothing. He is comforted – you should be, too!

• LUKE 23:43 Jesus answered him, "I tell you the truth, *today* you will be *with Me in paradise."*

Jesus spoke these words on Good Friday around 3:00 to the penitent thief on the cross. The man had just embraced Jesus as his Savior. Jesus said, "I tell you (what?) the truth." Folks, we don't want half-truths on this subject. We are not satisfied with the pious platitudes of churches. We are not interested in catechetics. We want the truth! Jesus says, "I tell you the truth." "Today you will be with Me in paradise." Paradise is another word that was used for the Garden of Eden. Heaven is Eden restored, only better! Heaven is paradise, the home of God, the home of angels, and the home of the redeemed.

What about the teaching of purgatory? If ever a man deserved to go to purgatory, if there were such a place, it would be this thief. I say this in love and do not wish to demean, but one of the saddest teachings of one church is their teaching of purgatory. Their church doctrine teaches that those who die in the state of grace must suffer the fires of purgatory before they can go to heaven. This time can be shortened, however, by prayers, masses, and indulgences. What a sad way to have to face your last hours on earth.

REVELATION 14:13 Then I heard a voice from heaven say, "Write: *Blessed* are the dead who *die in the Lord* from now on." "Yes," says the Spirit, "they will *rest from their labor*, for their *deeds will follow them."*

This is a continuation of John's vision of heaven. Above "blessed" write "totally happy." Only those who die with faith in Jesus as Savior have this joy. They enter heaven. They rest from their labor. All of their trials and sufferings are a thing of the past. Their good works done out of love for the Lord follow them into heaven as a testimony of their faith. Folks, when you experience the loss of a loved one who died believing in Jesus, please don't worry about them, and please don't wish them back again. In love I say, they wouldn't come back if they could.

One Saturday one of my members, John Gaidies, called. He asked me to come right out; something had happened to his wife, Phoebe. On arrival I found the children in the yard crying. John was in the bathroom, working on the body of his wife who had suffered severe heatstroke. I helped John, but it became apparent that she was dead. Our efforts were futile. We picked her body up, placed it on her bed, and called the funeral home. Before we asked the four children to come in John and I knelt at the foot of the bed in prayer. When we stood up I said, "John, honestly now, between you and me and God, what do you think?" He looked at me. Tears were running down both of his cheeks. He said, "Pastor, I'm so happy for Phoebe." She was only 38 years old. Again he said, "I'm so happy for Phoebe." I said, "Why?" "Well," he said with a quivering voice, "I and the children are going to miss her, but now she is with the Lord. She is happier with the Lord than she would be with us." You should know that the next morning, Sunday morning, at the first service, John and the four children were in church in the front pew. Where do you belong when the Lord has taken a loved-one home? In the Lord's house. Happy are those who die in the Lord!

1 PETER 3:19 He (Jesus) went and preached to the *spirits in prison.*

The Apostles' Creed says, "He descended into hell." Early Easter Sunday morning Jesus' spirit left heaven and was reunited with His body in the grave. His first act is His glorious descent into hell

167

> as described in verse 19. Above the word "preached" please write "heralded a proclamation." What did He do? He heralded a proclamation to the souls locked up in hell. Class, the gates to hell are always locked. No one has ever escaped. The gates to heaven are always wide open. No one has ever wanted to leave. What was the proclamation? His victory over sin, Satan, and hell!

At the moment of death the body begins to return to dust. The believer is at once received into heaven, and the unbeliever is at once imprisoned in hell.

> I want to emphasize once more that the soul of the departed is not in purgatory, not in limbo, not in the cemetery, not in the bosom of the earth, but the soul is either in heaven or in hell. Would you agree with me that the last words of a dying man or woman are worth listening to? Yes. People will sometimes say things in their last hour that friends and relatives should listen to carefully. We're going to take a peek at the last words of four different men as they stood at death's door.

What they said at death's door

Thomas Paine, American infidel and author: "I would give worlds, if I had them that 'The Age of Reason' had never been published. O God, what have I done to suffer so much? But there is no God! But if there should be, what will become of me hereafter? Stay with me, for God's sake! Send even a child to stay with me, for it is Hell to be alone. If ever the Devil had an agent, I have been that one."

> This is an interesting confession for someone who said he didn't believe in God. Now, at death, he believes, but it's not helping him. How sad it is that if you lived your life without Jesus the chances are great that you will die without Him, too.

Francis Voltaire, noted French infidel and writer said to his doctor: "I am abandoned by God and man! I will give you half of what I am worth if you will give me six months' life. Then I shall go to Hell; and you will go with me. O Christ! O Jesus Christ!"

> This is also interesting because Voltaire said he did not believe in God. Here, at death, it is so obvious that he does believe in the reality of God, but to no avail. Now contrast these first two confessions to the next two.

Dwight L. Moody, great preacher: "I see earth receding. Heaven is opening. God is calling!"

> Is this very different from the first two confessions? Just as men live differently they also die differently. I have seen many people die, and there is a huge difference between the two. I doubt that any of you have heard of the next man. You should know that he was so ill from disease he contracted on the mission field that his friends finally had to place him on a ship to bring him back home for treatment. He speaks these words on the deck of a ship on the China Sea.

Adroniaram Judson, great American missionary to Burma: "I go with the gladness of a boy bounding away from school. I feel so strong in Christ."

> How does the normal, typical boy leave school? "Ah, shucks, it's all over." Can you imagine that? You say, "Man, this kid is sick. Let's get him to the doctor. There's something wrong." It is sad that

some who confess to be Christians cannot say what Judson said. I hope you will be able to say it.

2. What does the Bible say about Christ's second coming?

I want you to jot a couple of figures down here. 1. One out of every thirty verses of the Bible talks about Jesus' second coming. 2. There are 318 New Testament references to the coming of Christ. 3. One third of the New Testament deals with the return of Jesus in some way.

ACTS 1:11 "Men of Galilee," they said, "why do you stand here looking into the sky? This same Jesus, who has been taken from you into heaven, *will come back in the same way* you have seen Him go into heaven."

The Lord led 120 believers to the hill of ascension. He gave them the Great Commission. He promised He would be with them until the end of the world. His final act: He blessed them; as He was doing so He slowly disappeared in the clouds. When He was gone holy angels came and spoke verse 11. From this verse and others we learn the following three points. Please jot them down. **Jesus will 1. Come back visibly. 2. Come back bodily. 3. Come in glory** and all the angels in heaven will accompany Him. This will be in stark contrast to the way He came the first time. His first coming in Bethlehem was quiet. His second coming will be noisy. Trumpets will be blown announcing His arrival. His first coming was in humility as He lay a little Baby on a bed of straw. He will come the second time in great majesty and power, as King of kings and Lord of lords.

REVELATION 1:7 Look, He is coming with the clouds, and *every eye will see Him*, even those who pierced Him.

Who drove the nails through His hands and feet? The soldiers did. But also the Sanhedrin which condemned Him to death. Your eyes will see Him and so will mine. It will be a joy for all believers to behold and a supreme moment of terror for all unbelievers.

ACTS 17:31 For *God has set a day* when *He will judge the world* with *justice* by the *Man* He has appointed.

God has set the Day. For the invasion of Europe in World War II the date was changed a number of times, and that has happened with a number of important events – dates are sometimes changed. The contractor changes the date when the building will be completed. The couple changes the date on which they will be married. The date for the end of the world, however, will not be changed. God has set that date.

On the Last Day God will judge the world with justice. It's very disconcerting for us to see the lack of justice in many of our courts today. Some people feel there was great injustice in the O. J. Simpson trial. No one will feel that way about Judgment Day. How come? Because of the Judge. Judge Ito and the jury may have made mistakes with O. J. Simpson. Who has God appointed Judge for the Final Judgment? The Man. Who is that? The Man, Christ Jesus. The divine and omnipotent Jesus with a glorified body will be seated on a throne.

It's going to be a big trial. Over twenty billion people have lived so far, and each of them will be judged. Some of you may be thinking, "Wow, that's going to be a long trial. We're going to stand in line a long time to wait our turn." Actually it will take no time at all because we're out of time and into timelessness. What will determine the verdict? The Judge will look for saving faith.

MARK 13:32-33 *No one knows* about that day or hour, not even the angels in heaven, nor the Son, but only the Father. *Be on guard! Be alert! You do not know* when that time will come.

Jesus is speaking these words on Mt. Olivet. What does He say? "No one knows" the date of His second coming. Jesus says that the angels in heaven do not know when the end of the world will take place. We are surprised, however, when Jesus says that even He does not know the date. The only way this mystery makes any sense is to think of the following. According to His divinity He knows all things. When speaking these words Jesus is in His state of humiliation, when He did not always use the attributes of His divine nature. It would appear that at this time, according to His human nature, He did not know the date of the End.

We do not know that date either. CNN will not break in to announce the End. Well-known reporters will not have any clue. Their cameras will not be pointed to the sky to present us with a "live" picture. What does Jesus, therefore, tell us to do? Be on guard, be alert. You don't know if it's going to be tonight before this class is finished. We might not even have a chance for our coffee break. You may never have to pay another tax bill. You may never get another tax refund.

2 PETER 3:10-11 The day of the Lord will come like a *thief*. (How does a thief come? Does a thief send you a card in the mail saying, *"Dear Dave and Heidi, we is going to rob your house next Monday night at 9:30. We would like for you to be gone from 9:30 to 10:30. Sincerely, Mike and Spud."* That kind of warning would never come. You don't expect a thief to strike. How many people are expecting the end of the world today? Percentage-wise it must be low. What will happen on that Day?) The *heavens* will *disappear* with a roar (that means that our universe vanish); the *elements* will be *destroyed* by fire, and the *earth* and *everything in it* will be *laid bare*. (Everything will destroyed by fire. Laid bare means there will be nothing left. That means your house is going to go. Your car is going to go. Your clothes, your diamond rings, your bank account, everything is going to go.) Since *everything will be destroyed* in this way, what kind of people ought you to be? You ought to *live holy* and *godly lives*.

> "Invest heavily in the only two things that will endure this fire: people and the Word of God"

We have a choice each day between physical things and spiritual things. So many times the physical wins out. We should, instead, opt more and more for the spiritual. We need some physical things to live in this world, but let's try to accent the spiritual things. Invest heavily, not in stocks, bonds, and mutual funds, but invest heavily in the only two things that will endure this fire: people and the Word of God. Then you will have something that will endure.

1 PETER 4:7 The *end* of all things is *near*.

According to the Bible the world is a little over 6,000 years old. The Old Testament era is about 4,000 years. For 4,000 years God's people waited for the **first coming** of the Messiah. In the New Testament era God's people have been waiting for the Lord's **second coming**. The Bible speaks of the time from Jesus' birth on as the **last times**, so, we have been living in the last times for 2,000 years. One of the marks of the first century Christians is that they believed in the imminent return of Jesus in the sky. They frequently greeted one another with the word, "Maranatha," which means, "The Lord is coming." **The belief in the millennium, the idea that Christ will reappear on earth where He will reign with the saints for 1,000 years, has no basis in Scripture**, although it seems to be taught in the apocryphal books.

Jesus will come again in great glory. Everyone will see Him. He will judge all men. The date, known only to God, will come suddenly and unexpectedly, and will bring an end to the world and the universe. We are encouraged to lead a godly life and stand in readiness.

3. What about the resurrection of the body?

JOHN 5:28-29 A time is coming when *all who are in their graves* will *hear His voice and come out* – those who have done good will *rise to live,* and those who have done evil will *rise to be condemned.*

Remember the incident of Lazarus? His body was dead and decaying. In John 4:43 we read, "Jesus called in a loud voice, 'Lazarus, come out!' The dead man came out, his hands and feet wrapped with strips of linen, and a cloth around his face." People were shocked at what they had just seen. Many Jews began to believe in Jesus because of this miracle.

Now try to imagine this scene. It is the Last Day. Jesus appears in great glory in the sky with all the holy angels. Suddenly and powerfully Jesus speaks to all the dead. What happens next? **All the bodies of all the dead, over 20 billion bodies, will be raised to life and will be reunited with their souls**. There will be, however, **two distinct classes** of people on the Last Day. **The first group has done good works out of faith in their Savior, and they will rise to live. The second group has done works that are evil because they come from unbelief, and they will rise to be condemned.** (You may want to jot down page 33, question 7, which describes what a good work is in God's sight.)

JOB 19:25-27 I know that *my Redeemer lives,* and that in the end He will stand upon the earth. And after my skin has been destroyed, yet *in my flesh I will see God*; I myself will see Him *with my own eyes* – I, and not another. *How my heart yearns within me!*

Follow closely now. Job concluded that God was punishing him for no good reason. He had even murmured against God. **He expected to die without God vindicating him before his death. Yet, despite all of his trials and weakness of faith, he makes this confession: "I know that my Redeemer lives."** He perceives His Savior slain and then resurrected, very much alive, and that He will stand upon the earth on the Last Day. Look at the words, "after my skin has been destroyed." Job had what some call "black leprosy." This turned his skin black like an elephant's skin. It was rough, wrinkled, and dry so that large pieces of skin would break loose and fall away leaving exposed flesh. Job knew he was approaching death, but what does he say? After my skin has been totally destroyed, "yet in my flesh I will see God; I myself will see Him with my own eyes – I, and not another."

What a confession of faith in the resurrection of a body that was decaying even before death! **You should know that when Job says he will see God he is really speaking about the Son of God.** Job knew all about this Seed of Abraham. Job says that even though his physical eyes close in death and turn to dust – yet, with those very eyes he will see God on the Day of Resurrection. You, too, should join Job in this confession: "I'm going to see Jesus, the Son of God."

You should know that God finally vindicated Job. Despite everything, he knew that God loved him. What do you suppose the last sentence means? "Oh, how anxious I am for that Last Day when this poor body is made alive and new, and I see Jesus!" That is the aspiration of every child of God. "I'm going to see Him." I hope that tonight you yearn for the day when you will see the Lord in great majesty. Maranatha! And what is your response? Maranatha!

PHILIPPIANS 3:20-21 (Underline the italicized words as we come to them.) Our <u>citizenship</u> is in heaven. And we eagerly await a Savior from there, the Lord Jesus Christ, who... will _transform our lowly bodies_ so that they will _be like His glorious body_.

Above "citizenship" write "commonwealth." What is a commonwealth? It is a body of people constituting a community in which the citizens have rights and privileges. Now apply that to heaven. That's your home, a community in which you will have rights and privileges. What does Paul say next? We are eagerly waiting for Jesus to come from there. Class, when Jesus comes from heaven on the Last Day, what will he do for us no matter what condition our bodies are in? He will transform these lowly bodies to be like His glorious body.

 1 CORINTHIANS 15:51-52 Listen, I tell you a mystery: We will not all sleep (some believers will still be alive on earth on the Last Day.), but we will _all be changed_ (Whether our bodies are dead or still alive.) – in a _flash_, in the _twinkling of an eye_ (Both "flash" and "twinkling" are used to emphasize how fast), at the last trumpet (Which marks the last moment of time.) For the trumpet will sound (Every person, dead or alive, will hear the trumpet.), the dead (The dead bodies in the graves.) will be _raised imperishable_ (What does imperishable mean? Immortal, never again given over to sickness, aging, and death.), and we _will be changed_.

At the split second of the end, when the trumpet blows, all believers will have new and glorified bodies. All mortal restraints will be removed from our bodies. There will be no imperfections of any kind. We will not wear glasses or contact lenses. We will be like new and even better than new!

On the Last Day all the dead will hear Jesus. They will be told to come out of their graves to be reunited with their souls. The bodies of the believers will change, have no more sin, sickness, or death. The same change will occur to the bodies of believers living on earth on this Day.

Consider the thought that Jesus would really make a very poor funeral director! 1. The funeral of Jairus' daughter. He raised the girl from the dead and ruined the funeral. 2. The son of the widow of Nain whose body was being carried to the cemetery. Jesus brought him back to life and presented him to his mother and ruined that funeral. 3. Lazarus, who died and was buried. Jesus brought him back to life and ruined that funeral. 4. He went to his own funeral, died, and was buried, but He brought His body back to life. He ruined His own funeral. 5. He will also ruin your funeral. On the Last Day He will bring your body back to life. Such is the power of the Son of God!

4. What will happen on Judgment Day?

2 CORINTHIANS 5:10 For _we must all appear_ before the judgment seat of Christ.

There are two judgments. **The first judgment is private** and takes place at the moment of death. The soul is either received into heaven or condemned to hell. **The second judgment is public.** It will take place on what is appropriately called Judgment Day. **How public will it be? It will be in the presence of all the holy angels and before all men who have ever lived.** Sometimes, when I do door-to-door canvassing, people will say, "Oh, I believe that my religion is a very private thing. I don't want to talk about it." These people are unaware that their religion or lack of it will be a very public thing on the Last Day. How strange that they do not want to talk about their faith. Why do you suppose that is? Because there is something wrong with it, and they know it.

Judgment Day will be a happy day and a sad day – happy for you as you see the Lord, happy for you as He judges you and finds you totally innocent of all sin (thanks to Him) and having kept the Holy Commandments of God perfectly (thanks again to Him). But it will be a sad day to see all those people, the vast majority, judged by the Lord and found guilty of sin and unbelief.

ACTS 17:31 For God has *set a day* when He will *judge the world* with *justice* by the *Man* He has appointed.

The date is set, the Judge is the Lord, and He will judge with justice!

JOHN 12:48 There is a *judge* for the one who rejects Me and does not accept My words; that *very word* which I spoke *will condemn him* at the last day.

What will be used to condemn unbelievers on the Last Day? The very words of Jesus that He spoke in His three year ministry on earth. There are, in reality, two times for judgment – the first is at the moment of death and the second is on Judgment Day. **The Judge will use His holy words for both judgments. The Word is the criteria for the judgments.**

MARK 16:16 Whoever *believes* and is baptized *will be saved*, but whoever *does not believe will be condemned.*

When a man comes to faith in the Savior he will also be baptized. What is it, however, that condemns a person to eternal death? Unbelief. It isn't sin that damns, but the rejection of the salvation which Jesus earned for us. **Biblical Christianity is the only religion in the world which does not demand that the sinner save himself or help in the process.**

MATTHEW 25:31-34,41 When the Son of Man comes in His glory (That is Judgment Day. "In His glory" means that Christ's divinity will fully shine through and out of His body.), and all the angels with Him (What an awesome sight to see Jesus in His full majesty surrounded by all His holy angels.), He will sit on His throne in heavenly glory. *All the nations* will be *gathered before Him* (The holy angels will gather the entire human race before Jesus), and He will *separate the people* one from another as a shepherd *separates the sheep from the goats* (The angels will then divide the human race into two groups.) He will put the *sheep on His right* and the *goats on His left* (This division before the actual judgment takes place will already be a judgment. It will be plain for all to see.) Then the King will say to those on His right, *"Come, you who are blessed by My Father* (Not a single sin of the believers will be mentioned by the Judge. He will only mention the good works which they performed out of love to their Lord. The Lord tells them that all this was possible because they were blessed by the Father who gave His Son to save them); take your inheritance, the Kingdom* (This is the Kingdom of Glory, heaven itself, where we will be kings and will rule and reign with Jesus.) *prepared for you since the creation of the world* (Even before the creation of the world, God, in foreknowledge, saw us, saved us through Jesus, and began preparing His House for our arrival.)" Then He will say to those on His left (Here are the saddest words any human being can hear), *"Depart from Me, you who are cursed,* into the *eternal fire* (This fire will never go out, but will burn people forever and, yet, not consume them.) *prepared for the devil and his angels* (The fire of hell was originally prepared for the devil and his evil angels as an appropriate punishment for their sin against God when they were in heaven.)"

What an awesome description of the activity of Judgment Day! The most wonderful word that you will hear on that Day are these words of Jesus, "Come, you who are blessed by My Father, take your inheritance, the Kingdom prepared for you since the creation of the world." **How happy you will be as you see Jesus looking right at you and speaking these words to you.**

The saddest words of that Day will be these words spoken to each unbeliever: "Depart from Me, you who are cursed, into the eternal fire prepared for the devil and his angels." **You will hear one of two messages – Either "Come, you who are blessed," or, "Depart from Me, you who are cursed."** Here is Scripture that you need to read to some of your unbelieving friends and relatives. You know some people who are not ready for this Day. How are they supposed to get ready for it unless they know about it, unless someone tells them about it? Sit down with them and read these verses and explain them.

LUKE 16:22-24 (This is a parable told by Jesus. Underline the italicized words as we come to them.) The beggar *died* (His body no doubt disposed of as if it were garbage, but watch the contrast as to the dispatch of his soul.) and the *angels carried him* to *Abraham's side* ("Abraham's side" is a Jewish expression for heaven. Notice the contrast. Men throwing his body away, but angels carrying his soul to heaven! I truly believe that angels will be by my deathbed and will carry my soul safely to heaven.) The rich man also *died* and was buried (Both men were alike in that both died, but there the similarity stops. While the poor beggar had his body thrown away, we can assume that the rich man had a royal funeral, a lot of mourning, a lot of people, but, no angels!") In *hell*, where *he was in torment* (Torment accurately describes what people in hell are experiencing.), he looked up and saw Abraham far away, with Lazarus by his side (This does not mean that people in hell and heaven really do see and speak to each other. It is so stated in order to teach us several basic truths.) So he called to him, "Father Abraham (All his life the rich man would have nothing to do with Abraham and his faith in the Messiah.), *have pity on me* (In this world the rich man had no pity on Lazarus, but now, in hell, he cries for pity. Watch this: THERE IS NO MERCY IN HELL.) and send Lazarus to dip the tip of his finger in water and cool my tongue (On earth he drank the finest wines and cooling drinks. In hell his request for mercy is small, a few drops of water to cool his tongue, and it is denied!), because *I am in agony in this fire*" (He is now in agony in the fire of hell, a fire millions of times worse than any fire on earth. Hell is now making a huge impression on him. I have a tiny idea of the fear, pain, and agony he had because, years ago, in St. Louis, I was caught in a hotel fire on the 17th floor. I thank a black bellhop for leading me to safety.)"

Folks, I realize that there are people around who laugh at this story told by Jesus. We who are believers should remind them that the day is coming when their laughing will turn to crying. Tonight hell is full of people who wish they hadn't dismissed the Bible teaching of hell, who wish that they were anyplace but there. When we read the rest of the story, Jesus says that the rich man in hell wanted to become a missionary. He asked Abraham to send Lazarus back to earth to warn his brothers so that they would not join him in hell. That request is also turned down. **Listen to me, children of God, if you want to be a missionary and bring the lost to Jesus, the time to do so is now.** How many people are there in hell tonight who wish that you and I would go and warn their friends and relatives so that they do not perish also? Many times, when Jesus taught on earth, He would say, "He who has ears, let him hear!" Please hear what Jesus is saying to you.

I believe in doing whatever I can to warn people of hell. Many years ago, at my first congregation, I had a junior confirmation class of 8th graders that I was teaching one cold Saturday in January. It was about 10:00 in the morning. It was 10 degrees below zero outside. I was in a basement classroom teaching this very Scripture to a class of twelve boys and girls. I spared no words in trying to portray the horrors of hell. When I finished I asked the kids if there were afraid of hell. All of them were scared of it except one little boy, Eddie Scheel. He was a really nice kid, but more than once he was a pain in my side. Eddie, being a big wheel, said to all the class: "Oh, I don't believe in hell." I said, "Eddie, you don't believe in hell?" "No," he said, "I don't believe it." I said, "Okay, let's stop. Everyone, put your books down, get in a straight line and follow me. Eddie, you are first right behind me. The rest of you line up behind him." They all got in line. I led them out of the classroom and into the furnace room. There was a huge gas furnace, about ten feet square. As we came into the room, the furnace turned on. We walked around to the front of the furnace, to the door. I opened the door, and I moved Eddie right in front of me so that he stood directly in front of the opening to the furnace. I grabbed him by his shoulders, pushed him down to the level of the opening, and then I shoved his ahead about ten inches into the hole so that his nose was only a couple of feet from the huge flames belching out. I said, "Eddie, do you believe in hell now?" He said, "I believe! I believe!" Folks, in this case, I "scared the hell right out of him" or maybe into him. I'm sure some of you are saying, "Are you sure you should have done something so dramatic as that?" I say, "With Eddie, yes!" I then had the other kids look into furnace, too. Believe me, it made a "burning" impression on their minds. I told the class, "Hell is even worse than the fire in that furnace." You should know that it wasn't too many years ago that Eddie called me long distance, and he told me how alive he was in Jesus in that same congregation. "Praise God!"

MATTHEW 10:28 Do not be afraid of those who kill the body but cannot kill the soul (The worst that people can do to you is to kill your body, but they cannot kill your soul.) Rather, be afraid of the One (Namely, God) who can *destroy both soul and body in hell* (That means the eternal destruction of body and soul in hell forever.)

A man can take a gun and shove it against your head with the threat, "Do this or I pull the trigger." He could pull the trigger and end your life. You say, "That's bad." Not at all when compared to what God can do to you! The Lord is saying that if you insist on having fear in your heart, then fear God who can destroy your body and your soul forever. Obviously this terrifying fear refers to the fear over the holy justice of God because of sin. Unbelievers can have that; believers should not have that. Look at the word "destroy." People who have terminal illness that involves pain often hope for relief by death. The people in hell have no such hope. It will go on forever!

ISAIAH 66:24 Their worm (guilty conscience) *will not die, nor will their fire be quenched,* and they will be *loathsome to all* mankind.

Heidi, how does it feel to have a guilty conscience? Really bad. Is it better or worse than bad breath? Worse. We cannot stand a guilty conscience for very long. Imagine all your guilty conscience experiences rolled into one and multiplied many times over – that is what the lost will experience in hell. If anyone you know thinks that hell isn't all that bad, just have him chew on this. Next, their fire will not be quenched. There are no fire departments in hell. Those in hell will be burned in great agony forever. This is the veritable truth of Holy Scripture.

The last part says they will be loathsome to all mankind. This means that those in hell will not be able to stand the sight or presence of the people around them. One day I was ringing doorbells. At one house a lady answered the door. I explained to her the Gospel message. Her response was: "I don't care if I go to hell." I said, "You're kidding." She said, "Oh, no, I'll have plenty of company there." She was brazen about it. I then quoted this verse to her with emphasis on loathsome. I said, "Lady, it will do you no good. When you get to hell, you may have many of your friends there with you, but it will be of no benefit to you. You will not be able to stand the sight of them nor they the sight of you. You'll be all alone." Her response? She closed the door in my face. **What's your response? Do you know of someone who needs to have this verse explained to them?**

MATTHEW 7:13-14 Enter through the *narrow gate.* (Why?) For *wide is the gate* and *broad is the road* (Like a broad freeway with hundreds of lanes.) that *leads to destruction* (It's easy to go through this gate because it's wide, and the road on the other side of the gate is wide. The problem is that people pay no attention to where the road is leading. It's leading to hell.), and *many enter through it* (That shows how inviting and how easy it is to chose this gate and road.) But *small is the gate* and *narrow the road* (What makes it small and narrow? It comes by repentance and faith in the Savior.) that *leads to life* (Eternal life in heaven.), and *only a few find it* (You don't have to look for the wide gate and broad road. It's right there in front of everyone. The narrow gate and narrow road must be found by the grace of God.)

"The road that leads to heaven is similar to a narrow footpath"

Some surveys indicate that over 95% of the American people believe they are going to go to heaven. Jesus teaches that the freeway that leads to hell is extremely wide and is jam-packed with humanity. Then He says that the road that leads to heaven is similar to a narrow footpath, and there are only a few people who are on it. The voice of Jesus seems sad as He speaks these words. How it must grieve the Lord to see so many people perish needlessly. Won't you try to help someone find the narrow gate and narrow road this week? Heaven is too wonderful, hell is too horrible, and eternity is too long to just let people wander on their own.

Everyone, all believers and all unbelievers, will stand before Christ for judgment. Jesus will look for saving faith and the fruits of saving faith. There are today and will be then only two camps: saved or unsaved, fruits of faith or lack of them, sheep or goats, blessed or cursed, the glory of heaven or the torment of hell.

5.   What will heaven be like?

Here are definitions of heaven by four little boys. **Eric Kinder** said, "It's a place where there's money laying around. You can just pick it up and buy things. I'm gonna buy a basketball and play basketball with my great grandmother." **Bobby Vogel** said, "It's a place down the road where you watch Jesus wash His heart 'cause He keeps it clean. Clean hearts, that's what heaven's all about." **Daniel Reagan** gave this definition: "It's like a blue sky with clouds, and it's really a fun place because you can play on the clouds. You have to stay away from the edges though or else – wow – you'll fall off!" **David Drennan** said, "Heaven is sort of big, and they sit around and play harps. I don't know how to play a harp, but I suppose I'd better start to learn how pretty soon." What is heaven like? Is it a Christian nirvana where we will do nothing but sit on the edge of a fleecy cloud, dangle our legs over the edge, and play a harp? These boys labored over their concept of what heaven is like. Fortunately, we have a more reliable source, the Bible. Let's go to it.

JOHN 14:2 In My Father's *house are many rooms*; if it were not so, I would have told you. *I am going there to prepare a place for you.*

Above rooms write "permanent residences." There is only one house in heaven, the Father's house. Everyone lives in this house. The picture is one of intimate fellowship with God and with everyone there. Jesus tells the disciples that He is going ahead of them to make everything ready.

1 JOHN 3:2 Dear friends, now we are children of God, and *what we will be has not yet been made known* (With our mortal and finite minds we cannot know or understand how beautiful heaven will really be.) But we know that when He appears, *we shall be like Him*, for *we shall see Him* as He is.

This we do know, that when Jesus appears in the sky and our bodies are resurrected, **these bodies will be changed to become glorious like Jesus' body. We will be ageless and never again will**

we experience the many bodily limitations we are now so familiar with.

Remember the name, John Bosshart, when you get to heaven. He really loved the Lord. He was a close friend in Jesus. One Saturday we went pheasant hunting and then squirrel hunting with his revolver. Never got any squirrels, but we sure scared a lot of them. John was in this class, a neat young man in his late twenties. He drove 600 miles on Sunday in order to make this class session. We were studying this verse. He had his elbows on the table and cupped his chin in his hands in deep thought. He raised his hand and asked: "What will heaven REALLY be like?" He wanted to know what was behind all these words. I said, "John, to really find out you are going to have to wait until you get there. There is no way I can explain what it is really going to be like." John was satisfied. There was an approving smile on his face. That was at 9:30 Sunday evening. After class he made plans to have his two daughters baptized the following Sunday. At 9:00 Monday evening he was at home and took the revolver we had hunted with off a shelf. In a way no one understands, there was a shell in the chamber, and it went off and struck him in the stomach. His wife called me. I found him lying on the floor of his bedroom unconscious. The ambulance rushed him to the hospital to surgery. There, at 9:30, exactly twenty-four hours after he asked his question about what heaven was really like, he left earth for heaven and discovered first hand. There is only one way you are going to know what heaven is like. Like John, you'll have to wait until you get there.

"Because of You, Lord we are here!"

REVELATION 7:9-10 Before me was a *great multitude* that no one could count, from every nation, tribe, people and language, standing before the throne and in front of the Lamb (<u>That is Jesus.</u>) They were wearing *white robes* (<u>Which symbolizes holiness. Their dirty robes were washed white by</u> the red blood of Jesus.) and were holding *palm branches* in their hands (<u>Which means that they had life, salvation, and peace.</u>) And *they cried out in a loud voice* (<u>Imagine how loud with the voices of many millions of the redeemed shouting in one loud refrain</u>): *"Salvation belongs to our God*, who sits on the throne, and *to the Lamb."*

Notice that no one in heaven takes any credit whatever for his being there. Not one single person takes credit for doing even one small thing to get there. This very night all the saints in heaven point to the Lamb and shout: "Because of You, Lord, we are here." And that, my friend, shall be our theme of praise to the Lamb forever and ever. We will never tire of it.

REVELATION 7:16-17 *Never again will they hunger*; never again will they *thirst*. The sun will not beat upon them, nor any scorching heat (<u>All of the hardships, trials, and pains of their earthly walk will be gone forever.</u>) For the Lamb at the center of the throne will be their *Shepherd*; *He will lead them to springs of living water* (<u>The Lamb is Jesus, and He leads His flock to clean, pure, living water. Think of Psalm 23</u>!) And *God will wipe away every tear from their eyes.*

God will wipe every tear from His children's eyes. It is the picture of a mother who wipes away her child's tears so that the child can smile and laugh again. As a faithful believer you may have to shed many a tear here on earth, but remember, soon God shall turn your tears into heavenly joy! Imagine the utter and unexplainable joy the saints have in heaven right now; soon it will be your turn!

REVELATION 21:3-5 And I heard a loud voice from the throne saying, "Now the *dwelling of God is with men*, and *He will live with them. They will be His people,* and God Himself will be with them and be their God (<u>Class, here is the fulfillment of the name Immanuel. What does that mean?</u>

God with us.) He will *wipe every tear from their eyes*. There will be *no more death or mourning or crying or pain* (All of this was the result of sin.), *for the old order of things has passed away."* He who was seated on the throne said, *"I am making everything new!"* Then He said, "Write this down, for *these words are trustworthy and true."* (For a more complete description read all of Chapter 21.)

John did not write these words on his own initiative. He wrote what the Holy Spirit moved him to write. Look at the last words. God is giving His seal of truth. We are not dealing with speculation or pie-in-the-sky. We may trust these words implicitly.

PSALM 16:11 You have made known to me the path of life; You will *fill me with joy in Your presence*, with *eternal pleasures at Your right hand.*

While David spoke these words, they were really the prophetic words of Someone greater than David, the Messiah. After His death, resurrection, and ascension the Lord made a prophetic statement about His return to heaven. What does He say? "Father, You will fill me with joy in Your presence. There will be eternal pleasures at Your right hand." What Jesus could say His children can also say. Many times we endure sorrow here, but in heaven God will fill you with joy. He will so fill you with heavenly joy that even He could not put one more ounce of joy in your cup. Frequently your pleasures on earth are momentary. In heaven your pleasure will endure forever. And yet some of you say, "Oh, I think I want to stay in Kansas longer." You've gotta be kidding!

PSALM 17:15 (While this is a confession of David, it is also a confession of Jesus following His resurrection and ascension into heaven. By faith it is our confession, too!) In *righteousness* (That means in holiness.) *I will see Your face*; when I awake (This is your bodily resurrection.), *I* (Both body and soul) *will be satisfied with seeing Your likeness* (That is, seeing the full glory of God.)

Have you ever been fully satisfied in this world? No! Even your best day on earth could have been better, because there are limitations here. You will not really be satisfied with that new home, with that trip to Hawaii, with your retirement. Who do you have to see, according to this verse, to be fully satisfied? God! **Notice that you will not be satisfied just because you are in heaven. You will be satisfied because you see God**. When you look at God you won't want to look at anything else. Anne Ross Cousin wrote:

> The Bride (Church) *eyes not her garment but her dear Bridegroom's face;*
> *I will not gaze at glory But on my King of grace. Not at the crown He giveth*
> *But on His pierced hand: The Lamb is all the glory of Immanuel's land.*

ROMANS 8:18 (Did St. Paul have a lot of suffering on earth? Yes, a lot. Let's read what he says about it.) I consider that our present sufferings (As Christians we may have to suffer some things. Some of us will lose some of our unbelieving friends. Some of our unbelieving friends will not go along with us as we walk with Jesus. We may have an abundance of normal sufferings which all men are subject to. Whatever the sufferings, what does Paul say about them? They) are not worth comparing with *the glory that will be revealed in us.*

Let's draw a scale on the marker board. On the left side let's write a large "S" to represent all the sufferings we go through on earth. On the right side let's put a "G" to represent the glory we will see and the glorified people we will be in heaven. Which side would go down first? The "glory" side. When the suffering side from this earth is compared to the glory side of heaven, the suffering side won't even move the scale. **Friends, let's spend less time accenting our sufferings, and more**

Heaven is God's home, a place of entrancing beauty. It will be filled with a huge crowd of people who came from all over the earth because salvation came to them, and now they offer perfect praise to God and the Lamb who made it all possible. We will be totally satisfied and happy and will live intimately with God. Our greatest joy in heaven will be the joy God's presence brings us. We shall live in indescribable joy and glory. Or...

> THINK
>
> Of stepping on a shore and finding it heaven;
> Of taking hold of a hand and finding it God's hand;
> Of breathing a new air and finding it celestial air;
> Of feeling invigorated and finding it immortality;
> Of passing from storm and tempest to an unbroken calm;
> Of waking up, and finding it Home!

6. To whom will God give eternal life?

JOHN 3:16 For God so loved the world that He gave His one and only Son, that *whoever believes in Him* shall not perish but have *eternal life.*

To whom will God give eternal life? Only to those who believe in His Son as their Savior.

JOHN 3:36 Whoever *believes in the Son* (Watch the next three words.) *has eternal life* (Has it right now), but whoever *rejects the Son will not see life*, for *God's wrath remains* on him.

If you believe in the Son you have eternal life now, but if you reject the Son, God's wrath remains on you. One of the saddest funerals I ever conducted was this one. There was a couple who went through a class like this. He weighed about a hundred pounds, and she weighed about 250 pounds. Remember the weight. They seemed to believe in the Lord. With time, however, they stopped reading their Bibles, stopped attending church, and gave up their Christian faith. We were in the process of starting church discipline when, suddenly, he died. Since they were still on the church rolls, I was obligated to bury him. I want to tell you something – it's a very difficult thing to conduct a funeral at church when the deceased was not a Christian. At the end of the service they moved his casket down the aisle while she followed right behind. Just as they passed the last pew she, in her uncontrollable grief, leaped up on the casket with all 250 pounds, screaming and crying. I thought, "Oh, no, she's going to break the casket and the whole mess will be on the floor." I have never witnessed such a spectacle in my life. The people who saw it were absolutely stunned. I want to tell you something: The way you live is the way you die. Be sure that you and your family live in Jesus so that you can die in Him and have everlasting life.

God gives eternal life only to those who believe on His Son, Jesus Christ, as their personal Lord and Savior.

7. What, then, should be some important goals in our lives?

- ACTS 16:31 *Believe in the Lord Jesus*, and you will be saved.

Write "Goal # 1" to the left of Acts 16. If we are to prioritize our goals according to the Bible, this would have to be number 1. Could anything be more important than that for us? This is basic to salvation, to life, to hope, to everything. It's basic for my children, for my neighbors, for my friends, for the world – everyday, every hour – to believe in Jesus!

REVELATION 2:10 *Be faithful, even to the point of death*, and I will give you the crown of life.

Write "Goal # 2" to the left of Revelation 2. Folks, I do not believe in the doctrine that is taught by some churches: "Once in grace, always in grace." If that teaching were Biblical, would Revelation 2:10 be necessary? No, we wouldn't need it. You can lose the crown of life. Who is saying so? No one less than Jesus. He says, "Be faithful to Me right up through death. If you are, I will give you the crown of life."

I want to make a confession. You know that I am happy for all of you, for the spiritual progress you've been making. I must tell you that for a number of weeks now I have gone into a new state of mental and emotional activity over you. I am concerned about you. You say, "You shouldn't worry, pastor." That's right, but I am very concerned. About what? About whether or not you are going to be faithful to Jesus until you die. I am thrilled that you confess Christ as your Savior and Lord. I am so happy for you, but I worry that the devil, the world, or your own sinful flesh is going to lead you off to where you were before, and for some of you, that was unbelief. Please don't let that happen. Please, please, please be a good Bible student at home and in worship and Bible class.

MARK 16:15-16 *Go into all the world and preach the Good News to all creation. Whoever believes and is baptized will be saved,* but *whoever does not believe will be condemned.*

Write "Goal # 3" to the left of Mark 16. When I look at Scripture and ask, "What should be my third goal?" I believe it is this passage. My third goal is to take that which I have spiritually and give it away, and the more I give it away, the more I'll have it. Who says so? Jesus! Go and share the Good News with everyone you can. I want to spend the rest of my life doing that.

REVELATION 22:20-21 He who testifies to these things says, "Yes, *I am coming soon."* Amen. *Come, Lord Jesus.* The grace of the Lord Jesus be with God's people. Amen.

Write "Goal # 4" to the left of Revelation 22. I heard of a man who, each night before he went to sleep, would go to his bedroom window and look up into the sky and say, "Perhaps tonight, Lord?" And in the morning, upon arising from bed, he would go to the same window and look up into the sky and say, "Perhaps today, Lord?" It would seem to me, if we are going to prioritize things, that goal # 4 would be the development and growth of the concept within ourselves, in our minds and hearts, that the imminent return of Jesus in the sky is about to take place! Unless I am operating with that kind of thinking, I'll spend too much time on peripheral piffle (Don't ask me how to spell that.) I'll be robbing myself of some of those good stewardship concepts that are rightfully mine as a child of God. The Lord Jesus will not be satisfied until He comes to take all His children Home. That should have a profound effect upon how I live, on how I act, on what I do with my life.

We should make absolutely sure that we believe on the Lord Jesus for salvation and that we remain faithful to Him to the end. We should do everything we can to personally win the lost for their Savior and heaven. All who believe in Him and are baptized will be saved. We should joyfully look forward to the time when Jesus comes to take us to our eternal Home. May each of us in this class pass through those pearly gates to live forever with our Lord, live with each other, and with all those we brought to Jesus.

Let's pray together

Lord Jesus, our precious Savior, we thank You with all our might for this Bible study course and in particular for this last Lesson. Thank You for warning us about the anguish of Hell. Thank You for telling us about the glory of Heaven. What a beautiful city Jerusalem must be. Thank You for describing what we will be like and for the description of the activity which takes place there continually. Please strengthen our faith in You in the days ahead through good Bible study. Please give us power to live for You. Please use each of us to tell others about You so that they may be saved, too. Finally, Lord, when life is over, take each of us to our beautiful home in Heaven where we will eternally thank and praise You, the Father, and the Holy Spirit. Hear us, Lord Jesus! Amen! Amen! Amen!

Let's sing together

> Abide with me, fast falls the eventide. The darkness deepens;
> Lord with me abide. When other helpers fail and comforts flee,
> Help of the helpless, oh, abide with me.
>
> Swift to its close ebbs out life's little day; Earth's joys grow dim,
> It's glories pass away. Change and decay in all around I see;
> O Thou who changest not, abide with me.
>
> I fear no foe with Thee at hand to bless; Ills have no weight,
> And tears no bitterness. Where is death's sting? Where grave thy victory?
> I triumph still if Thou abide with me.
>
> Hold Thou Thy cross before my closing eyes; Shine through the gloom,
> And point me to the skies; Heav'n's morning breaks, and earth's vain shadows flee;
> In life, in death, O Lord, abide with me.

Bible reading for the next few days

Revelation 19, 20, 21, 22, and Psalm 23

Worksheet no. 10

1. When we die _body_ and _soul_ separate. Our _soul_ goes to heaven, and our _body_ returns to dust.

2. True or _False_: Unbelievers are given another chance to be saved after they die.

3. A person says, "I don't really care if I go to heaven or not." How would you reply? _Some day you will care, and you will regret your decision forever. The better part of wisdom would be to think it over carefully now._

4. _True_ or False: Unbelievers will be condemned to everlasting death by Christ on Judgment Day for not believing in Him as their Savior and for not living their lives to His glory.

5. Read 1 Corinthians 15:56-57. Where does death get its power? _From sin_. Where do we Christians get our victory? _From our Lord Jesus Christ._

6. When Scripture speaks of hell as everlasting fire and punishment with intense pain and weeping (✖) it is an effort on God's part to make men fear ever going to such a place, ( ) it is an overstatement of truth, (✖) it is an effort to describe the true and terrible conditions of all those who die without Christ.

7. What passages from this Lesson prove that when Christ returns He will not reign on this earth for a thousand years (millennium) as some people believe He will? *2 Peter 3:10-11 and Matthew 25:31-34,41.*

8. What are some of the joys we will experience in heaven? *We will have glorified bodies like Jesus' glorified body. There will be no more tears or suffering. Our joy will be complete.*

9. *True* or False: Because Christ rose from the dead, all Christians are positively assured of their redemption, resurrection, and new life in heaven.

10. Read Daniel 12:3b. What, hopefully, will be one of your greatest joys in heaven? *To see those people that I was privileged to bring to Jesus.*

11. Survey your friends, acquaintances, people you know. Jot down the first names of just three of them who may not know Jesus personally as their Savior: _____

_____

Mention at least two things you can do to help them find Jesus:

a. *Invite them to church with me.*

b. *Informally share my faith in Jesus with them.*

12. If you knew you would die at the end of this year, how would your life change (try to mention specifics)? *I would try to be more loving. I would try harder to share the Gospel with my family and friends. I would desire to be on good terms not only with God, but also with men.*

_____

13. If you were granted just one wish, what would the wish be? *I would like to be in heaven with my family and Christian friends.*

How could this wish become reality? *By all of us being faithful to our Savior.*

14. In view of everything learned in this Bible study, mention at least four important goals for your life that you want to pursue from here on:

a. *That I believe in Jesus Christ as my personal Savior.*

b. *That I remain steadfast in this Christian faith to death.* _____

c. *That I share the Gospel of Jesus with other people.* _____

d. *That I joyfully and with anticipation look forward to the second coming of Jesus.* _____

PASTOR, ENCOURAGE YOUR PEOPLE TO STUDY THIS COURSE ON HEAVEN

Some groups, having completed *I Have Good News For You*, continue to meet weekly or every other week using the seven lesson Bible study, *The Many Wonders of Heaven* by Pastor Ginkel. Write to the address on page 1 for a descriptive brochure on this and other Bible studies.

Announcements: _____

_____

_____

_____

_____

_____

_____

_____

_____

_____

_____

The Many Wonders of Heaven

SEVEN LESSONS OF GOOD NEWS ON:

1. The Wonder of Entrance

2. The Wonder of God

3. The Wonder of the Saints

4. The Wonder of God's Family

5. The Wonder of Reward

6. The Wonder of Activity

7. The Wonder of the City

"Every valley shall be filled, and every mountain and hill shall be brought low, and the crooked shall be made straight, and the rough ways shall be made smooth; and all flesh shall see the salvation of God"
Luke 3:5-6

This is a Bible study that prompts a high level of interest. Usually class size doubles and even triples. People have a lot of questions about life after death. Here is an opportunity to find answers from Scripture.

A Time To Laugh... or Cry

Twenty Old Testament stories on the heroes of faith – each an occasion for God and man to laugh and cry. The thread of the Messiah is carefully followed from Genesis 3:15 to Malachi. Written by Pastor Ginkel using the NIV. While it was designed for preconfirmation classes and Christian Day Schools, it is being used even more frequently by adult Bible study groups. Each lesson begins with a contemporary introduction, hymn, prayer, and explanation of text, probing and practical questions for discussion, plan of action, daily Bible reading schedule, and Bible memorization plan. Humor is used throughout. A Leader's Guide makes teaching the course a pleasure.

He was oppressed, and he was afflicted, yet he opened not his mouth; like a lamb that is led to the slaughter ...
Isaiah 53:7

You will like this –

1. Conservative theology and Christocentric

2. Good "discussion starter" questions

3. Excellent notes and commentary

4. Adaptable. Students can "keep up" with flow
   of the class if they miss a session

5. A good dose of humor is used